# FIRST NATIONAL CITY BANK of New York.

# *Monthly Economic Letter*

## ANNUAL INDEX FOR 1963

### TABLE OF CONTENTS
**Arranged Serially**

### GUIDE TO PAGE NUMBERS

| | | | | | |
|---|---|---|---|---|---|
| Jan. | 1-12 | May | 49-60 | Sept. | 97-108 |
| Feb. | 13-24 | June | 61-72 | Oct. | 109-120 |
| Mar. | 25-36 | July | 73-84 | Nov. | 121-132 |
| Apr. | 37-48 | Aug. | 85-96 | Dec. | 133-144 |

## INDEX

# Monthly Economic Letter

## General Business Conditions

Business enters 1963 on a note of sustained high-level activity. Fears of a business recession this winter, so widespread six months ago, have been largely dispelled, and hopes have been aroused that tax cuts can be worked out to revitalize our economic growth. The Department of Commerce has offered a tentative estimate that the gross national product showed a further moderate increase in the fourth quarter, raising the 1962 total to about $554 billion.

Despite a scattering of strikes, and ominous threats of others of a more serious nature, total employment (including 2.7 million in the armed forces) has been holding at a seasonally adjusted annual rate of 70½ million. Christmas sales, when the figures are added up, evidently will compare favorably with the 1961 holiday season. The extra shopping day between Thanksgiving and Christmas helped offset the effects of unusually severe weather in the East and South and of newspaper strikes in New York and Cleveland. Sales of 1963 model cars, which started off so auspiciously in October and November, declined less than is normally expected in early December, supporting the industry's expectation of a second good year in a row. New truck sales have also been booming, with domestic deliveries in the first 11 months of 1962 greater than for any full year since 1955.

### Industrial Activity on a Plateau

Industrial production has moved along a high-level plateau since midyear. The Federal Reserve index (seasonally adjusted, 1957-59=100), which moved up into a range of 119 to 120 in July, held within this narrow band through November (119.5). Reports on new orders received by manufacturers and the relatively conservative level of inventories give promise of sustained industrial activity.

Businessmen have been cautiously adding to previously planned capital expenditure programs. According to the November survey of the Department of Commerce and the Securities and Exchange Commission, outlays on new plant and equipment in the second half reached an annual rate of $38.4 billion (seasonally adjusted), $0.6 billion more than had been envisaged in the August survey. Outlays in the fourth quarter were expected to be about the same as in the third. Anticipations for the first quarter of 1963 indicate a modest decline, but actual outlays may well turn out to be higher, as was the case in the preceding three quarters. This is supported by the announcement, since the survey date, of a number of major investment projects, including Bethlehem's plan for a $250 million steel-finishing mill in northern Indiana.

## Retrospect on 1962

As we look back, 1962 was a good year although it left a feeling of disappointment. Many new records were set. The gross national product picked up nearly 7 per cent over 1961. Total employment (including the armed forces) rose 1½ million and averaged more than 70 million persons for the first time. Industrial production increased 8 per cent, and so did new plant and equipment expenditures, which finally pierced the old record that had stood since 1957. While results for the fourth quarter remain to be reported, estimates of the Department of Commerce indicate that corporate profits for the nine months were running at an annual rate 11 per cent higher than in 1961.

Nevertheless, the year was disappointing. The hopes of the Administration, shared by stock market investors, had been for an even more vigorous expansion. The highly optimistic forecasts of personal income and profits on which federal revenue estimates had been based were quickly shown to be unjustified, and, since government spending was tailored to these expectations, another sizable deficit—officially estimated at $7.8 billion—is in the making for the fiscal year ending June 30.

The economy weathered a sequence of disturbing events—the steel-price controversy in April, the subsequent nose-dive in the stock market, and, in October, the Cuban crisis. Active expansion took a rest in the second half. But business, right up to the year-end, showed no clear symptoms of slipping off into a new recession.

### The President's Speech

The problem confronting the Administration and the new Congress, meeting this month, is to put new thrust into the economy. The business community was heartened by the clear understanding of the problem displayed by President Kennedy in his speech on December 14 before the Economic Club of New York. The President spoke of the accumulated evidence of the last five years that our present tax system—developed hastily in wartime to meet emergency needs—siphons out of the private economy too large a share of personal and business purchasing power and reduces the financial incentives for personal effort, investment and risk-taking.

Stressing this nation's capacity to do better, Mr. Kennedy pointed out that "the Federal Government's most useful role is not to rush into a program of excessive increases in public expenditures, but to expand the incentives and opportunities for private expenditures."

It is a welcome change to see emphasis given to economic stimulation by improving incentives to work and enterprise rather than by raising government expenditure totals. The President did not accept the view attributed to some of his advisers that the purpose of tax cuts should be simply to enlarge the deficit.

Promising to put brakes on expenditures, but accepting the inevitability of a deficit in present circumstances, he said our practical choice is between two kinds of deficits: "a chronic deficit of inertia, as the unwanted result of inadequate revenues and a restricted economy, or a temporary deficit of transition, resulting from a tax cut designed to boost the economy. . . . The first type of deficit is a sign of waste and weakness. The second reflects an investment in the future."

Mr. Kennedy reviewed other possibilities and found them wanting. To *raise* taxes in an effort to balance the budget would be self-defeating because "it would provide a heavy deflationary effect" and "move us into a recession at an accelerated rate." Intensification of the Federal Reserve's easy money policy might not give much stimulation to the economy and would risk an outpouring of funds abroad—"a hemorrhage in our balance of payments."

The President's budget and tax messages are awaited with uncommon interest. Chairman Wilbur D. Mills of the House Ways and Means Committee, which must originate tax legislation, has set as his goal a personal income tax rate schedule running from 15 to 65 per cent and a 47 per cent corporate rate, but insists that achievement of such reforms must hang on appropriate limitation of expenditures and enlargement of the tax base.

What is vital is getting started, reinspiring the business community and thereby moving the economy forward. As Mr. Kennedy said, "we cannot afford to do nothing":

> I do not underestimate the obstacles which the Congress will face in enacting such [tax] legislation. No one will be fully satisfied. Everyone will have his own approach. A high order of statesmanship and determination will be required if the possible is not to wait on the perfect.
>
> . . . This nation can afford to reduce taxes—we can afford a temporary deficit—but we cannot afford to do nothing. For on the strength of our free economy rests the hope of all free men.

## Changing Patterns of Population Growth

As the bells rang in the New Year, the census clock in Washington recorded a figure of 188,044,096 for the population of our fifty United States.

The estimated increase in population in the 33 months since the last actual count, in April 1960, is 8,037,096. In fact, we are adding each year a number equal to the population of the original thirteen states.

The estimated increase in population during 1962 was 2,754,096, or 1.5 per cent. Over the life of the nation the percentage rate of population growth has tended to decrease, though not steadily. The slowest rate of increase in population, 0.7 per cent per annum, was witnessed during the decade of the Thirties which embraced the Great Depression. After the unhappy interlude of World War II, population growth steepened to 1.7 per cent per annum during the decade of the Fifties.* The bumper crop of postwar babies, and the remarkable prolongation of the average life span, led to sizable upward revisions in Census Bureau projections of population growth. It also led to high expectations of business expansion during the decade of the Sixties as children go through their schooling, join the working population, marry, establish homes and raise families.

Population is no guarantor of prosperity, as countries like China and India can testify. As parents know so well, increase of population means more mouths to feed and rising expenses for clothing, allowances and education with each passing year. It is only when boys and girls are ready and able to take jobs, and add to the national production, that the strain is relieved.

The unbalanced age distribution of the population is a source of great interest among market researchers. Varying growth rates among particular age brackets have important effects upon markets for particular types of goods. In the February 1961 *Letter*, we reviewed population projections under the heading of "The Sixties—Problems and Potentials." Since then the Census Bureau has corrected its projections on the basis of the 1960 Census results and a slowing of the birth rate. Against this background, and with the passing of the years, it is useful to take a fresh look at the data.

### 200 Million in 1967

By 1970, according to the new projections, the total population of the United States will have risen from the 180 million counted in the 1960 Census to somewhere between 209 and 214 million. For 1980, a range of 246 to 260 million is indicated.

The Census Bureau in 1958 offered four sets of projections, based on different assumptions as to birth rates. The highest and lowest of these projections have now been discarded. Series I, which implied a rising birth rate, was already 1.3 million too high by 1960, after adjusting for Alaska and

* Alaska, with an April 1, 1960 population of 226,167, became a state on January 3, 1959; Hawaii, with 632,772, on August 21, 1959. The average percentage increase for the decade is calculated as though both had been states at the time of the 1950 census.

Hawaii. Series IV, the lowest, which assumed a marked decline in the birth rate, was 0.5 million too low by 1960. The one most nearly right so far, Series III, which assumed a moderate decrease in birth rate, has been used for the projections cited in this article. It has the population increasing at an annual rate of 1½ per cent during the entire decade of the Sixties, with the rate of growth quickening slightly to 1.6 per cent during the decade of the Seventies.

According to these figures, the nation's population should cross the 200 million mark about midyear 1967. The 100 million level was achieved in early 1915. In other words, the United States will have doubled its size in 52 years. We went from 25 million to 50 million between 1853 and 1880, a period of 27 years, and then on to 100 million in 1915, or 35 years. Immigration was a major factor in the more rapid population growth prior to 1915.

### The Postwar Baby Boom

The main point of interest in population statistics lies in the shifting composition. Markets are shaped by the way the population is made up—among babies, parents and grandparents, among workers, dependents and retired people, or among residents of cities, suburbs and farms.

The age composition of much of today's—and tomorrow's—population was built in over decades past. A relative "deficit" now exists in the 20 to 39 age group because the long-term decline in the birth rate was temporarily intensified by the Great Depression and World War II. With demobilization, the marriage rate jumped nearly 50 per cent in 1946. By 1947, the number of births was up by fully one third—a million more babies than in 1945.

After this first postwar surge, the birth rate slipped back—but not as much as population experts had expected. Part of the higher level of births was a catch-up from the past—making up for marriages and children postponed during the depression. At the same time, the tendency of people to marry younger and to complete families earlier appeared to be borrowing from the future. The birth rate, which peaked out in 1947 at nearly 27 per thousand population, remained around 25 until 1957 before resuming a decrease to an estimated 22.6 in 1962. In large part, however, this has merely reflected the declining proportion of women in the child-bearing ages in the total population—owing to the faster expansion of both younger and older age groups—and not a reduction in family size.

Over the past 15 years, various sectors of the economy have felt the stimulus of the growing population. It has not been a one-shot stimulus: not a wave which advances and then recedes, but

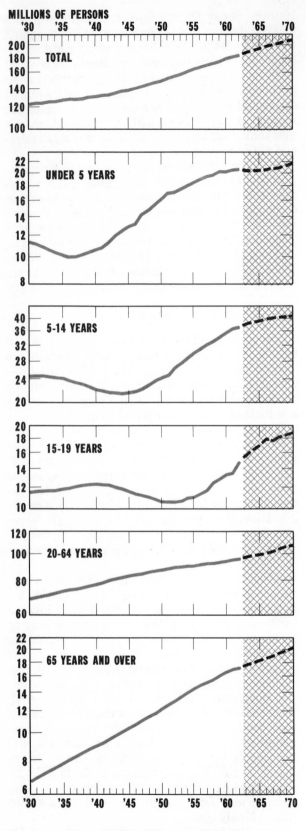

**MILLIONS OF PERSONS**

TOTAL

UNDER 5 YEARS

5-14 YEARS

15-19 YEARS

20-64 YEARS

65 YEARS AND OVER

**Total Population by Age Groups**
(Ratio scale to show proportionate changes.)

Source: U.S. Bureau of the Census, 1930-62, actual; 1965 and 1970 projection Series III; 1963-64 and 1966-69 interpolated by FNCB on basis of earlier Census projection.

a rapid surge to a new high level of demand. The accompanying chart shows the developing pattern of population changes, both the historical perspective and the expectations for the Sixties.

In 1947, the number of children under the age of 5 jumped more than 1 million, and large gains persisted through 1951. In that five-year period, the age group under 5 years expanded by 4 million—more than in the 45 preceding years put together. Another 3 million youngsters were added over the next decade, but expectations are that this group will remain at about the present size until the postwar babies' babies start showing up in the late Sixties. The demand for bassinets, baby food and books by Dr. Spock—booming a decade ago—is beginning to flatten out.

In 1952-56, the 5 to 9 year-old group experienced a similar expansion, with unprecedented pressures on the nation's elementary schools. In 1957-61, the same pressures developed in the group aged 10 to 14 and, consequently, on junior highs and high schools. In both these groups, as the chart shows, the rate of growth is expected to slow in the late Sixties.

### Expanding Markets

In 1963, the number of 16 year-olds will increase by more than 1 million. What this means to the economy can best be appreciated by parents of teenagers. Certainly it means more business for the grocer, the milkman and the clothing store. But that was also true at earlier ages. More importantly, it means that we are on the threshold of some major changes.

Two recent news items emphasize the shape these forces are already taking. In reporting a 500,000 increase in unemployment during November, the Bureau of Labor Statistics commented: "Mainly responsible was a greater-than-seasonal increase in the number of teenage job-seekers, more than half of them full-time students looking for part-time jobs." Whatever this implies about this country's concept and measurement of unemployment, it also warns of the growing pressures on the job market.

On the other hand, the automobile industry attributes a significant part of the record sales of new passenger cars in the fourth quarter to the support given by strong demand and relatively firm prices for used cars; these in turn are said to reflect increased demand for used cars by teenagers. In over two thirds of the states, 16 is the minimum age for a driver's license; demand from teenage drivers is expected to rise sharply in 1963 and the next few years.

This sort of impact will be repeated with increasing frequency in the years ahead. Colleges face a rise of as much as 50 per cent in enrolments in the next six years. The demand for buildings, equipment and teaching staffs will be unprecedented.

In 1965, the numbers reaching 18 will jump sharply. Many of these young people will be looking for at least part-time jobs and thinking of marriage. In early 1961, the Census Bureau estimated that 28 per cent of 18 and 19 year-old girls were married or divorced, compared with 71 per cent of those aged 20 to 24. Half of all girls who get married do so by the time they are 20⅓ years old; males, on the average, are 2½ years older.

New households create demands for all sorts of goods and services, for independent housing, furniture and appliances. But it should be noted that the main force of these demands will not be felt until 1965 or, more likely, 1967 when the postwar babies begin to reach 20. The initial growth of housing demand undoubtedly will be for apartments. Single-family homebuilding will not feel the main stimulus until the Seventies.

### Effects on the Labor Force

Even more important than the potential demands will be the ways and means of fulfilling them. In the years ahead, an increasing number of teenagers will be looking for full-time jobs. The Bureau of Labor Statistics has projected the total labor force for 1970 at 85.7 million, an increase of 12.6 million from 1960. Half of this rise is expected to come in the 14 to 24 age group, which comprised less than one fifth of the 1960 labor force.

Not all observers regard this influx of workers as an unmixed blessing. This group naturally will be among the least skilled and least experienced in the labor force. Young people already have trouble finding jobs; unemployment in the 14 to 19 age group was reported at 14 per cent in November 1962, compared with 5.3 for the total labor force. As the number of young labor force entrants rises sharply over the next few years, the task of assimilating them will constitute a real challenge.

If the national production is going to grow as fast as we want it to, the economy will need to make use of the services these young people have to offer. The challenge is for educational institutions to lay a solid foundation of knowledge, for parents to teach habits of industry, and for government to avoid minimum wage standards that will deny untrained beginners the opportunity for that important first job. Certainly it will be essential, through tax reforms, to improve the inducements to work and gain more recruits into the insufficient army of employers.

## Annual Gold Review

Over the past year, again, gold has figured prominently in financial developments and policies. Output in the Free World is running at the highest level recorded in history. Of these enlarged supplies, however, more has been absorbed into industrial uses and private holdings, and correspondingly less added to official stocks, than in any other year since World War II. The U.S. gold stock, although still representing some two fifths of world monetary gold outside Russia, has declined to its lowest level since 1939.

While gold has been very much in the news, it is sometimes difficult to fit isolated facts into a coherent and intelligible pattern. In particular, the U.S. gold position can be appraised sensibly and realistically only within the framework of the world picture. This review seeks to set world gold developments and policies into perspective.

### Output at Record Levels

In 1962, world gold output (excluding Russia, Mainland China, etc.) approached 37 million ounces, equivalent to $1.3 billion—2 per cent more than in 1940 when it had reached its peak following the universal currency devaluations during the Great Depression. Last year's output was 6 per cent higher than in 1961 and 52 per

| Estimated Gold Production in 1962 | | | | |
|---|---|---|---|---|
| | In Millions of Dollars | Per Cent Change from: 1961 | 1953 | 1940 |
| South Africa | $ 890 | +11% | +113% | +81% |
| Canada | 145 | −7 | +2 | −22 |
| United States | 55 | 0 | −20 | −68 |
| Australia | 35 | −8 | −8 | −40 |
| Ghana | 30 | +3 | +15 | −3 |
| Southern Rhodesia | 19 | −5 | +6 | −35 |
| Philippines | 14 | −7 | −18 | −64 |
| All Others* | 102 | −2 | −15 | −61 |
| Total* | $1,290 | +6% | +52% | +2% |

* Excluding Russia, Mainland China, and countries in their spheres, for which figures are not reported.

cent above 1953, when the post-World War II rise in production began.

As in earlier years, the rise in world gold output was attributable to a further increase in South Africa, which accounts for a little more than two thirds of world production outside Russia. Rich new discoveries, improved techniques, and production in association with uranium explain the growth. In Canada, the second largest producer, output dropped somewhat despite a rise in the Canadian dollar price associated with devaluation. Production in the United States, which still holds third place, remained practically unchanged.

Russia's production continues to be blanketed in secrecy. Western observers put it variously at $350-600 million. We are less in the dark regarding the gold Russia sells in Europe to balance its international accounts. Import statistics of the United Kingdom show gold imports from Russia at $68 million during the first ten months of last year, as against $183 million during the comparable period of 1961; Russia also ships gold to the Continent. Exports, of course, do not necessarily coincide with sales. Russian sales were stepped up in late October and in November; even so, it appears that they were smaller in 1962 than in the five preceding years when they averaged $240 million annually. Despite the rise to new heights in South African output, therefore, total new gold supplies in the Free World last year were of the same order as in 1961—some $1.5 billion.

### Private Demand in the Limelight

A comparison of new gold supplies with year-to-year increases in the total of official gold stocks makes it possible to get an approximate idea of the varying amounts of gold absorbed by the arts, industry and private holders.

In the United States, uses in the arts and industry have been expanding in recent years. Net consumption in 1961 amounted to $97 million—somewhat less than in 1960 but almost twice as much as only five years ago. With production covering only three fifths of consumption, the U.S.

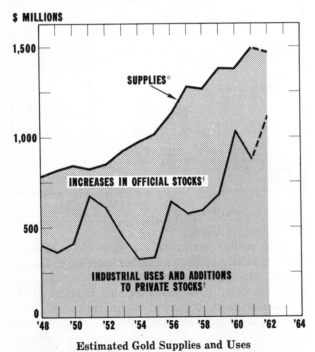

**\$ MILLIONS**

SUPPLIES*

INCREASES IN OFFICIAL STOCKS†

INDUSTRIAL USES AND ADDITIONS TO PRIVATE STOCKS†

'48  '50  '52  '54  '56  '58  '60  '62  '64

**Estimated Gold Supplies and Uses**

* Excluding Russian output but including reported Russian gold sales. †Excluding Russia, etc.
Note: Plottings for 1962 are based on preliminary estimates.

gold stock is being drawn upon in a degree by domestic needs. In addition to traditional uses, some entirely new industrial applications have been developed in recent years; the gold- and silver-plated spacecraft Mariner II, which reached its rendezvous with Venus two weeks ago, is a striking illustration. Contrary to the practice in most other countries, where gold coins and medals are available as stores of value, there is no gold coinage here and residents are not allowed to hold gold in monetary form except for coins of recognized numismatic value minted before April 5, 1933.

In the world around us, with few exceptions, gold is held and traded privately, serving its age-old function as the citizen's favorite hedge against paper-money inflation. As the chart shows, more gold moved in 1962 into private uses and holdings than in any other postwar year. The tentative figure works out at $1.1 billion or some $250 million more than in 1961. Thus, somewhat over three quarters of total new supplies went into private uses and holdings.

In the broad perspective shown in the chart, these developments in 1962 appear as the third postwar wave of greatly enlarged private gold absorption. The first of these waves dates back to 1951, the accompaniment of the Korean inflation; the second was in 1960, the year of the great fright over the dollar and the London gold rush. In last year's circumstances, there was a persistent demand for gold in Latin America as well as in the Far and Middle East; but the bulk of hoarding can be traced to what may best be called investment demand in Europe. Declines in American and European stock markets, along with wage-price spiraling on the Continent, reinforced the demand for gold last spring; the Cuban crisis led to a sharp but short-lived flurry in late October.

Although under pressure during most of last year, the London gold price at no time exceeded $35.20 an ounce; this is minimal in comparison with the $40 momentarily reached in October 1960. To keep the price on an even keel, gold sales had begun to be made in late 1960 from British reserves under a broad understanding that the Bank of England could replenish in the United States gold it sold on the London market. In early 1962, when renewed pressures developed on U.S. gold stocks, this "gold bridge" was supplemented by a wider informal cooperation among central banks to refrain from buying gold in London when the supply is short and to participate with the United States in channeling gold to the market.

The strength of demand from people of moderate means has increased premiums of coins over bar gold. To meet demand, quite a few nations have resumed the minting of gold coins, though for sale as a commodity rather than for circulation as money. Last year, South Africa joined the parade with a new two-rand piece.

### The Anatomy of Official Gold Flows

As a result of the enlarged private gold absorption, much less from current gold supplies was left for additions to official gold stocks than in most other postwar years. In fact, during the first nine months of 1962 for which estimates could be made at this writing, official stocks in the aggregate increased by only around $200 million. During the last quarter, with the London price most of the time below the U.S. Treasury selling price of $35.0875 (in part as a result of reported Russian sales, as already noted), central bank buying probably increased; but, even so, 1962 was not a good year. As the world has learned the hard way, confidence in currencies must be maintained if gold is to flow into international reserves to buttress international liquidity.

The following table traces the magnitude and origin of changes in official gold stocks from October 1961 through September 1962.

Several significant facts stand out clearly. Of the $1.3 billion of U.S. gold sales, over half went to the United Kingdom but only part of it seems to have been added to British stocks. Four continental countries—France, Spain, Belgium and Austria—bought $779 million of gold from the U.S. Treasury during the twelve months ended September 1962. France, which now has the larg-

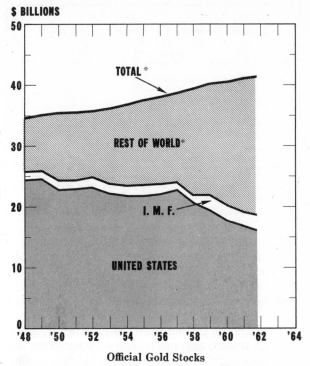

$ BILLIONS

TOTAL *

REST OF WORLD *

I. M. F.

UNITED STATES

'48  '50  '52  '54  '56  '58  '60  '62  '64

**Official Gold Stocks**

\* Excluding Russia, etc.
Note: Latest plotting September 1962.

est balance-of-payments surplus in Europe, will—as the Finance Minister, M. Giscard d'Estaing, stated—use future dollar accumulations to pay off debts it owes to the United States; last year, it thus prepaid $470 million. On the other hand, Continental nations acquired comparatively small amounts of gold in the London gold market and from other non-U.S. sources; this contrasts sharply with large acquisitions outside the United States during previous years.

Two other factors greatly influenced international gold flows last year. During its exchange crisis in the spring, Canada sold a sizable amount to the United States, incidentally easing our position. On the other hand, South Africa, using part of its new production to rebuild its reserves depleted during the payments difficulties of 1960-61, supplied less gold.

Most of the European nations keep the bulk of reserves in gold. The ratio of gold in British reserves, shown in the table as of June 1962, was sharply increased after the United Kingdom had repaid, in July, the remainder of its indebtedness to the International Monetary Fund. In the British view, a country which is an international financial center should hold most of its reserves in gold. For Germany, the ratio is lower than in most neighboring countries, but in absolute amount its gold stock is the largest after our own.

Until 1961, the United States kept its international reserves entirely in gold. Today, it also holds modest amounts of convertible foreign currencies

| Changes in Official Gold Stocks, Oct. '61-Sept. '62 (In Millions of Dollars) | | | | |
|---|---|---|---|---|
| | Additions through Transactions with: | | Gold Stock Sept. '62 | As % of Gold & For. Exch. Reserves |
| | U.S. | Other* | Amount | |
| United Kingdom... | $ 712† | $—512† | $2,600‡ | 76%‡ |
| Common Market: | | | | |
| Germany ....... | 0 | 24 | 3,668 | 57 |
| France ........ | 356 | 1 | 2,481 | 70 |
| Italy .......... | 0 | 15 | 2,241 | 69 |
| Netherlands .... | 0 | 0 | 1,581 | 89 |
| Belgium ....... | 144 | 32 | 1,341 | 82 |
| Switzerland ...... | —47 | 28 | 2,453 | 93 |
| Portugal ......... | 0 | 32 | 469 | 61 |
| Spain ........... | 166 | — 15 | 428 | 41 |
| Austria .......:.. | 113 | 8 | 419 | 40 |
| Canada .......... | —190 | — 48 | 689 | 28 |
| South Africa .... | 0 | 283 | 488 | 79 |
| All for. countries¶ | 1,321 | 205 | 23,093 | 52 |
| Int'l Mon. Fund.. | 0 | 129 | 2,175 | |
| United States..... | | | 16,082 | 97 |

\* Residual figures; including gold from new production, Russian sales, etc. †July 1961-June 1962. During Oct. 1961-Sept. 1962, additions through transactions with the U.S. amounted to $721 million. ‡ June 1962. ¶ Excluding Russia, etc.

Sources: Derived from data in *Federal Reserve Bulletin* and International Monetary Fund's *International Financial Statistics.*

| 1958-62 Decline in U.S. Treasury Gold Stock | | |
| (In Millions of Dollars) | | |
| | Unadjusted Decline | Adjusted to Exclude Transactions with IMF* |
| --- | --- | --- |
| 1958 ................ | $2,247 | $2,247 |
| 1959 ................ | 1,078 | 1,034 |
| 1960 ................ | 1,689 | 1,989 |
| 1961 ................ | 878 | 1,028 |
| 1962† ............... | 911 | 911 |
| Total ............. | $6,803 | $7,209 |

* Among these transactions were gold sales by the IMF with the right of repurchase, the proceeds of which are invested in U.S. Government securities; they amounted to $300 million in each of the years 1959 and 1960, following a similar $200 million transaction in 1956. † Through December 26.

($338 million as of last October). The thought is that present arrangements among leading nations for reciprocal currency holdings contain within themselves the possibility of wider and more general application that will tend to improve the working of the international currency system.*

How far the United States is prepared to go in holding foreign currencies, and how far other nations may be ready to move toward holding smaller proportions of reserves in gold, is not at all clear. The President of the German Federal Bank, Dr. Karl Blessing, mentioned at the IMF's annual meetings last September that nations might consider agreeing on some "common attitude toward the composition of currency reserves." Professor S. Posthuma, a member of the managing board of the Netherlands Bank, suggested two months ago a ratio of 60 per cent in gold to 40 per cent in "key" currencies, including—in addition to the dollar and the pound sterling—the currencies of the European Common Market nations. Such mutual currency holdings would be endowed with guarantees of reimbursement in the event of devaluation. These are provocative ideas but an arrangement of this sort would not necessarily ease the U.S. gold position.

### The U.S. Gold Position

During 1962 (through December 26), the U.S. Treasury's gold stock declined by $911 million. This approximates the losses in 1961 and 1959 but was much less than those in 1958 and 1960.

The U.S. gold stock on December 26 amounted to $15,978 million, lowest since 1939 but still 39 per cent of the Free World's monetary gold stock; in 1949, when the U.S. gold stock was at its peak, the ratio was 70 per cent.

People who speak in terms of a threatening gold deficiency often cite the fact that the U.S. gold stock is now less than U.S. liabilities to foreign

* See "The Dollar in the World Today" and "The Question of Gold Guarantees" in the September and October 1962 issues of this Letter.

countries and international financial bodies. This is not, however, the whole story. As Dr. Max Iklé, member of the managing board of the Swiss National Bank, remarked last fall, a world banker— just like any other banker—cannot keep 100 per cent liquid:

> In order to assess whether . . . a run [on the U.S. dollar] is likely, it is necessary to take a closer look at the creditors. The world's central banks hold short-term claims to a total of $12 billion and the international institutions to a total of $5 billion, so that only $8 billion consists of private claims.
>
> Since the purpose of international institutions is to overcome monetary crises, they would not take part in a run on the dollar. It would be just as pointless for the central banks to do so, as they have a stake in the maintenance of the present monetary system and would in the event of a monetary crisis be called upon to provide assistance through the machinery of the IMF. Not the least important function of private holdings of short-term dollars is, for various reasons, their use as working balances, so that these claims, too, are more stable than their short-term character might suggest.

Dr. Iklé also noted that a comparison of U.S. gold stock with short-term liabilities to foreigners overlooks the $7 billion of short-term claims on foreigners held by American banks, business and individuals. It also forgets that U.S. long-term private investments abroad exceed the long-term investments of foreigners in our own country by $28 billion. The U.S. Government holds foreign government obligations; some of these are being repaid in advance of maturity to reduce the U.S. payments deficit.

While the international balance sheet of the United States shows, despite the loss of gold, a respectable surplus of assets over liabilities, this must not make Americans complacent. For no nation can run up its floating obligations indefinitely.

Confidence in the U.S. dollar is also an indispensable condition for the proper functioning of our international currency system. Over the past year, fears and suspicions have brought about enlarged gold hoarding and, as a result, official gold stocks have increased by less than 1 per cent out of new production. With firm confidence in the dollar and other leading currencies, official gold stocks could increase each year by as much as $1 billion—or 2½ per cent—assuming quite generously that, out of the $1.5 billion of new gold supplies, some $500 million were used in industry and the arts.

The Managing Director of the International Monetary Fund, Dr. Per Jacobsson, speaking in New York on December 12, expressed the belief that "the gold markets next year will see less demand for hoarding purposes, and therefore should become in 1963 a useful supplier of monetary gold and a real alternative to the U.S. Treasury in this respect."

# Corporate Profits Statistics

This Bank published its first comprehensive tabulation of corporate profits in the *Monthly Letter* for April 1928, showing results for 709 companies for the year 1927 in comparison with 1925-26. These summaries were the outgrowth of earlier articles which gave profit tabulations for selected industries, starting with steel and sugar in March 1924 and later expanded to include rubber, meat packing, automobiles and tobacco.

It is natural for a bank to follow figures on profits. Profitability is a test of creditworthiness. But it has become well understood that profits have broader and deeper significance. Viewed comprehensively, profits are a barometer of fluctuations in production and employment; they provide a reading of the incentive for business expansion.

There are more than eleven million business enterprises in the United States, as measured by the number of tax returns filed with the Internal Revenue Service. Nine out of ten are individual proprietorships or partnerships. But a million-odd enterprises, including all the biggest ones, are organized in the corporate form. These firms generate more than half of the national income and provide about half of the jobs.

Over the 35 years since we started publication of corporate income figures,* a number of government agencies have developed other sets of data, applying different techniques and offering estimated totals for all corporations or all manufacturing corporations. Because of divergences among the statistical series, we have had numerous inquiries as to how these differences arise. The present article represents an effort to explain these differences.

### Methods Compared

From the beginning, our main idea has been to get figures out promptly with a minimum of time-consuming statistical refinement. The data we published on April 2, 1928 lagged just three months after the close of 1927. The comprehensive data of the Internal Revenue Service (then the Bureau of Internal Revenue) for 1927 were not available until November 1929, a lag of 22 months. Meanwhile, we had published indicated directions of change for 1928 and the first three quarters of 1929.

The Internal Revenue Service (IRS) has a far bigger job to do, tabulating figures on tax returns

for a million corporations. It provides a broad benchmark record of corporate profits back to 1916, three years after the corporate income tax was first put in force. Our data, drawn from published reports to stockholders, do not necessarily agree with figures the same corporations supply to the IRS; the rules of tax accounting sometimes depart from the practices which accountants consider appropriate for normal bookkeeping and reporting to shareholders.

One major discrepancy between stockholder reports and tax returns stems from different methods of reporting depreciation, depletion and amortization allowances. Many companies, particularly in the extractive industries, have been taking advantage of the accelerated amortization provisions of the 1954 Revenue Act in their tax returns while applying straight-line depreciation methods in reports to stockholders. Looking ahead, it is likely that similar discrepancies will arise as a result of the different ways in which the recently enacted 7 per cent investment tax credit and the new guidelines and rules for depreciation are treated in reports to the tax collector and shareholder.

Another area of difference is in the reported earnings of foreign subsidiaries. For U.S. tax purposes, only the remitted dividends of foreign subsidiaries have been reported, while for stockholder reports unremitted earnings have often been included.

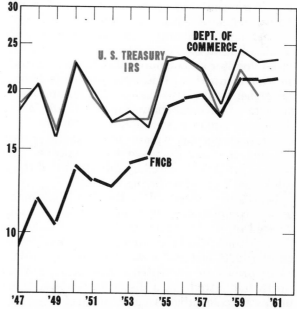

**Profits, U.S. Corporations**
(Ratio scale to show proportionate changes.)

Note: Figures of FNCB are affected by double-counting of profits represented by dividends paid to domestic corporations. IRS data are adjusted to exclude intercorporate dividends.

---

* A comprehensive record of profits figures published by this Bank is available in *Understanding Profits* by the late Claude Robinson (Van Nostrand, Princeton, New Jersey, 1961).

Our publication schedule calls for reporting of first, second and third quarter results in our May, August and November issues, respectively—in other words, with a one-month lag. In the March issue we report on results for both the fourth quarter and the year for corporations issuing quarterly statements. In April, we publish a more comprehensive and detailed tabulation currently covering over 3,500 companies classified by 65 industry groups.

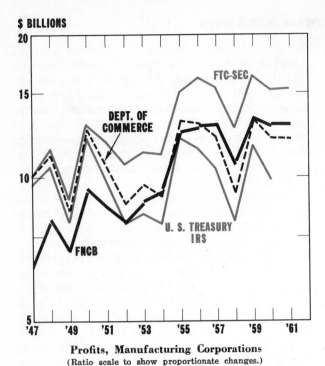

**$ BILLIONS**

**Profits, Manufacturing Corporations**
(Ratio scale to show proportionate changes.)

Note: Figures of FNCB and FTC-SEC are affected by double-counting of profits represented by dividends paid to domestic corporations. IRS data are adjusted to exclude intercorporate dividends.

These are just two of the ways in which variances between tax and management accounting can result in divergences between profits reported to the tax collector and to shareholders.

A more obvious difference is that our figures cover only a fraction of 1 per cent of the million corporations active in the United States today. We record the figures of companies which publish regular financial reports—in other words, corporations which have been able to achieve public distribution of their securities. As the experienced investor knows, public distribution of stock does not insure that a firm is going to make money. Nevertheless, it is true that our figures are biased in favor of success, embracing practically all of the largest and most successful corporations. This bias toward success explains in considerable part the discrepancies discussed below between the rates of profits calculated by this Bank and those calculated from other bodies of data.

Less well understood is the fact that many profits compilations—including ours—are exaggerated by double counting. Income represented by dividends paid by one domestic corporation to another gets included twice. This is appropriate where profits are calculated as a percentage of net worth but introduces a distortion of level when profits are calculated as a percentage of sales.

### Movements Over Time

The year-to-year movements of our figures conform quite closely to IRS and other data, although

at different levels. There has, however, been an upward bias in our series over a longer time span. This shows up in the first chart on profits of all corporations. Also noteworthy is a failure of our figures to show the 1960 downturn which emerges in the preliminary IRS report for that year, made available last month.

The IRS figures, as charted, exclude intercorporate dividends, a fact that helps explain the $21 billion level of profits we reported for 1960 against a shade less than $20 billion for the IRS. But this is not the whole explanation. IRS data show a sharp increase in losses of unprofitable corporations, the great majority of which are not included in our tabulations. In 1960, losses amounting to $6.9 billion were reported by 470,000 corporations, compared with $4.9 billion recorded by 404,000 corporations in the previous year. In a typical year, two out of five corporations show red ink on their tax returns, but the $6.9 billion of losses recorded for 1960 has been exceeded in only two previous years, 1931 and 1932, when there was massive unemployment.

Another interesting difference appears in the timing of the 1955-57 peak. The IRS shows it in 1955, the Department of Commerce in 1956, and our tabulation in 1957.

The Department of Commerce data, which form an integral part of the national income accounts, are based historically on IRS figures and are carried forward by estimation. The Department seeks to measure corporate earnings accruing to U.S. residents, without deduction of depletion charges and exclusive of capital gains and losses. Profits accruing to residents are measured by eliminating intercorporate dividends from profits of domestic corporations and by adding net receipts of dividends and branch profits from abroad. In other major respects, the definition of profits is in accordance with federal income tax regulations.

### Profits in Manufacturing

Interest in profits data tends to focus on earnings of manufacturing corporations—both in the aggregate and for comparisons among various lines of activity. The most comprehensive quarterly figures are tabulated jointly by the Federal Trade Commission and the Securities and Exchange Commission (FTC-SEC) which, since 1943, have been publishing *Quarterly Financial Reports for Manufacturing Corporations*. The FTC-SEC uses a sample of some 10,000 corporations to estimate the total for all manufacturing corporations, currently some 165,000 in number. The FTC-SEC reports, issued about three months after the close of each quarter, provide considerable detail on income accounts and balance sheets as well as rates of return on stockholders' equity and margins on

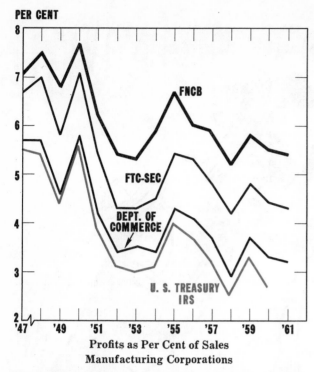

**Profits as Per Cent of Sales**
**Manufacturing Corporations**

Note: Figures of FNCB and FTC-SEC are affected by double-counting of profits represented by dividends paid to domestic corporations. IRS data are adjusted to exclude intercorporate dividends.

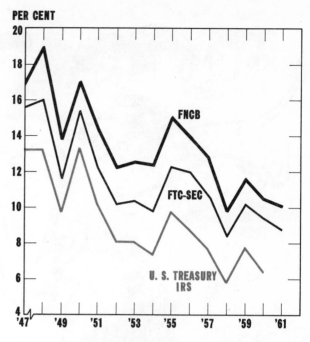

**Profits as Per Cent of Net Worth**
**Manufacturing Corporations**

Note: The profit numerators include intercorporate dividends.

sales, classified by asset size and industry groups. The profits figures published by the FTC-SEC correspond essentially to those shown in shareholder reports.

The FTC-SEC figures run about one fifth higher than those compiled by this Bank for manufacturing. Over the postwar period, our figures have tended to move closer to the FTC-SEC data and both sets of figures have grown relative to the compilations of the Department of Commerce and IRS. All figures move in reasonable conformity with one another although, as in the case of all corporations, there is lack of agreement on the timing of the 1955-57 peak.

### Profit Rates

In a growing economy based on private enterprise, profits should move higher with the passing of the years, the growth in volume of business handled and enlargement of invested capital. Since World War II, corporate profits have not kept up with the expansion in gross national product, sales or invested capital. Hence the widespread discussion of a "profit squeeze" and the related disappointing growth performance of the entire economy.

The final pair of charts gives the picture for manufacturing. In the calculation of returns on net worth, all three sets of figures include intercorporate dividends. The figures run along rather neatly together save for differences of level. From the IRS figures, supplemented by what we know of behavior since 1960, it appears that manufacturing corporations as a group have earned less than 8 per cent on net worth for six successive years running back to 1957.

In the chart relating profits to sales, the curves again move in a fairly parallel way. But the differences in level are even more pronounced than in the case of return on net worth. This is partly because the IRS and Department of Commerce data, as shown in the chart, exclude intercorporate dividends partly because our data are biased toward more successful enterprises. From the IRS figures, considered together with other compilations for years since 1960, it would appear that average profits for manufacturing corporations have been down somewhere around 3 cents per sales dollar ever since 1957. This is the period during which—in the words of Chairman Heller of the President's Council of Economic Advisers—we have been suffering our case of "tired blood" evidenced by "persistent underutilization of our human and physical resources."

## FIRST NATIONAL CITY BANK

*the nicest things happen
to people who carry . . . . ✳*

# Monthly Economic Letter

## General Business Conditions

The economy has been marking time in the opening weeks of 1963, while the major news affecting business was being made in Washington and Brussels. With much of the nation buffeted by severe storms or disrupted by labor disputes, economic visibility was sharply reduced. Such fresh statistics as were available on production and trade pointed toward a continuation of an upward drift, exciting neither high hopes nor gloomy apprehension. The biggest question marks for American businessmen were posed by President Kennedy's tax reform and spending proposals, while France's rejection of Britain's bid to join the Common Market created new uncertainties abroad.

An erratic weather pattern bringing arctic blasts to the United States and other countries of the Northern Hemisphere hampered economic activity through much of January. Heavy snows and low temperatures discouraged shoppers, slowed industrial activity, disrupted transportation and wrought heavy damage to fruit and vegetable crops. Compounding these difficulties were numerous strikes. The most costly was the long-shoremen's walkout which tied up Atlantic and Gulf coast shipping for 34 days at an estimated loss of up to $800 million. Local disruptions were caused by newspaper strikes in New York and Cleveland and by the transit dispute in Philadelphia.

Nevertheless, tentative January data are encouraging. Retail sales in the first three weeks of 1963 averaged 11 per cent higher than a year earlier, influenced by a 16 per cent gain in new car sales. The spotty influence of strikes, however, is apparent in department store sales. A nationwide rise of 6 per cent over a year ago contrasts with declines of 32 per cent in downtown Philadelphia, 6 per cent in Cleveland and 5 per cent in New York City during the week ended January 19.

Sub-zero cold and icy roads kept workers home, helped hold gains in steel production below seasonal expectations, and caused shutdowns of auto assembly lines. On the other hand, petroleum refinery runs and electric power production advanced to meet heating demands. Both the crop freeze and the dock strike are adding to the housewife's food bills.

Meanwhile, the business and financial community had mixed reactions to the President's proposals for tax reduction and record spending. The stock market continued to react buoyantly to the prospects of tax cuts. The Dow-Jones industrial average touched 684 on January 29, capping a 22 per cent increase during the last three months and a recovery of nearly three fourths of the ground lost between December 1961 and June 1962. However, businessmen were

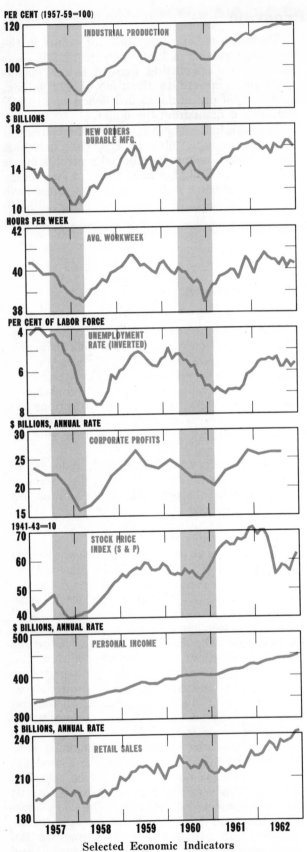

PER CENT (1957-59=100)

**INDUSTRIAL PRODUCTION**

$ BILLIONS

**NEW ORDERS
DURABLE MFG.**

HOURS PER WEEK

**AVG. WORKWEEK**

PER CENT OF LABOR FORCE

**UNEMPLOYMENT
RATE (INVERTED)**

$ BILLIONS, ANNUAL RATE

**CORPORATE PROFITS**

1941-43=10

**STOCK PRICE
INDEX (S & P)**

$ BILLIONS, ANNUAL RATE

**PERSONAL INCOME**

$ BILLIONS, ANNUAL RATE

**RETAIL SALES**

**Selected Economic Indicators**

Shaded areas represent recession periods as determined by the National Bureau of Economic Research. All figures, except stock prices, are seasonally adjusted.

deeply disappointed in the failure of the tax reform proposals to carry through on promises to improve incentives for work and enterprise.

### The Administration's Forecasts

In his Economic Report, President Kennedy described the outlook for continued moderate expansion as favorable. He said he did not expect a fifth postwar recession to interrupt our progress in 1963. Yet the bright optimism of last year's Economic Report has been replaced with a much more cautious appraisal and an emphasis on the failure of the economy to achieve full employment and rapid growth in the years since 1957. He expressed confidence that his tax program would correct these conditions by 1965.

For 1963, the Council of Economic Advisers forecasts an increase in gross national product of $24 billion, or 4 per cent, to $578 billion, understood as the midpoint of a $10 billion range. Such an advance, according to the President, "will leave the economy well below the Employment Act's high standard of maximum employment, production, and purchasing power." Most private forecasts for 1963 have tended to cluster at or somewhat below the lower end of the $573-583 billion range projected by the Council.

This more cautious view is prompted by the behavior of some of the more widely followed indicators of business activity, as shown in the accompanying chart. One index after another rose in 1961 and early 1962 and then showed little further progress during the remainder of the year. For example, the Federal Reserve index of industrial production (seasonally adjusted, 1957-59=100) advanced to 119.3 in July, held between 119 and 120 during the remainder of the year, and ended up at 119.6 in December. On the other hand, personal income and retail sales are still setting new highs.

A curious omission from the President's messages—noted by Congressmen on both sides of the aisle—was any proposal for dealing with disruptive strikes. The forced settlement of the recent dock strike raised immediate fears that an unfortunate precedent had been set for the numerous major contract negotiations scheduled for 1963. After an 80-day Taft-Hartley cooling-off period and federal mediation efforts failed to produce agreement, the President appointed a special three-man panel which worked out a two-year contract calling for added wage and fringe costs of 37½-39 cents per hour. This translates into increases of more than 5 per cent per year, far out of line with the "guideposts" for non-inflationary wage behavior set forth by the Administration.

# The Tax Program

It has been a long time since a President's messages to a new Congress have been more eagerly awaited than was the case this January. The same central theme dominated all of them: the need to create jobs and growth by cutting income tax rates. A special message on taxes offered specific proposals.

President Kennedy urges that individual income tax rates, which now range between 20 and 91 per cent, be reduced to a range of 14 to 65 per cent; that the corporate tax rate be reduced from 52 to 47 per cent; and that these reductions be coupled with selected structural changes, effective in 1964, concentrating the main benefit of the rate reduction on persons already subject to the lowest rates of tax.

The program would be phased out over three years, but the benefit to larger corporations, in terms of cash flow, would be delayed until 1969 by a proposal to speed the timing of corporate income tax payments.

The whole package is calculated to give up revenues in the amount of $13.6 billion a year gross or $10.2 billion net. These, however, are theoretical figures which fail to allow for expansion in the base of taxable income, acceleration of corporate payments, and scheduled step-ups in social security levies, such as the $2 billion increase that went into force January 1. The budget document predicts that revenues will actually keep rising, with the proposed income tax reductions helping to encourage growth of the economy and the base of taxable income.

## Perils of Deficit Financing

Many people are shocked by the idea of cutting taxes when, as a result of continuously rising outlays, there is already a deficiency of more than $8 billion to cover expenditures and no end of deficits is clearly in sight. The President does not endorse the idea that tax reductions should be enacted for the specific purpose of enlarging the deficit. He accepts deficits as inevitable, for the next few years, and proposes tax cuts as an alternative to bigger increases in spending:

> No doubt a massive increase in federal spending could also create jobs and growth, but in today's setting, private consumers, employers, and investors should be given a full opportunity first.

The business community—indeed all working people—will welcome the first opportunity to demonstrate what they can achieve in a climate oriented toward stimulation of private enterprise. There are many who apprehend that, if tax reform founders, the political alternative will be more government spending, taxing and controlling —a repudiation of the American way of life.

There are unhappy memories of events in the business recession of 1958 when the decision was made against tax cutting. Instead, federal spending soared upward to the tune of $11 billion, leading to a peacetime record deficit of $13 billion, and a flight from the dollar.

The situation was salvaged by retrenchment in spending in fiscal '60—the last year in which the Federal Government enjoyed a surplus. Since then cash spending has been rising at an average rate of $7 billion a year. Even though prices have been holding broadly stable, under the influence of competition from abroad and some slowing in the rate of wage increases here, the balance-of-payments problem remains with us and also talk of eventual inflation.

We have our own experience, and that of innumerable foreign nations, to illustrate the perils of running big deficits to accommodate unbridled increase in government expenditure. In our limited modern experience with tax cuts, we have never suffered inflation as a consequence. But our previous tax cuts have been preceded or accompanied by retrenchments in federal spending.

While not arguing for deficits *per se*, the President offers reassurances that "monetary tools are working well" and that the "balanced approach that the Treasury has followed in its management of public debt can be relied upon to prevent any inflationary push." Our balance of payments, he has said, would be helped by tax reductions which would make investment in America more profitable, increase plant efficiency, cut costs and improve our competitive position in world trade.

Discussing the same theme, Federal Reserve Board Chairman William McC. Martin has pointed out that:

> . . . accelerated growth will presumably lead to larger internal investment and credit demand, and so to some gradual rise in interest rates, not through the fiat of restrictive monetary policy, but through the influence of market forces. With rising credit demand pressing on the availability of credit and saving, the flow of funds from the United States to foreign money markets will be more limited. In addition, a closer alignment of interest rates internationally can be expected to result and this will help to reduce the risk of disturbing flows of volatile funds between major markets.

These considerations and assurances, coming from such respected quarters, justify a bold approach to desperately needed income tax rate reforms. We should improve management of the public debt. We must be prepared to pay higher interest rates as necessary to put the damper on inflationary influences and expectations. But this is not enough. We will have to sweep away the idea that government expenditures inevitably must increase to the tune of billions of dollars each passing year. Loosening restraints on private spending logically demands a new sense of caution on public spending.

### Structural Changes

The emphasis which the President has given to tax reforms insures early and thorough study by the House Ways and Means Committee, which originates tax legislation. Action will be held back for two reasons: the over-all budgetary situation, and needs for lengthy hearings and deliberation on the proposed "selected structural changes."

There is a horrible waste—millions of man-hours—in the time people now spend trying to figure out what the law is, what they owe, and what methods are open to them to minimize tax liabilities. The penalties for faulty homework are heavy.

The Ways and Means Committee can perform a great public service by resisting the addition of new gadgets. People cannot accurately report their tax liabilities when the statutes become so complex that even the experts and the courts are confused as to what the language is intended to mean.

A year ago the President had promised that a major program of reform would be aimed among other things at simplification of our tax structure. This objective has got lost in the shuffle. Some of the proposed structural changes would simplify tax accounting; others would introduce new inequities and complexities.

The Committee will want to give particular thought to the proposed "minimum standard deduction" and "floor under itemized deductions of individuals." The minimum standard deduction is a device to excuse several hundred thousand people from paying any tax; it would make deductions dependent upon family status, just as personal exemptions already are.

### Itemized Deductions

The floor under itemized deductions is not a floor at all but a boom unmercifully and indiscriminately cracked down on the heads of people who itemize deductions. It would make the first 5 per cent of lawful deductions unlawful.

Citizens who itemize deductions are found in all income brackets—the man who has his home broken into or burned down, the man who suffers abnormal medical bills by reason of sickness in his family, the man whose generosity to church, schools, and eleemosynary institutions exceeds that of his neighbors, the man who unavoidably has exceptional state and local taxes to pay.

Up to $10,000 of income, a person may take a 10 per cent deduction without need to justify it. At this level and higher, the taxpayer is under compulsion to itemize deductions to gain the reliefs intended by law. Specific deductions, if abused, ought either to be repealed by statute or disallowed in the process of administration.

There is no excuse for such a shotgun attack, covertly repealing present equitable provisions and stripping rate reductions of practical meaning for many people.

### One Package?

The President wants the entire tax revision program "promptly enacted as a single comprehensive bill":

> The sooner the program is enacted, the sooner it will make its impact upon the economy, providing additional benefits and further insurance against recession.

For this reason, the question arises as to whether it will not prove wiser to break the legislation into two pieces and enact moderate reductions applicable to 1963 quickly, to clear uncertainties and give tax shaving a chance to show what it can do toward economic stimulation as an alternative to greater expenditure increase. Meanwhile, Congress may ponder structural reforms and, by actions on appropriations, set a base for further cuts.

This is particularly necessary if the final objective is to cut the initial rate as low as 14 per cent. The initial rate is the most expensive to cut. It is the one that everybody pays. Thus it must be most closely related to the proposed levels of government expenditure.

### The Human Equation

Many people look at the budget in easy terms of arithmetic: so much deficit, so much stimulation. Overlooked all too frequently is the human equation. What damage does a program of tax-free handouts do to the self-reliance and employability of the beneficiary? Conversely, what damage do 30, 40, and 50 per cent federal income tax rates—on top of still other levies on income—do to the desire of industrious people to seek advancement? The President, in advocating tax reform as "the most urgent task confronting the Congress in 1963," showed understanding of the system of incentives which makes an individual enterprise system work:

> This net reduction in tax liabilities of $10 billion will increase the purchasing power of American families and business enterprises in every tax bracket. . . . It will, in addition, encourage the initiative and risk-taking on which our free-enterprise system depends—induce more investment, production, and capacity use—help provide the 2 million new jobs we need every year—and reinforce the American principle of additional reward for additional effort.

Unfortunately, the specific proposals have lost sight of fundamental objectives—reinforcing the American principle of additional reward for additional effort. They have been distorted by conflicting desires to release purchasing power into the hands of consumers on a massive scale with the effects of pushing a greater proportion of the cost of government onto the shoulders of people in the middle and upper income brackets.

What the Congress will need to do is to give attention to the progression of rates—which as proposed would remain steep—and consider the desirability of making it more worthwhile for people to earn more taxable income for the benefit of themselves and the nation.

As the President states so eloquently:

> These are not domestic concerns alone. For upon our achievement of greater vitality and strength here at home hang our fate and future in the world—our ability to sustain and supply the security of free men and nations—our ability to command their respect for our leadership—our ability to expand our trade without threat to our balance of payments—and our ability to adjust to the changing demands of cold war competition and challenge.

## *Taxation and Diminishing Returns*

The reform that has the most to commend it in terms of equity and common sense, but the least in terms of political appeal, is a reduction in the personal income tax progression. The present rate structure starts at 20 per cent and rises in 23 quick steps all the way to 91 per cent— so far as we know, the roughest income tax rate in all the world. In the steep climb to this punitive levy, applicable to taxable income beyond $200,000, the federal government takes 26 per cent of taxable income above $4,000, 50 per cent above $16,000, and 65 per cent above $32,000. The President has proposed that the 91 per cent be cut to 65 per cent, an upper limit widely accepted by proponents of rate reform. This is about as high as most other countries go in taxing increments of income. Other rates would be cut more or less proportionately.

While the severity of the present rates is mitigated by innumerable special provisions, three points stand clearly in favor of reform:

• First, it is offensive to American conceptions of personal liberty and justice to ask a man to give up so much of the fruits of additional effort. Unreasonable exactions are linked with despotism, not freedom. Our war for independence was fought to be rid of the "multitude of New Offices" and swarms of Officers sent to "harass our people, and eat out their substance."

• Second, the steep rate progression poaches upon the rewards for working hard and accepting additional responsibility. It undermines private capital accumulation, wrecks the normal working of compound interest, and tells enterprising people that it is less useful to build taxable income than to search out ways to get around the tax laws and limit their tax liabilities. Being human, people respond to this perversion of incentive.

• Third, the higher personal income tax rates do not in fact produce significant amounts of revenue. They drive potential income away. In other words, the rates run well beyond the point of diminishing returns. Reduced rates, given time, would benefit the revenues.

How did we ever come to accept this lopsided rate structure?

Income taxation became established as a permanent source of revenue by the 16th Amendment to the Constitution ratified in 1913. Following British example, rates in excess of 50 per cent were invoked during World War I and continued through 1922. After cutbacks by 1925 to a top of 25 per cent, applicable to income beyond $100,000, even steeper increases were put in force during the Great Depression and World War II. The top rate was jumped to 63 per cent in 1932, 79 per cent in 1936, 88 per cent in 1942 and 94 per cent in 1944. Interestingly, the top rate in some of these earlier years applied only to income beyond $1,000,000 or $5,000,000. Now there is not enough income out yonder to warrant carrying the progression beyond $200,000. (A ceiling on the percentage of total tax to taxable income makes 87 per cent the marginal tax rate on taxable income beyond $629,500.)

We have never gotten very far away from the extreme rate progression invoked during the World War II emergency. In fact, the present structure is even harsher than the one in force during that war because the shrinkage in the value of the dollar has raised the effective rates.

Rates were shaved in 1946 and 1948 to a scale of 16.6 to 82.13 per cent but moved up again during the Korean War to a range running from 22.2 to 92 per cent effective in 1952-53. The present range, from 20 to 91 per cent, has been in force since 1954.

The chart gives a picture of rate progressions in force in 1913, 1925-28, 1932-33, 1948-49, and 1954 to date, as well as that proposed for 1965. The slightly higher rates in force during the latter years of of World War II and during the Korean War are not shown on the chart; they follow along so closely with the schedule now in force that they would scarcely be distinguishable. In short, we are still living with an emergency structure jerry-built in the depression—when "soak the rich" was a popular cry—and during World War II and the Korean War. The wartime rates reflect an effort to restrain private investment; their retention saps the strength of the nation and its ability to wage today's cold war.

No one planned the tax system this way. As Richard V. Carpenter, professor of law at Loyola University, Chicago, points out in the December issue of *St. John's Law Review:*

> It has tended to grow like Topsy, pulled and pruned one way or another by political forces which may be ascendant at one time or another. By and large such forces have not been impressed by the importance of encouraging profits, particularly the profits of big business.
>
> For thirty years in this country there have been too many bureaucrats, writers and teachers of influence who purport to downgrade the profit motive as something rather vulgar and selfish—a curious attitude due, perhaps, in some part to snobbery, in part to a psychological lack of empathy on the part of men in professions motivated in greater degree by satisfactions other than financial gain, and in part by pure envy. It is the same spirit which frequently finds expression in terms of Fabian Socialism or state capitalism.
>
> Yet we must face the fact that men generally will invest only when they can hope for reasonable compensation for the use and risk of their money. All the appeals in the world to socialist theory or human benevolence will not alter this mainspring of human conduct.

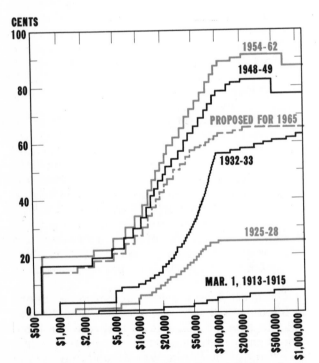

**Taxation of One Additional Dollar of Income As Related to Net Income of an Individual**

(Logarithmic scale for net income brackets)

Note: The 1965 curve does not allow for proposed arbitrary increase in taxable income (in the amount of 5% of adjusted gross income) for persons itemizing deductions; this would be equivalent to an increase of more than 5% above scheduled tax rates as shown in the chart for 1965. The 1925-28 curve does not allow for limited earned income credit.

## Equality vs. Opportunity

If we should want to make equality of income and wealth a central goal of our society, and stifle growth and initiative, we should by all means keep the present rate structure. The socialist-communist ideal of a classless, egalitarian society has an emotional appeal to many people, including some Americans. But this kind of society does not work—as the Russians have learned the hard way. We could still strive for this goal, but at the cost of giving up our claim to world leadership and our priceless heritage as a land of opportunity and of individual rights.

The growing popularity of tax-free handouts of public funds—robbing selected Peter to pay collectivist Paul—is one of the most disturbing features of present-day American life.

By accident, if not design, we have fallen in with a tax structure that breaks down the motive power of our economy—individual effort and enterprise. Karl Marx was right when, in the *Communist Manifesto*, he foresaw the possibility of using the "heavy progressive or graduated income tax" as the means of making "despotic inroads on the rights of property, and on the conditions of bourgeoisie production."

But the people as a whole have never endorsed the kinds of tax rates we have in our system. In a survey by the American Institute of Public Opinion earlier this year it was found that the public would cut rates further than the Administration proposes.

## Gifts to the Rich?

Nevertheless, flattening out the steps will encounter resistance. No doubt it will be described as "a gift to the rich." The calculation may be offered that a cut in the top personal income tax rate from 91 to 65 per cent will make a dollar of income after tax in this bracket worth 35 cents instead of 9 cents while most taxpayers will have to be content with an increase of five or ten cents per dollar of taxable income.

It is strange that anyone should talk of an income tax reduction as a "gift." The implication is that what people earn is not theirs but the property of government.

If we want to maintain our form of society, and the freedom of people to save and build great enterprises, we must think straight on questions of property rights. What a man earns is fundamentally his own—subject to reasonable tax levies to support essential government services. If we view the matter any other way, we deprive him not only of property but also of incentive for earning income and opportunity for accumulating property. And that is where our tax system has gone sour. We need strong incentives, not to avoid taxes as now, but to work and to build enterprises that create jobs.

We do not need bigger federal deficits and bigger supplies of money to raise the levels of effort and production and the rate of growth of our economy. We can gain these ends by tax reforms that will make it more inviting for people to take jobs and employers to hire them. Then we can get balanced increase of production and consumption at a stable price level.

The object of cutting back the income tax progression is neither to give anything away nor to increase the deficit. It is to restore incentive to earn more. A person who can make 15, 30 or 50 thousand dollars a year is a rare individual. We need more of these individuals, and more incentive for others to work to successively higher levels of income and responsibility. The prospect of becoming a slave to income tax at an early age, and at a comparatively moderate income level, is not inviting.

### A Common Misunderstanding

Contrary to most impressions, a high tax bracket today does not mean that a man is rich; it may simply mean that he is being prevented from becoming rich. An unmarried Congressman with no other income but his government salary may find himself in the 56 per cent tax bracket. But that does not make him rich in terms of accumulated property. All that is certain is that he has more than $7,000 of income tax liabilities and many nondeductible expenditures which society expects a person in his position to shoulder. The doctor, lawyer, plant superintendent—community leaders all over the country—are in the same boat.

As a matter of fact, a man or woman who actually is wealthy has better opportunities, as by judicious gifts of property, to keep income out of the higher brackets. We have growing up a whole new generation of people who, while making good money, have never had a fair chance to realize the aim of financial independence. Successful people in business, the arts and professions do have some property but it is apt to be limited to their homes, the accouterments of modern living, rights to pensions upon retirement and rights to insurance benefits on death. These assets are not available for taking a flyer in business.

Many crocodile tears are shed for small business these days. But how can a small individual enterprise grow—the normal way, out of reinvested profits—when the 50 per cent rate takes effect at a taxable income level of $16,000?

Certainly it would be easier for people to climb the ladder of success if the income tax steps were not so steep. The step to 50 per cent is the hardest. It is at this point, if not sooner, that people weary at the prospect of working for the primary benefit of government and reconsider the value of attempting to earn additional taxable income. By unconscionable greed, government debilitates the energies of its people, the progress of the nation and its own revenue flow.

## Budgeting for Tax Reform

Intense interest had built up in the weeks preceding the unveiling of the Administration's budget plans for fiscal 1964 because the fate of President Kennedy's tax reform proposals in Congress was thought to depend on how effectively expenditures are restrained and the prospective deficit minimized. The President's Budget Message on January 17 therefore aroused disappointment when he projected expenditures of $98.8 billion and a deficit of $11.9 billion.

The spending total not only tops estimates for fiscal '63 by $4.5 billion and fiscal '62 by $11 billion but also exceeds the previous record of $98.3 billion set in fiscal '45 at the decisive stage of World War II. The estimated $11.9 billion deficit follows on the heels of deficits of $8.8 billion in the current year and $6.4 billion in 1962 and has been exceeded in peacetime only by the red ink figure of $12.4 billion in 1959.

The President described his spending plans as "frugal," "severely limited," and the "minimum necessary to meet the essential needs," and promised to strive for greater efficiency in government operations. Nevertheless, a number of Congressional leaders promptly labeled the proposed budget as "discouraging" and "extraordinarily high" and called for hefty cuts in spending.

As the President had promised previously, overall spending other than for National Defense, Space, and Interest, which together are up $4.5 billion, is shown as declining in the budget—by a nominal $300 million. But observers were quick to note that the apparent decline was based on a mixture of hope and juggling, that civilian payrolls were being swollen, and that most items of expenditure on the domestic side continued to show a strong upward trend. Further sharp increases beyond fiscal '64 are foreshadowed in new programs proposed in such fields as education, youth opportunities, mental health, missile defense and medicare for the aged.

Far less controversial and almost escaping notice in the press was the fact that the Government's financial plan primarily stresses the "consolidated cash budget," embracing both the traditional "administrative budget" and the accounts

**Federal Expenditures by Major Function**
**Fiscal Year 1964**
(In Millions of Dollars)

| | Fiscal '64 Estimated | ——Change from—— Fiscal '63 Estimated | Fiscal '62 Actual |
|---|---|---|---|
| National Defense .......... | $ 55,433 | +2,429 | +4,330 |
| International Affairs & Finance .................... | 2,679 | — 195 | — 138 |
| **Total Defense** ............ | **$ 58,112** | **+2,234** | **+4,192** |
| Space Research & Technology. | 4,200 | +1,800 | +2,943 |
| Agriculture ................. | 5,696 | —1,035 | — 199 |
| Natural Resources ......... | 2,503 | + 123 | + 356 |
| Commerce & Transportation . | 3,388 | + 63 | + 614 |
| Housing & Community Development .............. | 276 | — 249 | — 73 |
| Health, Labor & Welfare... | 5,613 | + 698 | +1,089 |
| Education ................. | 1,537 | + 176 | + 461 |
| Veterans Benefits & Services . | 5,484 | — 61 | + 81 |
| Interest ................... | 10,103 | + 321 | + 905 |
| General Government ....... | 2,195 | + 154 | + 320 |
| **Total Nondefense** ........ | **$ 40,995** | **+1,990** | **+6,497** |
| Allowance for Contingencies & Pay Adjustments....... | 375 | + 300 | + 375 |
| Less: Interfund Transactions .................... | 679 | + 33 | + 46 |
| **Total Budget Expenditures.** | **$ 98,802** | **+4,491** | **+11,015** |
| Trust Fund Expenditures (incl. Govt.-sponsored Enterprises) .............. | 28,382 | +1,107 | +3,181 |
| Less: Intragovt. Trans., etc. | 4,707 | — 105 | — 571 |
| **Total Cash Outlays.......** | **$122,477** | **+5,703** | **+14,768** |

Note: Details may not add to totals because of rounding.

of trust funds and government enterprises, which previously had been shown as outside the "regular" budget. Many business and academic economists had recommended the change because the cash budget more faithfully reflects the impact of government spending, taxing and borrowing on the economy and financial markets.

As the tables show, spending in the cash budget is slated to rise by $5.7 billion to $122.5 billion in fiscal '64, while cash receipts are expected to be $3.8 billion higher at $112.2 billion. The anticipated cash deficit of $10.3 billion compares with shortfalls of an estimated $8.3 billion in the current fiscal year and $5.8 billion in fiscal '62.

### Defense and Space Outlays Boosted

Outlays for National Defense loom largest in the budget at $55.4 billion, up $2.4 billion from the current year and $9.7 billion from fiscal '60. Contrary to the popular impression, however, the continuing increase in defense spending does not reflect rising costs of missile hardware and manned aircraft—which are now declining with virtual completion of the Atlas and Titan I programs and suspension of Skybolt—but bigger outlays for conventional weapons, expanded development of anti-missile missile systems and an $885 million package of proposed military pay boosts. Military

assistance abroad is slated to decline by $300 million to $1.4 billion as more aid is supplied under existing authorizations.

Spending under the heading of International Affairs and Finance is shown as dropping from $2.9 billion to $2.7 billion, but this is more apparent than real. Economic aid is scheduled to rise by $200 million, primarily for the Alliance for Progress. This is more than offset by lower net outlays for the Export-Import Bank, which is expected to sell off more of its seasoned loans to private and foreign lenders.

Rocketing upward with an increasing thrust of dollars is the program for Space Research and Technology, which is slated for a further boost of about 75 per cent to a total of $4.2 billion. With the aim of reaching the moon by 1970, spending for manned space flight will almost double to $2.7 billion, while meteorological and scientific projects will get smaller increases. In the last five years, space spending has increased almost 30-fold.

### Other Expenditures Undiminished

On the domestic front, outlays are scheduled to continue upward almost across the board, though this fact is somewhat shrouded by the bookkeeping involved. For Agriculture, the figures show a $1 billion decrease to $5.7 billion. Most of this decline, however, is based on the hope that textile mills, which are currently withholding cotton purchases in expectation of new legislation to lower fiber prices, will come back into the market next year and relieve the government of some support costs.

Activities listed under Natural Resources are budgeted for a rise of $123 million to $2.5 billion, while outlays for Commerce and Transportation are scheduled to go up $63 million to almost $3.4 billion as higher postal rates help balance off increases in other types of spending. Expenditures out of the highway trust fund are expected to grow by $391 million to $3.4 billion. The budgeted total for Housing and Community Development is almost halved from $525 million this year to $276 million, but the saving is to be accomplished by having the Federal Housing Administration shift from lending its own money to guaranteeing private mortgages in sales of properties acquired on defaulted loans. Actual outlays for urban renewal, public housing and special programs are scheduled to grow further.

Programs under Health, Labor and Welfare are also expanded almost uniformly, up $700 million to $5.6 billion under the administrative budget; with payments from social security and other trust funds going up $1 billion to $22.8 billion, the overall cash total is expected to reach $27.4 billion. Further increases are planned for the National Institute of Health, for manpower development and for the Federal Government's share of expanded welfare programs. Outlays for Education are booked to rise $176 million to $1.5 billion, with most of the growth stemming from a proposed new program for federal aid to education. Veterans Benefits and Services are shown as dipping $61 million to $5.5 billion largely because of declining readjustment benefits, but pensions and medical care costs continue to increase.

Growth of the public debt is expected to boost interest costs by $321 million to $10.1 billion under the administrative budget, but almost $1.8 billion of this money will be paid to the trust funds, thus helping to limit cash outlays to $7.7 billion. General Government costs are slated to rise by $154 million to $2.2 billion, with the biggest increase going to the Internal Revenue Service to enlarge tax collection machinery.

### Tighter Reins on Spending

The weak point in the new budget is not revenues—expected to grow despite phased-out tax cuts—but the continuous rise in spending. Chairman Wilbur D. Mills of the House Ways and Means Committee had earlier called for "better control of the rises in expenditure" as a prerequisite to tax-rate reductions.

Both Congress and the public are rightly concerned that since the last recorded surplus, in fiscal '60, we have had a string of cash deficits, each larger than the one before for a three-year total deficit of $16.4 billion. The proposed budget plan would bring the accumulated red ink to $26.7 billion. In this connection, an inescapable fact is that since fiscal '60, nondefense spending has soared 37 per cent while defense expenditures have risen 22 per cent.

What is needed is a determined effort to trim expenditures down the line, particularly on non-

| Federal Cash Receipts From and Payments to the Public (In Billions of Dollars) | | | |
|---|---|---|---|
| Fiscal Year | Payments | Receipts | Deficit (—) or Surplus (+) |
| 1948 ................ | $ 36.5 | $ 45.4 | + 8.9 |
| 1949 ................ | 40.6 | 41.6 | + 1.0 |
| 1950 ................ | 43.1 | 40.9 | — 2.2 |
| 1951 ................ | 45.8 | 53.4 | + 7.6 |
| 1952 ................ | 68.0 | 68.0 | * |
| 1953 ................ | 76.8 | 71.5 | — 5.3 |
| 1954 ................ | 71.9 | 71.6 | — 0.2 |
| 1955 ................ | 70.5 | 67.8 | — 2.7 |
| 1956 ................ | 72.6 | 77.1 | + 4.5 |
| 1957 ................ | 80.0 | 82.1 | + 2.1 |
| 1958 ................ | 83.4 | 81.9 | — 1.5 |
| 1959 ................ | 94.8 | 81.7 | —13.1 |
| 1960 ................ | 94.3 | 95.1 | + 0.8 |
| 1961 ................ | 99.5 | 97.2 | — 2.3 |
| 1962 ................ | 107.7 | 101.9 | — 5.8 |
| 1963 Estimated ........ | 116.8 | 108.4 | — 8.3 |
| 1964 Proposed ........ | 122.5 | 112.2 | —10.3 |

\* Less than $50 million surplus.

defense items, in order to limit the size of the deficit and make room for tax reductions. We cannot have our cake and eat it too. Some encouragement that spending will be trimmed may be found in statements of leading Congressmen on both sides of the aisle. Thus, Chairman Clarence Cannon of the House Appropriations Committee promised: "We will look for and find places to cut it substantially without impairing national security." Congressman Leslie C. Arends took the same view, noting that such cuts "need not be drastic but they could be substantial. This is simply a matter of close scrutiny."

There is basic truth in President Kennedy's view that a temporary deficit stemming from a bold tax reduction program can lead to budget surpluses in future years. But those surpluses will never come about unless real self-discipline is shown now in holding down nonessential spending.

## The U.S. Treasury in the Long-Term Bond Market

Early last month, an officer of the Federal Reserve Bank of New York slit open four sealed envelopes and announced the results of the first underwritten sale of United States Treasury obligations in 68 years. A 75-member syndicate of government securities dealers, banks and investment houses had won the $250 million offering by bidding $275 more than the next group— about one tenth of a cent per $1,000 bond.

The winning bid for the 30-year bonds, which are callable in 25 years, was 99.85111 with a 4 per cent coupon, establishing a net interest cost to the Treasury of 4.008210 per cent. The next bid, 99.85100 with a 4 per cent coupon, would have established a net interest cost of 4.008216 per cent. Reoffered to the public at par, the issue was a quick sellout and moved to premium. In

the wake of this initial success, the Treasury on January 30 announced plans for a second competitive long-term bond offering in April.

The financing last month had unusual features. The amount of $250 million is the smallest sum the Treasury has sought since 1937 on an offering of marketable bonds to the public for cash. Limiting the amount that could be offered was the fact that, for the first time in recent memory, the Treasury was experimenting with a technique which has become standard practice for private utilities and state and local governments—selling long-term bonds competitively on a single price, "all-or-nothing" basis to underwriters who assume the risks and responsibilities of placing the bonds with ultimate investors. A competitive sale meant that several syndicates had to be organized, each of which had to be strong enough to take up the total $250 million issue. In terms of the underwriting resources currently available in the bond market, $250 million is close to the practical limit which could be sold competitively.

In the first decade of the present century, to help finance the Panama Canal, and again in the middle 1930s, the Treasury tried competitive bidding in an attempt to sell long-term obligations. In both instances the issues were not underwritten, but were offered at tender to anybody wanting to put in a subscription, the same way Treasury bills are sold every week. This method of selling bonds did not prove popular with investors. For the last 28 years, offerings of Treasury bonds for cash subscription have been open to anyone (save for occasional restrictions on commercial bank participation). By the customary procedure, cash offerings of bonds, notes and certificates are thrown open to professional investors and the general public on the same terms; when subscriptions exceed the full amount of the offering, bonds are allotted to subscribers on a percentage basis.

### Postwar Unfunding

During the depression and World War II, as the public debt soared from $16 billion on June 30, 1930 to a peak of $279 billion on February 28, 1946, the Treasury relied on long-term bonds for a sizable part of its financing. At the close of 1946, private holders owned $54.7 billion of bonds due beyond 10 years and $38.7 billion due beyond 20 years.

The benefit of the debt-funding efforts during the depression and World War II was sacrificed by the practice, beginning in 1942, of pegging bond prices at or above par. As holders of bonds wanted their money, they sold in a market supported by the Federal Reserve. The result was that the bonds lost their character as long-term investments and became equivalent to interest-bearing cash. The Treasury attempted no long-term offerings under these artificial conditions.

After bitter controversy, the Federal Reserve in March 1951 announced withdrawal of the pegs, thus restoring long-term bonds to their basic investment character. To take the weight of potential offerings from the market, the Treasury offered nonmarketable investment series bonds, convertible at the choice of the holder into five-year notes, in exchange for specified issues. By the end of 1952, as a result of purchases by the Federal Reserve, exchanges into the convertible bonds, absence of new offerings and passage of time, public holdings of marketable Treasury bonds due beyond 10 years had been reduced to $24.8 billion and those due beyond 20 years to nothing at all.

Since 1952, the Treasury has made a succes-

sion of probing efforts to restore for itself a place under the sun in the long-term investment market. But despite these attempts, the amount of marketable bonds due beyond 10 years in the hands of the public fell to $16 billion by the end of 1962. This amount pales in significance in comparison with the vast amounts of long-term financing accomplished each year to support home building and other construction activity, and to support expansion of private utilities and other needs of private business. The market has certainly been big enough; the question has been one of willingness to take a continuing place in the long-term investment market and pay the rates required to hold that place.

### Previous Efforts

The first effort in debt funding was made by the Eisenhower Administration which, upon taking office, put out a $1.6 billion issue of 30-year 3¼ per cent bonds. Although 3¼ per cent would seem very reasonable by present-day standards, the Treasury, castigated for paying an excessive rate, waited two years before trying again.

A series of innovations were begun in the second Eisenhower Administration and carried forward under the Kennedy Administration. Since June

| Structure of U.S. Public Debt, Year End, 1946 & 1962 | | | | |
|---|---|---|---|---|
| | Dec. 31, 1946 | | Dec. 31, 1962 | |
| | Amt. In Billions | % of Pub. Issues | Amt. In Billions | % of Pub. Issues |
| Savings bonds and notes .......... | $ 55.5 | | $ 47.5 | |
| Treasury bills ..... | 17.0 | | 48.3 | |
| Treas. certificates, notes and bonds due within 1 year | 37.8 | | 39.0 | |
| Other oblig. due or redeemable within 1 year .......... | 0.5 | | 1.0 | |
| Total due or redeemable within 1 year ......... | 110.8 | 47.5% | 135.8 | 53.1% |
| Treas. notes and bonds due in 1-5 years ........... | 24.8* | | 65.9† | |
| Total due or redeemable within 5 years ........ | 135.6 | 58.2 | 201.7 | 78.9 |
| Treas. bonds due in 5-20 years ...... | 54.0 | | 38.6 | |
| Total due or redeemable within 20 years ....... | 189.6 | 81.3 | 240.3 | 93.9 |
| Treas. bonds due after 20 years... | 43.6 | | 15.5 | |
| Total public issues ........... | 233.1 | 100.0 | 255.8 | 100.0 |
| Noninterest-bearing and matured debt | 1.5 | | 4.3 | |
| Special issues to govt. trust funds | 24.6 | | 43.4 | |
| Total public debt | $259.1 | | $303.5 | |

*Including Armed Forces Leave Bonds. †Including nonmarketable 2¾s of 1975-80 convertible on demand into 1½% five-year Treasury notes and nonmarketable Foreign Currency Series.

Note: Details may not add to totals because of rounding.

1960, six advance refundings—"operations leap-frog"—have been accomplished. Bondholders have been invited, usually well before maturity, to exchange securities for longer-dated issues.

In announcing last month's underwriting experiment, Treasury officials said a principal reason for attempting a syndicate offering was the absence of opportunities in the years immediately ahead for achieving significant maturity extension through more advance refundings. Additionally, it was hoped to obtain a broader distribution of long-term Treasury obligations by enlisting the sales efforts of corporate and municipal bond dealers, as well as banks and investment houses regularly in the market for U.S. securities.

A further aim was to test the premise that interest costs to the government could be shaved by inviting competition for long-term Treasury obligations. Some members of Congress, notably Senator Paul Douglas of Illinois, argued that the Treasury could cut its borrowing costs by selling bonds competitively. He hailed the experimental syndicate offering, not commenting on objections that smaller investors who previously could subscribe directly on equal terms with all others now were forced to buy bonds from a member of the winning syndicate and pay a dealer's markup.

### When to Sell Bonds?

Many economists favor the issuance of long-term Treasury bonds in periods of business boom, to help tighten up the supply of credit. This runs into the objection from cheap money advocates that the rates which must be paid in those circumstances are relatively high and the Treasury would be saddled with unnecessary interest costs for decades ahead. A desire of the Eisenhower Administration to put out some long-term bonds in 1959, when heavy deficit financing was required and inflationary fears were running rampant, was defeated by the unwillingness of the Congress to raise the 4¼ per cent limit on the coupon the Treasury may offer on bonds.

The opposite point of view is that Treasury bonds should be sold when business is in a slump and interest rates are relatively low. This encounters the objection that the Treasury, by entering the long-term market, will be cutting into the availability of funds to finance construction activity and corporate capital outlays. Thus the ideal time for the Treasury to put out long-term bonds has been "never" or "hardly ever."

The right answer, however, would seem to be "always." We are going to have a huge federal debt for a very long time to come. There is an agreed need to put some of the debt in long-term form and restore to the Treasury its proper substantial place in the investment market. Treasury bond offerings in periods of boom can help restrain

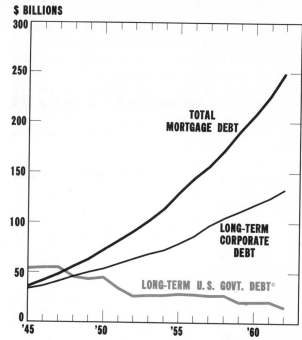

$ BILLIONS

TOTAL MORTGAGE DEBT

LONG-TERM CORPORATE DEBT

LONG-TERM U. S. GOVT. DEBT*

**Long-Term U.S. Government Debt, Total Mortgage Debt, and Corporate Debt (Nonmortgage)**
(December 31 Dates)

* Marketable interest-bearing public debt, excluding official holdings, maturing in over 10 years. All issues classified to final maturity except partially tax-exempt issues which are classified to earliest call date.

inflationary pressures and cut down on the amount of debt in the "near money" form of Treasury bills. In periods of slump, offerings can tap part of the excesses of investment funds in the market, reducing its long-term borrowing costs somewhat.

From the investors' standpoint, the Treasury has prejudiced its opportunities in the long-term market by not establishing a firm schedule of periodic offerings. Pension funds, for example, in working out their investment plans, have been discouraged from allocating funds for investment in U.S. obligations because they have had no assurance that additional new offerings would be forthcoming. Many institutional investors have gotten into the habit of totally ignoring U.S. bonds and allocating all funds to the mortgage and municipal and corporate bond markets. A large task of education is required. But the habits of investors can be changed if the Treasury will commit itself to periodic offerings, with amounts and rates adjustable to market conditions when the time arrives.

The task is a big one but it can be accomplished in moderate steps by keeping at the job.

**FIRST NATIONAL CITY BANK**

# HIGHLIGHTS OF 1962

*from the Annual Report of*

## FIRST NATIONAL CITY BANK

## In Our 150th Anniversary Year:

► for the first time total resources exceeded $10 billion.

► an increase of $770 million in deposits brought the total to $9.1 billion at the year end.

► these additional funds were put to work mostly by expanding loans to $5.0 billion, a new high.

► depositors were paid $67 million in interest on domestic time and savings deposits.

► salary and related payments totaled $115 million to 19,800 staff members here and abroad.

► taxes paid or set aside in the U. S. and overseas amounted to $54 million.

► net operating earnings were $74 million, equal to $5.80 per share of capital stock, compared with $5.70 in 1961, based on the 12,784,496 shares outstanding at the year end.

► cash dividends continued at the rate of $3.00 per share and a 2% stock dividend was distributed.

► the bank became one of less than a dozen U. S. companies which have paid cash dividends consecutively for 150 years.

► an addition of $20 million to capital funds increased the book value of each share from $63.28 to $64.86, based on the number of shares outstanding at the year end.

► 16 branches were added to our network of offices serving the New York metropolitan area, bringing the total to 104.

► seven new offices were opened overseas, making the total abroad 91 in 32 countries.

*For copy of complete Annual Report, write the Public Relations Department,*
*First National City Bank, 399 Park Avenue, New York 22, New York.*

# Monthly Economic Letter

## General Business Conditions

Business is holding a steady course, extending along the high plateau of late 1962. Clear signs are absent either of resumed advance or of impending decline. The business attitude is one of watchful waiting for portentous decisions in the area of fiscal policy. The encouragement inspired by plans to reduce income tax rates has been offset to a considerable extent by the disappointment, confusion and irritation aroused by specific proposals.

With the economy moving sideways in recent months, it took very little to tilt many business indicators slightly downward in January. Storms and strikes hampered activity, and industrial production, retail sales, and working hours in manufacturing all declined moderately from December after seasonal adjustment. Outdoor activities, including housing starts, have been particularly hard hit.

Nevertheless, the lack of forward thrust in over-all business activity since mid-1962 cannot be blamed on the weather. Industrial production, as measured by the Federal Reserve index (seasonally adjusted, 1957-59=100) eased 0.2 to 119.0 in January, the lowest figure recorded since June though still only a shade below the 119.8 peak touched in September. Speaking to a symposium sponsored by the American Bankers Association on February 25, President Kennedy described the economy as continuing in a phase of expansion but predicted that, if taxes are not cut, "the country will, in the not too distant future, be struck by its fifth postwar recession, with a heavy loss of jobs and profits, a record-breaking budget deficit, and an increased burden of national debt."

### Consumer Spending vs. Capital Spending

The present situation is best described as mixed. Consumer expenditures have continued to advance. Seasonally adjusted retail sales have held above a $240-billion-a-year rate since November, despite cold weather and newspaper and transit strikes. Surveys show an increase in the number of families planning to make major purchases in the months ahead.

On the other hand, business spending on new plant and equipment—basic to economic growth —has been flattening out. Moreover, businessmen do not appear to be planning much of a rise in outlays from current levels during the year ahead. Hence, many observers have found it surprising that the principal and most immediate stimulus of the Administration's tax program is directed at consumers. These proposals offer little stimulus for several years to come to the larger corporations responsible for the bulk of business capital investment.

Slowdown in inventory accumulation was one of the main influences holding back the rise in gross national product in the latter part of 1962. Stockbuilding declined from an annual rate of nearly $7 billion in the first quarter of 1962 to a rate of about $1 billion in the third and fourth quarters. One big question for the first half of 1963 is whether or not the steel stockpiling pattern of early '62 will recur.

At new car dealers, buildup of stocks in anticipation of the spring selling season is under way. Through February 20, car sales maintained a 13 per cent lead over 1962 and were 1 per cent ahead of 1955. Favorable sales reports have encouraged auto manufacturers to step up first quarter production schedules to 1,950,000 cars. Dealer stocks rose from 827,000 on January 1 to more than a million units by late February.

The steel mills also have experienced concurrent increases in production and inventories. By the week ended February 23, output was up to an annual rate of 108.8 million tons, compared with the January rate of 98.7 million. Until now, very little of this increased production has represented demand by steel users for additional stocks as a hedge against a possible strike this summer.

However, on February 20, General Motors announced its intention of adding 1 million tons of steel to its normal inventory by the end of July. Some other steel customers are following suit.

The steelworkers union has not yet announced whether it will exercise its option of reopening the two-year contract entered into a year ago. The union has the right to do so any time after April 30 and to strike 90 days after such reopening. Here is a case where every sensible consideration dictates a wage standstill. The problem in steel is not inadequate wages, but to reduce costs and get more business. The American Iron and Steel Institute calculates that the industry in 1962 had employment costs of $4.16 per hour, high in comparison with most other American industries and three to six times the costs borne by foreign competitors. It does not make sense for the union to seek higher and higher wages for fewer and fewer workmen.

### Concerns of the Business Community

The continuing pressure being brought to bear by organized labor to force wage increases is one of the prime concerns of the business community. Among labor contracts covering 5,000 or more workers, the U.S. Bureau of Labor Statistics has counted 94 which expire in 1963, and an additional 77 which provide for wage reopening. Altogether, these 171 contracts cover nearly 3 million workers in such important industries as steel, railroads, communications, construction and electrical products.

Recent labor disputes have tended to be prolonged, and some settlements—as in the case of the longshoremen's dispute settled by government intervention—have run far beyond proportions consistent with price stability. Any tendency to base a wage pattern on the longshoremen's contract would inevitably mean a squeeze on profits—and a dampening of the incentive to increase capital investment which the Administration has been seeking to stimulate.

These wage pressures are closely related to a second major concern of business—the balance-of-payments problem, which remains with us despite the success we have had in enlarging foreign exchange income from exports and overseas investments. Speaking at New York University on February 19, Per Jacobsson, Managing Director of the International Monetary Fund, expressed the opinion that the U.S. balance-of-payments deficit, at $2.2 billion for 1962, would be lower this year. This hope is founded, among other things, on some further narrowing of wage differentials as a result of exceptional increases in wage costs being shouldered by Western European and Japanese competitors. Certainly, immense help could be given to the balance of payments, and to the increase of employment opportunities here, if we were to accept his suggestion and seek a respite from wage increases until unemployment has been reduced.

### Doubts About Tax Reductions

A third concern is with the uncertainties of fiscal policy. The business community eagerly wants and needs income tax rate reforms, to relieve tax cost pressures as well as to improve incentives for enterprise. Here the President's fiscal program raised serious doubts as to whether there will be, after all, meaningful tax reductions.

It seemed incongruous that continuing expansion in expenditures and sizable tax rate reductions should be proposed at one and the same time. Even if better restraint on spending can be assumed, the tax program as submitted appeared to have lost focus on needs for increasing incentives for work and reducing incentives for tax avoidance. The emphasis instead was placed on increasing purchasing power and excusing hundreds of thousands of people from paying any income taxes at all. Every citizen needs a personal reminder of the high costs of government and of the benefits it disperses "for free."

Business opposition was further aroused by the suggested deferral for years of effective reduction in rates of income tax payments by larger corporations, and numerous reform innovations that would further complicate the law and take away much of the meaning of the apparent rate reductions. The President has taken a conciliatory point of view, and on February 25 indicated his willingness to drop the reforms from the package and correspondingly to narrow the rate cuts if necessary to get action. Expressing concern that Congress might enact tax cuts of less than $10 billion, the President said that "if we are going to do this, we might as well do it right or not do it at all. . . . I would say the most important thing is to get the bill this year. Whatever is necessary to get that bill, I would support."

## Fiscal Policy Debate

The Administration's fiscal program aroused every variety of criticism. From trade union quarters, unconcerned with budget deficits, emanated criticisms that we should have bigger spending increases and also big tax cuts concentrated even more on relief for people whose income tax liabilities are already the smallest. This would be to deny that marginal rates of income (i.e., after tax) have anything to do with productive effort.

Other critics were disturbed by the failure of the Administration's tax package to give paramount attention to the improvement of incentives to work and enterprise. With a cash deficit now running beyond $8 billion a year, it is a gamble to program major tax reductions. The gamble is safe only under two conditions: that the rate reductions give maximum stimulation to the economy and hence to the base of taxable revenues; and that restraint is brought to bear on expenditures so that a regenerated economy can bring the budget back into balance sooner than the present target date of fiscal '67.

Assurances have been given by high officials, including the Secretary of the Treasury and the Chairman of the Federal Reserve Board, that efforts will be made to insure noninflationary financing of the sizable deficits with which we are confronted. This is right and proper. But, as these responsible officials appreciate, monetary policy standing alone cannot preserve the value of the dollar against the erosive action of undisciplined government expenditure. If the objective of permanent income tax rate cuts is to be achieved, there must be a wholly new attitude toward spending.

### Tax Cut with Trimmings

The necessity of holding 1964 budget expenditures at the 1963 level to make way for tax reduction was stressed by a number of economists and business leaders testifying before the Congressional Joint Economic Committee last month. Concern was voiced not only over the $4.5 billion increase in administrative budget spending to $98.8 billion, but also over the request for $107.9 billion in new obligational authority. In testimony before the Ways and Means Committee, Treasury Secretary C. Douglas Dillon acknowledged that this implied continuing increases in outlays.

Suggestions for specific reductions in spending have not been lacking. Cutbacks are particularly urged in such fields as farm subsidies, foreign economic aid, federal credit programs and housing. Professor Neil H. Jacoby of the University of California at Los Angeles told the JEC that courageous action was needed to put activities in these categories on a "Metrecal" diet since they yield little public welfare per dollar. Other suggestions for trimming include the space program, public power construction, area redevelopment activities and foreign aids. Looming large in obligational authority for new programs are requests for $1.2 billion for omnibus aid to education, $100 million for youth employment opportunities and $100 million for urban mass transportation improvements.

The dangers in the spending trend were brought home dramatically before the JEC by Dr. Arthur F. Burns, president of the National Bureau of Economic Research. He calculated that if federal spending continued to climb at the rate of $5 billion a year, even an economic growth rate of 6 per cent a year could still mean a cumulative deficit of $75 billion before the budget was finally brought into balance around 1972.

Budget Director Kermit Gordon promised the Ways and Means Committee that the Administration would put a lid on nondefense spending and foresaw a balanced budget by fiscal 1967. He predicted that growth in defense and space outlays would be slower in coming years while nondefense outlays would be restrained through a four-point program of cutting down existing programs, increasing government efficiency, levying fees and user charges for services and substituting private credit for government loans.

### Alternative Fiscal Measures

While both the income and outgo sides of the President's budget proposals have evoked widespread criticisms, the case for cutting taxes remains just as strong as ever. Speaking for the Committee for Economic Development, Theodore O. Yntema of the Ford Motor Company suggested that an immediate cut of $6 billion—$4 billion for individuals, $2 billion for corporations—be made to stimulate the economy, and an additional cut of $5 billion be made if government expenditures are held at the fiscal '63 level. Alternatively, Dr. Burns pointed out that part of the revenue lost could be made up by a "sales tax or some other form of indirect taxation."

The substantial consensus that exists for tax reductions was well expressed in statements to the JEC by Dr. Jacoby and Dr. Burns, both of whom served as economic advisers in the Eisenhower Administration:

### Dr. Jacoby:

It seems to me quite evident that our economy has too large a margin of unemployed resources, resulting from a sluggish over-all growth of demand and an insufficient flexibility in adapting to technological changes. It is equally apparent that the primary cause of this condition is an overburdensome and absurdly complex system of federal taxation.

### Dr. Burns:

We can and should carry out this reform without subjecting our nation to the risk of long-range deficits. Other countries of the world—Japan and the nations of Western Europe—have kept redesigning their tax systems throughout the postwar period in the interest of stimulating investment. It is high time that we did the same and on a substantial scale.

Whether we like it or not, financial incentives are a powerful force in economic life. Even countries like Sweden and Yugoslavia, which have social systems that differ from our own have recently revised their tax laws so as to give greater recognition to this fact of human nature. I do not think the United States can afford to act otherwise.

The problem now is to conciliate differences and get on with the job.

## Corporate Earnings in 1962

An unexpectedly good performance in the fourth quarter made 1962 a better year for profits than the business community had been counting on only a few months ago. Compared with 1961, when earnings rose quarter by quarter, the rate of improvement had been shrinking steadily as the year progressed; by the final quarter, the margin of increase was expected to disappear entirely since profits in fourth quarter 1961 were already at an advanced level. But the closing quarter, affected by numerous year-end adjustments, showed a renewed upturn that carried earnings moderately above the year-ago level. Thus, while falling far short of the 23 per cent gain projected by the Administration at the start of the year, earnings for 1962 as a whole still showed a welcome improvement.

Our preliminary tabulation of reports issued by 2,511 corporations shows combined after-tax income of $20.0 billion, an increase of 13 per cent from 1961. For manufacturing companies alone, profits were up 16 per cent.

The improvement was broadly shared. Seventy-one per cent of the companies showed increased earnings over 1961. Cyclical industries, except for steel, tended to set the pace. Most manufacturing lines were joined by the services and transportation groups in reporting substantial gains. The smaller increases were generally turned in by companies in the mining, trade, utilities and financial fields.

Increases in earnings were largely the result of expanding sales volumes and did not represent a basic change in the trend of profitability. Preliminary indications are that profit margins and rates of return on investment were somewhat higher last year, but the degree of improvement was disappointingly small. Intense competition continued to be the rule in most lines of business. In fact, enlarged volumes were frequently accompanied by some weakening of prices, even in industries in which excess capacity was being absorbed. International companies generally benefited from the continuing expansion of business abroad, but the hazards in such operations were brought home by currency depreciation in a number of countries—including Canada, Argentina and Brazil—which not only reduced earnings but also asset valuations.

### Year-End Adjustments

Year-end adjustments for the investment tax credit and the switch-over to shorter depreciation lives permitted under the new Treasury Department guidelines appear to have had no systematic effect on reported earnings. Unless offset by matching entries, faster depreciation write-offs tend to reduce earnings, while the investment credit tends to raise them. (Exactly how the

**Net Income of Leading Manufacturing Corporations for the Fourth Quarter, 1962**
(In Thousands of Dollars)

| No. of Cos. | Industry Groups | Fourth Qr. 1962 | Per Cent Change from Fourth Qr. 1961 | Per Cent Change from Third Qr. 1962 |
|---|---|---|---|---|
| 39 | Food products .......... | $85,667 | + 8 | + 8 |
| 17 | Beverages ............... | 33,974 | + 3 | + 13 |
| 8 | Tobacco products ........ | 72,850 | +10 | + 6 |
| 44 | Textiles & apparel........ | 39,482 | ± 6 | + 23 |
| 18 | Rubber & allied products.. | 47,369 | — 3 | + 21 |
| 41 | Paper & allied products... | 69,766 | + 8 | + 8 |
| 23 | Printing & publishing.... | 15,085 | — 4 | — 29 |
| 54 | Chemicals, paint, etc...... | 262,973 | + 8 | + 6 |
| 34 | Drugs, soap, cosmetics.... | 131,528 | + 7 | — 1 |
| 58 | Petroleum prod. & refining | 849,389 | +16 | + 16 |
| 42 | Cement, glass & stone... | 120,210 | 0 | — 10 |
| 48 | Iron and steel............ | 139,014 | —42 | + 77 |
| 29 | Nonferrous metals ....... | 93,096 | — 5 | + 29 |
| 51 | Fabricated metal prod..... | 64,687 | + 6 | — 17 |
| 90 | Machinery .............. | 161,131 | +16 | + 10 |
| 96 | Elec. equip. & electronics.. | 187,110 | — 3 | + 39 |
| 31 | Automobiles & parts...... | 733,428 | +31 | +151 |
| 25 | Aerospace & rwy. equip... | 57,638 | +18 | + 3 |
| 77 | Other manufacturing .... | 129,015 | — 3 | + 2 |
| 825 | Total manufacturing .....| $3,293,412 | + 8 | + 28 |

investment credit should be handled in corporate accounting remains a point of controversy in the accounting profession and among regulatory commissions.) With the notable exception of the railroads, public utilities and the steel industry, the impact on earnings in most industries appears to have been moderate. In steel, the net effect of the changes was to lower earnings, particularly in the fourth quarter, but no clear-cut trend emerged among public utilities because of conflicting rules issued by various federal and state commissions. For the railroads, however, earnings were raised considerably by the new depreciation rules and investment credit because, under ICC regulations, the saving in taxes results in increased earnings.

A more complete tabulation of corporate profits will appear in the April *Letter*. Along with our usual compilations of profit margins and rates of return by industry, the article will also present statistics on cash flow items which were published for the first time last year.

### Trends in Manufacturing

Among manufacturers, reports of 825 companies show an increase for the fourth quarter of 8 per cent from the year-earlier quarter and a largely seasonal rise of 28 per cent over third quarter 1962. The seasonally adjusted percentage of companies reporting increased earnings over the preceding quarter rose from 46 per cent in the third quarter to 53 per cent in the fourth.

The auto industry had an excellent fourth quarter, as the new 1963 models met with a favorable reception. Though trailing 1955 in unit volume, sales and profits in dollar terms set new records for the year. In addition to good car sales, however, auto makers also benefited from strong demand for trucks.

The steel industry, in contrast, repeated the roller-coaster pattern that has become familiar in years of wage negotiations, with a big first quarter followed by a slump thereafter. Earnings of rubber companies declined despite sharply increased tire demand for new cars and replacements, as price-cutting at retail narrowed profit margins. Results for the major glass companies showed little change. Aluminum producers, who had earlier shown substantial gains with increasing volume, ran into a rash of price cuts in the final quarter. The petroleum industry capped a good year at home and abroad with an excellent fourth quarter performance, as prices showed some strengthening from previously depressed levels.

In the broad electrical equipment and electronics group, year-to-year improvement was narrowed considerably, partly because of year-end adjustments in the fourth quarter. Machinery manufacturers extended their gains throughout the year, with makers of office machinery, farm and construction equipment, and industrial machinery sharing in the upswing. Larger domestic orders offset declining exports as machine tool makers posted better results.

Weak prices were a problem through much of the year in chemicals and paper, but both industries finished the year with gains over 1961. Shoe industry earnings rose sharply from the depressed 1961 level. Year-to-year increases in the food and beverage group narrowed somewhat in the fourth quarter, while tobacco companies came out ahead after trailing in earlier quarters.

| | | Reported Net Income After Taxes | | Per Cent |
|---|---|---|---|---|
| No. of Cos. | Industry Groups | 1961 | 1962 | Change |
| 114 | Food products ........ | $438,556 | $464,701 | + 6 |
| 29 | Beverages ........... | 142,158 | 144,789 | + 2 |
| 10 | Tobacco products .... | 263,730 | 266,433 | + 1 |
| 48 | Textile products ..... | 110,209 | 144,671 | +31 |
| 55 | Clothing and apparel.. | 50,466 | 54,942 | + 9 |
| 22 | Shoes, leather, etc..... | 24,848 | 45,915 | +85 |
| 35 | Rubber & allied prod... | 242,972 | 237,238 | — 2 |
| 20 | Lumber & wood prod.. | 57,639 | 70,134 | +22 |
| 21 | Furniture & fixtures.. | 16,453 | 18,551 | +13 |
| 54 | Paper & allied prod... | 257,891 | 284,840 | +10 |
| 45 | Printing & publishing. | 61,124 | 67,438 | +10 |
| 85 | Chemicals, paint, etc.. | 1,099,663 | 1,231,445 | +12 |
| 49 | Drugs, soap, cosmetics | 451,570 | 461,193 | + 2 |
| 92 | Petrol. prod. & ref.... | 3,105,652 | 3,350,787 | + 8 |
| 59 | Cement, glass, stone... | 366,447 | 384,644 | + 5 |
| 55 | Iron and steel......... | 694,520 | 579,251 | —17 |
| 35 | Nonferrous metals ... | 283,423 | 316,516 | +12 |
| 106 | Fabricated metal prod. | 220,618 | 272,442 | +24 |
| 194 | Machinery .......... | 620,296 | 785,553 | +27 |
| 230 | Elec. eq. & electronics. | 658,590 | 762,811 | +16 |
| 40 | Automobiles & parts.. | 1,405,352 | 2,160,147 | +54 |
| 43 | Aircraft & rwy. equip. | 58,736 | 279,412 | + * |
| 122 | Other manufacturing.. | 374,151 | 412,235 | +10 |
| 1,563 | Total manufacturing.. | 11,005,064 | 12,796,088 | +16 |
| 6 | Metal mining ........ | 15,284 | 17,348 | +14 |
| 24 | Other mining, quarry. | 91,417 | 96,573 | + 6 |
| 30 | Total mining ........ | 106,701 | 113,921 | + 7 |
| 37 | Chain stores—food ... | 199,299 | 201,833 | + 1 |
| 46 | Chains—variety, etc... | 56,272 | 55,046 | — 2 |
| 57 | Dept. & mail order.... | 124,089 | 127,359 | + 3 |
| 122 | Wholesale & misc..... | 128,468 | 137,411 | + 7 |
| 262 | Total trade ......... | 508,128 | 521,649 | + 3 |
| 103 | Class I railroads (ICC) | 384,000 | 574,000 | +50 |
| 28 | Other transportation.. | 26,613 | 38,646 | +45 |
| 131 | Total transportation .. | 410,613 | 612,646 | +49 |
| 152 | Elec. power, gas, etc.. | 1,672,643 | 1,837,145 | +10 |
| 13 | Telephone & telegraph. | 1,421,242 | 1,537,375 | + 8 |
| 165 | Total public utility.... | 3,093,885 | 3,374,520 | + 9 |
| 41 | Amusements ......... | 35,858 | 35,577 | — 1 |
| 16 | Restaurant and hotel.. | 11,010 | 12,836 | +17 |
| 80 | Other bus. ser. & const. | 97,252 | 118,587 | +22 |
| 137 | Total services ....... | 144,120 | 167,000 | +16 |
| † | Commercial banks .... | 1,713,000 | 1,689,000 | — 1 |
| 164 | Investment trusts .... | 638,112 | 711,356 | +12 |
| 34 | Sales finance ........ | 39,318 | 40,485 | + 3 |
| 25 | Real estate .......... | 9,278 | 9,933 | + 7 |
| 223 | Total finance ........ | 2,399,708 | 2,450,774 | + 2 |
| 2,511 | Grand total ......... | $17,668,219 | $20,036,598 | +13 |

**Preliminary Summary of Net Income of Leading Corporations for the Years 1961 and 1962**
(In Thousands of Dollars)

* Increase over 200% not shown. † Federal Reserve Board preliminary tabulation for all member banks; the number of these banks (6,050) is not included in total number of companies.

# The Corporate Income Tax Rate

Of the annual revenue of around $10 billion proposed to be given up under the Administration's tax program, one fourth, or $2.6 billion, would be allocated to corporations. But a proposed speed-up of the tax payment schedule, applicable to corporations with tax liabilities in excess of $100,000 a year, would hold off for six years—until 1969—the full reduction in corporate tax payments. Indeed, as the table suggests, the percentage of income required to be paid by larger corporations would be higher in 1964 and 1965 than under the present rate and payments schedule. The Treasury figures that the payment speed-up will add $1.5 billion a year to the revenues.

### Proposed Corporate Tax Rates and Payment Rates

| Year | Normal Tax | Surtax on Income Over $25,000 | Total on Income Over $25,000 | Payment Rate Applicable to Large Corporations* |
|------|-----------|-------------------------------|------------------------------|------------------------------------------------|
| 1962 | 30% | 22% | 52% | 52% |
| 1963 | 22 | 30 | 52 | 52 |
| 1964 | 22 | 28 | 50 | 56 |
| 1965 | 22 | 25 | 47 | 52.9 |
| 1966 | 22 | 25 | 47 | 51.7 |
| 1967 | 22 | 25 | 47 | 51.7 |
| 1968 | 22 | 25 | 47 | 51.7 |
| 1969 | 22 | 25 | 47 | 47 |

* Tax payments as a per cent of taxable income for a corporation which keeps its accounts on a calendar year basis and has an even flow of taxable income. This does not allow for underpayments as may be permitted.

The Administration proposes for 1963 that the normal and surtax rates be reversed. The normal tax applies to the first $25,000 of taxable income; both normal and surtax apply to income beyond that level. Thus the eight-point reduction in the normal rate would give a slight benefit, up to a maximum of $2,000 per corporation, beginning this year. The benefit could be sizable to large enterprises operating through chains of separately incorporated units. To take away the incentive for "proliferation of corporate units," the Administration would, over a transitional period, restrict members of an affiliated group to one $25,000 surtax exemption. The 2 per cent penalty on the filing of consolidated returns would be eliminated and also the tax on dividends received from subsidiaries.

The plan is to have the combined corporate rate drop from the present 52 per cent to 50 per cent in 1964 and 47 per cent in 1965 and thereafter. This will benefit reported profits in 1964-65 and encourage shareholders to expect higher dividends. But the acceleration of payments will, in these next two years, be increasing the cash drain for tax payments. For calendar year corporations this added drain will begin on April 15, 1964. April will become a new corporate tax payment date, making five corporate tax payment dates a year.

Secretary Dillon has minimized the effect of payment acceleration on corporate cash positions. He has pointed out that some corporations —General Motors and Du Pont are prime examples—acquire and set aside short-term government securities to cover their income tax liabilities. For such corporations, acceleration can simply mean loss of interest on funds accumulated to pay taxes.

Yet it is more common for corporations to combine their accrued tax liabilities along with other current obligations. Until payment falls due the money is available to meet current payrolls and carry inventories and accounts receivable. Here acceleration of payments will require a company to go out and raise more funds. If dividends were to be increased at the same time, needs for raising additional funds would be intensified.

## Back to Pre-Korea

The President in his tax message spoke of the proposed drop in the combined corporate rate from 52 to 47 per cent as "ending the role of the government as a senior partner in business profits." This is certainly overdue. In fact, the rate is already scheduled by existing law to go down to 47 per cent effective July 1, 1963. Technically, the Administration is proposing deferral of the 47 per cent rate until 1965.

The Revenue Act of 1951 enacted the 52 per cent rate as a temporary measure, due to drop to 47 per cent on March 31, 1954. While personal income tax increases embraced in that law were allowed to expire in 1954, and also the Korean War excess profits tax, the scheduled drop to 47 per cent in the corporate tax rate has been postponed year after year, most recently in June 1962 when the 52 per cent rate was extended still once again to June 30, 1963. Thus the direct way to get the corporate rate down to 47 per cent is simply to refrain from extending the 52 per cent any further.

Many people have referred to 47 per cent as the pre-Korean corporate tax rate. Actually, the rate before Korea was 38 per cent, set by the Revenue Act of 1945 and kept in force down to September 23, 1950 when, after the outbreak of the Korean War, the Revenue Act of 1950 advanced the rate to 42 per cent, retroactive to January 1, 1950. As the accompanying table shows, the Revenue Act of 1950 and the Excess

### Combined Corporate Income Tax Rates*

| | 1946-49 | 1950 | 1951 | 1952 | Enacted |
|---|---|---|---|---|---|
| Revenue Act of 1945..... | 38% | 38% | | | Nov. 8, 1945 |
| Revenue Act of 1950..... | | 42% | 45% | | Sept. 23, 1950 |
| Excess Profits Tax Act.... | | | 47% | | Jan. 3, 1951 |
| Revenue Act of 1951..... | | | 50¾% | 52% | Oct. 20, 1951 |

* For calendar year corporations. Excludes excess profits taxes when applicable.

Profits Tax Act of 1951 successively hiked the 1951 rate to 45 and then 47 per cent. That is where the 47 per cent rate got into the law.

But the 47 per cent rate was superseded before it could become generally and fully effective. On October 20, the Revenue Act of 1951 increased the rate to 50¾ per cent, retroactive to January 1, 1951, and to 52 per cent for 1952 with an expiration date of March 31, 1954.

### Impact of the Corporate Tax Rate

Against this background, the most obvious flaw in the corporate tax rate proposals is that, with the acceleration of payments, the full benefits of the proposed reductions will be deferred until 1969. If we want an energetically expanding economy we should be thinking of still lower rates long before that. Except for excess profits taxes, which destroy themselves with their complexities, distortions and manifest inequities, the history of corporate tax rates is that they go up but rarely down.

As the chart shows, the corporate tax rates invoked during World War I were never undone. And the same is true of increases during the Great Depression, World War II and the Korean War. Now we are having to face the consequences of what these cumulative increases are doing to the structure of our economy, the economics of capital investment and our capacity for competitive industrial growth. Rates like 50 per cent, whether they apply to corporations or individuals, bring some strange perversions of incentive. Yet, although many scholarly studies point to the unwisdom of taxing corporations so heavily, there is only limited public understanding of the effects.

Perhaps the most logical case can be made in favor of not taxing corporate profits as such at all. President Franklin D. Roosevelt in 1936 seemed to have something like this in mind when he suggested that "the aim, as a matter of fundamental equity, should be to seek equality of tax burden on all corporate income whether distributed or withheld from the beneficial owners." The simplest approach to this objective might be, as some students have suggested, to make dividends deductible on the corporate income tax form just as interest is at present. Thus profits distributed as dividends would be taxed solely under the personal income tax structure and the undistributed profits would be taxed at an undistributed profits tax rate. What the late President had in mind was somehow applying personal tax rates to undistributed profits but this would run into serious practical difficulties.

Meanwhile, it should be noted that the Administration proposes repealing the dividends received exclusion and credit. These, enacted in 1954, offer a modest relief from double taxation of corporate profits distributed as dividends. Even with the dividends received credit, federal taxes on corporate profits paid out in dividends reach up to 93.8 per cent, not to mention state and local levies on the same income. Certainly it would take some big cuts in personal and corporate income tax rates to bring this extreme rate of taxation down to a sensible level.

### A Tax on Investment

There are, of course, those who argue that the corporate income tax is not borne by the shareholder at all but rather by the consumer. People of this mind nevertheless must see that high rates of tax on corporations organized for profit puts them at a serious disadvantage *vis-a-vis* domestic cooperatives and also overseas competitors. We will simply erode the base of revenue if we put excessive penalties on profit-seeking enterprise as

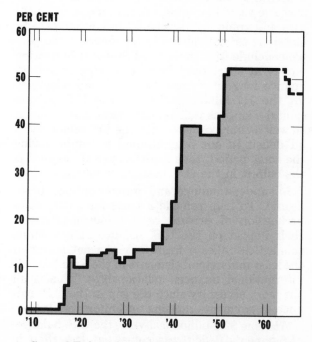

**General Federal Income Tax Rate for Corporations**

Note: The rates shown are the standard rates on taxable corporate income over $25,000. No account is taken of excess profits taxes. The 1909-12 levy on income was called an excise tax.

though encouragement of nonprofit ventures were our highest policy aim.

However the burden of corporate taxation is distributed, it has undeniable distorting effects upon the economy. Since profits represent a return on investment, heavy taxation of corporate income represents an appropriation from return on capital. A capital investment has to be twice as profitable before tax to be profitable at all after tax. Thus the result is to cut down the range of profitable investment opportunities. And the investments that became uneconomic in this way could have brought cost reductions and thus permitted increase in the national product, decrease in prices and stronger competitive power of American products in world markets. The more capital an industry can use economically the more it is discriminated against.

### Dr. Schmidt's Testimony

Dr. Emerson Schmidt, Director of Economic Research for the U.S. Chamber of Commerce, told the Congressional Joint Economic Committee on February 15 that "should a tax cut fail this year, the economy may well be retarded."

He added:

If the tax program goes through in its proposed form, corporation tax collections will be greatly accelerated and, to some extent, this will impair the working capital and interest earnings of corporate enterprises.

The suggested cuts and collection acceleration will mean that, in the above sense, the corporate tax rate will not fall below 52 per cent until 1966 and will not reach the proposed figure of 47 per cent until 1969.

\* \* \*

The corporation income tax has virtually no defenders except those who view it through the eyes of the revenue collectors and those who see it as something of a recession snubber.

Its incidence is capricious and uncertain. It raises the general price level. It is largely a disguised sales tax. It has put the corporate form of doing business at a disadvantage. . . . It retards new investment. It reduces investment per worker. It raises the average age of plant and equipment. . . .

It distorts investment decisions because of its severe bite. It consumes an enormous amount of time of high-priced talent in problems of compliance and efforts to avoid its burden. Virtually all major business decisions are tax-oriented.

In the face of these points, it is hard to understand the tardiness with which any cut was proposed, the smallness of the cut proposed in January 1963, and the spread of the cut over three years.

## Private Capital in Our Balance of Payments

Some people blame our persistent balance-of-payments deficit on private capital outflows. Weighing the $7 billion directly invested by American businesses in foreign countries over the past five years in mining, oil, manufacturing, utilities and trade against the $7 billion increase in our short-term liabilities to foreigners, these people conclude that the United States is borrowing money at short term from its foreign friends to finance long-term investments abroad. Comparing the $17 billion total outflow of U.S. private capital—long- as well as short-term, and recorded as well as unrecorded—with the $16 billion overall deficit in our international accounts during the same period, they say that private capital is the culprit in the U.S. balance of payments.

Misunderstandings and misconceptions beget legend. To help provide a basis for better comprehension of private capital movements and their impact on the U.S. balance of payments, this article takes a fresh look at what is one of the least understood elements in the Free World's international financial relationships. This is all the more necessary since the gap in the U.S. balance of payments remains uncomfortably large.

At some $2.2 billion last year, the U.S. balance-of-payments deficit was somewhat less than in 1961 (and roughly $1.5 billion less than the average for 1958-60). But last year's results reflect a number of special receipts, including prepayments

by foreign governments of debts to the U.S. Government, advance payments on German military

### Private and Government Sectors in the U.S. Balance of Payments, 1960-62
(In Billions of Dollars)

| | 1960-61 Avg. | | 1962* | |
| | Private | Govt. | Private | Govt. |
|---|---|---|---|---|
| Exports | $17.7 | $2.0 | $18.2 | $2.5 |
| Income on investments.. | 3.1 | 0.4 | 3.6 | 0.5 |
| Other services | 3.9 | 0.5 | 4.1 | 0.7 |
| Long-term capital inflows | 0.5 | .. | 0.5 | 0.5† |
| Repayments to U.S. Govt. | .. | 1.0‡ | .. | 1.3‡ |
| **Total Receipts** | 25.1 | 3.9 | 26.4 | 5.5 |
| Imports | —14.6 | .. | —16.2 | .. |
| Services | — 5.4 | —0.9 | — 5.7 | —1.0 |
| Private l.-t. investments | — 2.6 | .. | — 2.4 | .. |
| Military cash outlays.... | .. | —3.0 | .. | —3.0 |
| Govt. grants and loans.. | .. | —3.8 | .. | —4.3 |
| **Total Payments** | —22.6 | —7.6 | —24.3 | —8.3 |
| **Basic Position** | 2.6 | —3.8 | 2.1 | —2.8 |
| U.S. short-term capital outflows: Increase (—) in private sh.-t. assets abroad.... | — 1.4 | .. | — 0.6 | .. |
| Unrecorded outflows .. | — 0.6 | .. | — 0.9 | .. |
| **Over-all Position** | $ 0.6 | $—3.8 | $0.6 | $—2.8 |

\* Educated guesses based on preliminary and incomplete data.
† U.S. Treasury medium-term borrowings in Italy and Switzerland and other special transactions. ‡ Includes debt prepayments: $689 million in 1961 and $666 million in 1962.

Source: Derived from U.S. Department of Commerce, *Survey of Current Business*.

purchases here and the U.S. Treasury's medium-term borrowings in Italy and Switzerland. Without these special receipts, singled out in the table, last year's deficit would have been of the order of $3 billion—practically the same as in 1961. Such special receipts have not "solved" our problem; they merely have slowed the rise in amounts of dollars held abroad and have temporarily lightened the strains until we succeed in bringing our payments into better shape.

In the table, the conventional statistics are arranged to split the private and government sectors of the balance of payments. We can see clearly the large surplus generated by the U.S. private economy on commercial goods and services (i.e., excluding those financed by government aid). For the past three years, the commercial surplus has averaged some $4.5 billion. It covers by a comfortable margin U.S. private capital outflows of all sorts and those outflows, in turn, build investment income for the support of the balance of payments in the future.

In short, in the accounts that are affected primarily by market forces, the United States has a surplus. The trouble is that the surplus earned by private enterprise is not big enough to cover also the U.S. Government's military outlays abroad and the foreign exchange cost of U.S. aid.

### "Hide and Seek"

A further rearrangement in the balance-of-payments statistics, as computed by the U.S. Department of Commerce, throws additional light on private capital movements. For a variety of reasons, U.S. private short-term capital outflows are treated, in the official bookkeeping, quite differently from foreign private short-term capital inflows into the United States. When an American citizen makes a deposit in a Canadian bank or buys a Canadian Treasury bill, the transaction is recorded as a capital outflow; but when a Canadian makes a deposit in a U.S. bank or buys a U.S. Treasury bill, the transaction is considered as one means of "measuring" and "financing" the U.S. balance-of-payments "deficit." (In official parlance, terms like these are carefully avoided; but in plain English this is what it is all about.) The other means of financing the deficit —and, perhaps, the truly meaningful ones—are sales of gold and additions to liquid dollar assets in the hands of foreign governments, central banks and the International Monetary Fund.

Statistics rely on the concepts and educated guesswork of statisticians. The yardstick for "measuring" the payments deficit has been designed to encompass all foreign-held liquid dollar assets—whether official or private—on the ground that they are all potential claims on the U.S. gold stock. This approach is undoubtedly helpful in appraising the over-all international liquidity position of the United States, but it tends to obscure the nature of foreign private short-term capital inflows. It treats them as if they were merely a passive consequence of the state of the balance of payments. They are, in fact, the result of active decisions of foreign commercial banks, businesses and investors to place deposits in U.S. banks or make short-term investments in our market; these now total $8 billion.

Foreign private short-term capital inflows are influenced by international differences in interest rates as well as by differences in availability of lendable funds and credit needs, here and in the main financial centers abroad. In the same way, U.S.-owned private short-term funds move into and out of the United States. We can place foreign inflows side-by-side with U.S. outflows.

The practice of the United Kingdom and some other countries is to net private short-term capital inflows against private short-term capital outflows. By reason of the special position of the dollar as the currency to which other nations relate the value of their monies, we have a different way, as described above, of calculating our balance-of-payments position. But it is relevant to note that if we followed the British practice, our over-all payments deficit would be distinctly smaller than on present official reckoning: the average figure for 1960-61 works out at $2.4 billion, instead of $3.2 billion, and for 1962 at $1.9 billion.

The economic significance of short-term capital flows is, of course, in no way affected by the methods used to compile statistics. Such flows are sometimes regarded as "footloose" or "hot"

---

### Private Capital Movements
(In Billions of Dollars)

|  | 1950-55 Avg. | 1956-57 Avg. | 1958-59 Avg. | 1960-61 Avg. | 1962* |
|---|---|---|---|---|---|
| **Short-term** | | | | | |
| U.S. outflow ...... | $—0.2 | $—0.4 | $—0.2 | $—1.4 | $—0.6 |
| Foreign inflow† ... | +0.3 | +0.6 | +1.0 | +0.8 | +0.3 |
| **Long-term** | | | | | |
| U.S. outflow: | | | | | |
| Direct investment | —0.7 | —2.0 | —1.2 | —1.6 | —1.2 |
| Portfolio securities, etc. ...... | —0.3 | —0.7 | —1.2 | —0.9 | —1.2 |
| Total .......... | —0.9 | —2.7 | —2.4 | —2.5 | —2.4 |
| Foreign inflow .... | +0.2 | +0.4 | +0.3 | +0.5 | +0.5 |
| **Summary** | | | | | |
| U.S. outflow ...... | —1.1 | —3.1 | —2.6 | —3.9 | —3.0 |
| Foreign inflow .... | +0.5 | +1.1 | +1.3 | +1.3 | +0.8 |
| Errors and omissions‡ .......... | +0.3 | +0.7 | +0.5 | —0.6 | —0.9 |

* Estimated. † As measured by increases in liquid assets held in the U.S. by foreign commercial banks, international financial bodies other than the IMF, and other foreigners. ‡ This item is believed to reflect mainly short-term capital flows.

Source: Derived from U.S. Department of Commerce, *Survey of Current Business*. Data for foreign short-term capital inflows during 1950-59, which are not available from U.S. Government publications, are based on estimates published by Hal B. Lary in *Problems of the United States as World Trader and Banker*, National Bureau of Economic Research, 1963.

money hopping from country to country in search of gains from exchange speculation. At times of uncertainty about major currencies, some short-term capital flows across national boundaries in search of protection against currency depreciation. But, in the ordinary course of business, such funds—whether U.S.- or foreign-owned—represent responses to trade fluctuations and interest-rate differentials. Sometimes, as when the United Kingdom, Canada and Japan have invoked tight money to meet balance-of-payments crises, resultant outflows of U.S. private short-term capital have served to relieve intolerable strains on the official reserves of other countries.

### Bricks and Mortar

A substantial part of U.S. private long-term capital outflows is for direct investment in productive enterprise—bricks and mortar. Such outflows reached a peak in 1956-57, when new funds going to Canada and Latin America were exceptionally large. These subsequently declined, but at the same time flows were increased into Europe under the stimulus of the vigorous economic growth of the Common Market. More recently, U.S. direct investments in Europe have shown signs of leveling off as costs there have been rising and profit margins narrowing, and as productive capacities in some industries have moved temporarily ahead of demands.

These outflows of new funds, as recorded in the balance-of-payments statistics, are not, however, the full measure of the contribution made

**Private Long-term Investments, Europe and U.S., 1961**

(In Millions of Dollars)

|  | U.S. Investments in Europe | European Investments in the U.S. |
| --- | --- | --- |
| Direct Investments .... | | |
| Common Market ..... | $ 3,041 | $ 1,558 |
| France ............ | 840 | 175 |
| Germany .......... | 1,170 | 120 |
| Netherlands ....... | 308 | 1,023 |
| United Kingdom ..... | 3,523 | 2,484 |
| Switzerland ......... | 408 | 830 |
| Total Europe ........ | 7,655 | 5,129 |
| Portfolio Investments* | | |
| Total Europe ........ | 3,685 | 10,150 |
| Total ................. | $11,340 | $15,279 |

\* Corporate stocks, corporate, state and municipal bonds, and others.

Sources: U.S. Dept. of Commerce, *Survey of Current Business,* August 1962; *Foreign Business Investments in the United States,* 1962.

by American business to capital formation in host countries. In addition to new funds going abroad, American business year after year invests about $1 billion of its earnings abroad in expanding foreign operations. When capital flows, shown in the table on the preceding page, are combined with undistributed profits, it follows that in recent years about $2.5 billion has been added annually to direct investments abroad. If depreciation and depletion funds are added to fresh capital outflows and reinvested earnings, a figure of close to $5 billion is obtained—perhaps the most realistic measure of American gross investment abroad.

American business brings home large and growing amounts of earnings; last year, such receipts were up about 6 per cent from 1961. Indeed, remittances of income from direct investments abroad are much larger than outflows of new funds going into plants abroad. Over the past ten years, remitted income has exceeded the outflow of new funds by $9 billion. It is—next to exports —the largest single source of income in the balance of payments.

### A Two-Way Street

In the world today, business is becoming more and more internationalized. Long-term capital is flowing not only from here abroad but also from the rest of the world into the United States. A number of major companies operating here are foreign-controlled; American stocks and bonds are widely held abroad. Interestingly, Europe's private long-term investments here, at some $15 billion, are larger than the $11 billion of U.S. private long-term investments in Europe.

American investment and American know-how are welcome, especially when they lead to modernization of plant and higher productivity. Inflows of U.S. capital have played a part, both di-

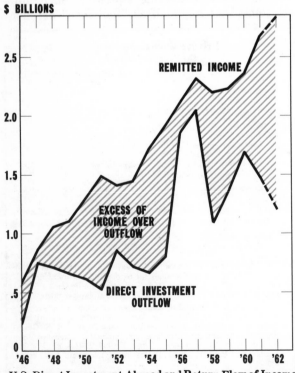

**\$ BILLIONS**

REMITTED INCOME

EXCESS OF INCOME OVER OUTFLOW

DIRECT INVESTMENT OUTFLOW

U.S. Direct Investment Abroad and Return Flow of Income

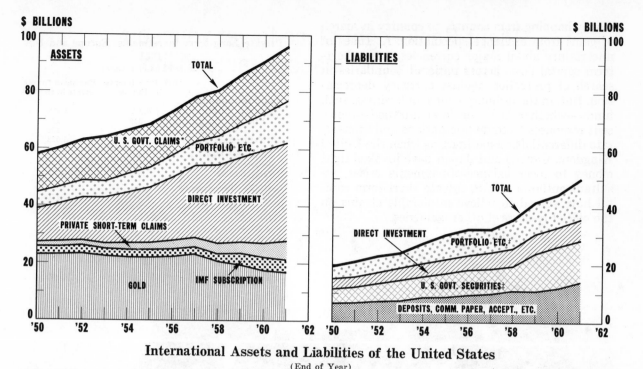

## International Assets and Liabilities of the United States
### (End of Year)

\* Excluding U.S. Government short-term claims, the bulk of which is in foreign currencies, and also World War I loans. † Other than U.S. Government bond and note holdings. ‡ Including holdings of international financial institutions ($4.6 billion in 1961) and estimated foreign holdings of U.S. currency ($0.9 billion in 1961).

rectly and indirectly, in the improvement of the balances of payments of many European countries. If, as it appears, there may now be some doubts about the benefits of foreign investment, it should be recalled that this is nothing new. In the mid-19th century, a Senator from South Carolina put the case in these terms: "No man . . . can deny that foreign capital, ay, *British capital*, has been the pap on which we fed; the strong aliment which supported and stimulated our industry, even to the present day; the Southern people, although they have received the goods and sold their crops to British agents and British factors, whether in their own cities or those further north, are not the less republican, nor the less independent in their politics, nor the less free from foreign partialities."

It has been hinted, here as well as abroad, that the U.S. Government should informally control U.S. long-term direct investments abroad as well as capital issues for foreign account in the New York market. The Administration has—rightly— rejected such suggestions. Whatever immediate advantage might be gained for our balance of payments by controls over U.S. long-term capital outflows would be more than offset by the damage such controls would do to the standing of the dollar as a reliable and freely usable currency.

To provide some relief to our capital account, the U.S. Government has properly urged other countries to free and broaden their own capital markets and make them more easily accessible to

domestic as well as to foreign borrowers. At the same time, as President Kennedy has suggested, we can, by reducing income tax rates to stimulate our economic growth, make the United States more attractive to foreign investors.

### Our International Balance Sheet

From recorded capital movements and certain other data, it is possible to construct a balance sheet for the United States, showing private and governmental international assets and liabilities.

The balance-of-payments deficit has not resulted in a loss of our international wealth. Our losses of gold have been more than offset by increases in earning assets held overseas. U.S. private long-term investment abroad exceeds the long-term investment of foreigners in our own country by $27 billion. In addition, the U.S. Government holds foreign government obligations, some of which are being repaid more rapidly to reduce our payments deficit.

Yet, the strength of our international balance sheet must not make us complacent about the major job that remains to be done to bring our international payments into better order. With our economic resources, skills and productivity, our task may well be easier than that many other nations must face year in and year out; but we can succeed only if we safeguard the real value of the dollar—measured, as it must be, by what it will buy in commodity markets and earn in investment markets.

**FIRST NATIONAL CITY BANK**

# Right Bank–right place to get your son started on the financial facts of life

SESSION IN SECURITY

One of our officers is showing two customers around the Bank—First National City, that is. "The Story of Banking" display invariably proves of genuine interest to customers and friends of all ages. △ Earlier, Dad enjoyed a meeting upstairs to review his personal financial planning. He was anxious to arrange his corporate executive benefits advantageously, and to coordinate these  with other family assets. Experienced people in our Trust Division are glad to help get these matters organized. △ Could you use a bit of help? (A surprising number of busy executives have given this important subject little thought.) A suggestion: Write or call for a copy of our new booklet titled "Executive's Guide to Personal Financial Planning." No obligation. **FIRST NATIONAL CITY BANK**

TRUST DIVISION, DEPARTMENT F, 399 PARK AVENUE, NEW YORK 22, NEW YORK          MEMBER FEDERAL DEPOSIT INSURANCE CORPORATION

# Monthly Economic Letter

## General Business Conditions

Winter has passed and spring has arrived without the business slump so widely feared last summer. It is true that the Bureau of Labor Statistics' unemployment rate edged up to 6.1 per cent in February, compared to a 5.6 per cent average for the year 1962. It is also true that stockpiling of steel, raising March production of the metal to an annual rate around 115 million tons, is adding a spurious element to industrial activity. Nevertheless, counterbalancing favorable forces are undeniable: a projected further increase in business spending for plant and equipment, the maintenance of employment at a record level, and new peaks for retail trade. The impression in the investment community is that corporate profits for the first quarter will show no more than a seasonal decline from the good results of fourth quarter 1962. This would tend to corroborate expectations of a slowly rising curve of plant and equipment spending.

Figures for February, when adjusted for recurrent seasonal fluctuations, show a picture of broadly sustained levels of activity. Retail sales for the month, as in January, ran 7 per cent ahead of the corresponding period of 1962. New car sales through March 20 maintained a 13 per cent lead over 1962. People keep adding to their savings accounts, and thus indirectly are helping to finance construction activity, state and local government outlays, and business borrowings. At the same time, they themselves have not been reluctant to borrow for specific purposes of buying homes and cars. Suspicions that some persons may be anticipating tax cuts, and spending ahead, cannot be confirmed although there is no question but that failure of action on taxes would have an unfavorable reaction.

The Federal Reserve index of industrial production (seasonally adjusted, 1957-59=100), at 119.1 for February, held within the remarkably narrow band of 118.9 to 119.8 that has prevailed now for eight months. Likewise, employment shows a sideways pattern on a seasonally adjusted basis; except for a dip in November, the total (including the armed forces) has held close to 71 million for seven months dating back to August.

### Recession or Advance?

Businessmen and economists have the challenging task of evaluating the risks and probabilities of a business recession. Officials of the Administration, from the President down, have warned that the period of business expansion, dating from the last cyclical low point in February 1961, is two years old. It may be observed that, in the eight peacetime cycles since 1919, the economy on the average has turned down after

28 months of expansion. Yet business fluctuations have never been evenly rhythmical, either in durations of time or amplitudes of fluctuation. The average cycle is one that never happened, an average of different sizes and shapes.

Some observers entertain a suspicion that when the statistics are all in, and converted from preliminary to final forms, it may be found retrospectively that business did indeed make a peak sometime this spring or even last winter. But this is far from the commonly accepted view. The general expectation is sustained activity, founded not only on continuing moderate expansion of trade and incoming orders but also on the conservatism of business inventories in relationship to sales and the ready availability of credit. Relatively tight money has preceded most important downturns in activity.

Expectations that the next phase may be one of renewed advance in production and employment have been strengthened by the latest survey of business plans for plant and equipment spending. The survey, by the U.S. Department of Commerce and the Securities and Exchange Commission, indicates that such outlays this year may reach $39.1 billion, 5 per cent higher than the 1962 total of $37.3 billion and 6 per cent above the old peak of $37.0 billion back in 1957. The survey results are supported by corporate announcements of stepped-up investment programs, better rates of new order inflow for machinery builders, and continuing rise in capital appropriations as reported by Conference Board—Newsweek tabulations.

## The Investment Lag

For several years now, the pressure of underutilized capacity in certain lines has fostered competitive price shaving and has blunted management's desire for additional capital investment. However, the economy appears to be gradually growing up to the capacity installed in the capital-spending boom of 1955-57 which followed the 1954 tax reductions. Moreover, with the high cost of labor as well as sharply competitive conditions in most markets, business managements are under pressure to improve cost controls and to minimize work forces by investment in modernized labor-saving equipment.

While investment to save on labor utilization may reduce employment, the process of investment actually enlarges employment opportunities. This is apparent when one considers that it typically takes years for a company to get back, through current cost savings, the money spent on cost-reducing investments. The investments themselves largely go to meet payrolls in capital goods industries.

Even though prospective plant and equipment spending for 1963 will achieve a record level, the rate of investment is a source of dissatisfaction to the Administration. Viewed in perspective of the total economy, business fixed investment in producers' durable goods and private nonresidential construction has been lagging for years. This is brought out in the chart which compares business and consumer investment since 1947, with the influence of rising prices eliminated by deflation of the figures into 1954 dollars.

In 1962, after adjusting for price inflation, business fixed investment was lower than it was in 1956 or 1957 and only 27 per cent greater than it was fifteen years earlier. Consumer expenditures for durable goods and homes were up more than one fifth in the past five years and approximately doubled over the fifteen years 1947-62.

This analysis supports the businessman's point that the emphasis in reforming taxes should be on incentives to produce, invest and offer employment. This is the kind of a tax bill we will have to have if we are to achieve the objectives of invigorated economic growth and fuller utilization of our labor force without precipitating a wave of inflation and a worsening of our international balance-of-payments position.

The hope in the business community is that the Congress, in fashioning tax legislation, will keep its eye on the goal of strengthening incentives and avoid being distracted by political considerations into giving up revenues on a massive scale for the sheer purpose of inflating amounts of money looking for goods to buy.

**BILLIONS OF 1954 $**

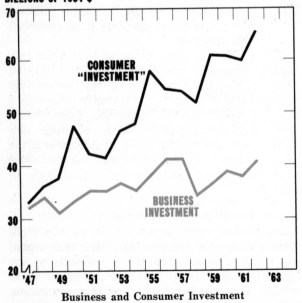

**Business and Consumer Investment**

(Annually in constant 1954 dollars)

Note: Consumer "investment" consists of expenditures on consumer durable goods and private residential construction. Business fixed investment consists of producers' durable goods plus private nonresidential construction.

# Review of Corporate Profits in 1962

The more comprehensive financial reports becoming available in the past month confirm the improvement in aggregate profits indicated by our preliminary tabulation for 1962. Nevertheless, returns on sales and net worth remain at the relatively depressed levels of the past five years.

With the inclusion of additional reports that have raised the number of corporations to 3,831, this bank's tabulation now shows combined net income of $23.9 billion, an increase of 13 per cent from 1961. Among manufacturers alone, 2,316 corporations have reported profits of $14.7 billion, up 16 per cent from the preceding year.

Outside of manufacturing, increases were shown in all the major divisions, though size of gain varied considerably. Profits barely topped 1961 results in finance, rose moderately in the utilities, mining, trade and services, and climbed sharply among railroads (in considerable part as a consequence of ICC accounting technicalities).

Despite the improvement in profit totals, analysis of the data indicates that the pressure on earnings that became intensified after 1957 has been only partially relieved. For all nonfinancial corporations included in our tabulation, the average margin on sales edged up from 5.5 cents per sales dollar in 1961 to 5.7 cents last year. The pattern is similar but even less favorable when earnings are figured as a return on investment. At the beginning of 1962, book net assets (also known as net worth, stockholders' equity, or capital and surplus) of reporting companies totaled $263.9 billion, an increase of 8 per cent from the previous year. Earnings, calculated as a return on this investment, rose from 8.7 per cent in 1961 to 9.1 per cent.

For a variety of reasons described in the January 1963 issue of this *Letter*, our figures for profits on sales and return on investment considerably overstate the results that will emerge from the fully comprehensive tabulations of the Internal Revenue Service about November 1964 when *Statistics of Income* for corporations, 1962, is due to be published. In the simplest terms, our figures are biased in favor of success, embracing almost all of the largest and most profitable corporations. Moreover, our figures unavoidably are affected by double counting of dividends paid by one domestic corporation to another.*

If our figures are used as a guide to movements in the IRS figures for 1961 and 1962, it would appear that the IRS figures may show a margin on sales for all nonfinancial corporations

* In calculating margins on sales, we do adjust General Motors' dividends out of net income of Du Pont.

of 2.3 per cent for the five years 1958-62, compared with 2.7 per cent for 1953-57 and 4.5 per cent for 1948-52. Similarly, the IRS data on rate of return on net worth for all corporations would come out to 5.7 per cent for 1958-62, compared with 7.6 per cent for 1953-57 and 9.7 per cent for 1948-52.

For manufacturing corporations, which account for about three fifths of reported earnings in this bank's tabulation, rates of profit exhibit the same general tendencies. As shown in the table, profit margins last year increased from 5.2 cents per sales dollar in 1961 to 5.5 cents, with 26 out of 41 industry groups showing improvement. Figured as a return on net assets, manufacturers' profits rose from 9.9 per cent in the preceding year to 10.9 per cent in 1962. On the IRS levels, profits of manufacturers in 1962 were apparently about 3 cents on the sales dollar and around 7 cents on the invested dollar.

Such calculations as these explain why many corporations still complain of the profit squeeze even though profit totals have reached a new peak. In terms of money invested and amounts of business done, earnings have yet to show the real pickup needed to spur investment and the whole economy.

### Accounting Changes and Cash Flows

The difficulties in estimating corporate earnings totals and calculating rates of profitability have been compounded in the past year by the Treasury Department's issuance of new depreciation guidelines and the enactment of the 7 per cent investment tax credit (3 per cent for most public utilities). On the whole, however, the impact on reported earnings from these changes has not been large, except in the case of railroads, steel and public utilities. The great majority of companies have treated the investment tax credit, in effect, as a saving in cost of new equipment with all or part of the benefit spread over the life of the asset. On the other hand, firms adopting shorter equipment lives for both tax purposes and shareholder reports typically have experienced some reduction in current earnings.

The changes in federal tax policy, as reflected in the shorter depreciation lives and the investment credit, are expressions of the growing recognition of the importance of the internal generation of cash in business finance. Cash flow—here defined as the sum of depreciation charges and retained income—is more and more regarded as a basic factor in determining the financial capabilities of business to meet growing working capital requirements and to replace and expand plant and equipment investment.

# Net Income of Leading Corporations for the Years 1961 and 1962

### (Dollar Figures in Thousands)

| No. of Cos. | Industrial Groups | Reported Net Income After Taxes 1961 | Reported Net Income After Taxes 1962 | Per Cent Change | Book Net Assets Jan. 1-a 1961 | Book Net Assets Jan. 1-a 1962 | % Return on Net Assets-a 1961 | % Return on Net Assets-a 1962 | % Margin on Sales-b 1961 | % Margin on Sales-b 1962 |
|---|---|---|---|---|---|---|---|---|---|---|
| 16 | Baking | $ 58,993 | $ 61,144 | + 4 | $ 608,533 | $ 624,113 | 9.7 | 9.8 | 2.7 | 2.7 |
| 12 | Dairy products | 104,026 | 109,367 | + 5 | 947,991 | 1,031,140 | 11.0 | 10.6 | 2.6 | 2.7 |
| 21 | Meat packing | 45,350 | 53,570 | +18 | 975,603 | 991,699 | 4.6 | 5.4 | 0.6 | 0.6 |
| 13 | Sugar | 30,020 | 35,308 | +18 | 453,445 | 448,819 | 6.6 | 7.9 | 3.0 | 3.4 |
| 91 | Other food products | 439,541 | 464,454 | + 6 | 3,423,275 | 3,647,434 | 12.8 | 12.7 | 4.3 | 4.3 |
| 17 | Soft drinks | 68,149 | 74,462 | + 9 | 435,884 | 467,920 | 15.6 | 15.9 | 6.8 | 6.9 |
| 17 | Brewing | 37,353 | 38,572 | + 3 | 395,007 | 416,838 | 9.5 | 9.3 | 4.1 | 4.1 |
| 14 | Distilling | 114,938 | 115,199 | ..† | 1,414,746 | 1,478,579 | 8.1 | 7.8 | 4.0 | 3.9 |
| 15 | Tobacco products | 277,441 | 281,891 | + 2 | 1,878,980 | 2,004,533 | 14.8 | 14.1 | 6.1 | 6.0 |
| 62 | Textile products | 128,450 | 167,458 | +30 | 2,231,152 | 2,286,735 | 5.8 | 7.3 | 2.7 | 3.1 |
| 79 | Clothing and apparel | 70,290 | 80,617 | +15 | 656,960 | 715,327 | 10.7 | 11.3 | 3.5 | 3.6 |
| 27 | Shoes, leather, etc. | 25,990 | 47,887 | +84 | 477,701 | 478,595 | 5.4 | 10.0 | 1.8 | 3.1 |
| 47 | Rubber and allied products | 249,992 | 245,451 | — 2 | 2,440,895 | 2,586,690 | 10.2 | 9.5 | 4.1 | 3.7 |
| 27 | Lumber and wood products | 76,961 | 90,905 | +18 | 1,165,019 | 1,198,986 | 6.6 | 7.6 | 5.3 | 5.3 |
| 34 | Furniture and fixtures | 24,382 | 24,795 | + 2 | 342,832 | 359,213 | 7.1 | 6.9 | 3.3 | 3.1 |
| 80 | Paper and allied products | 394,162 | 425,503 | + 8 | 4,874,873 | 5,126,476 | 8.1 | 8.3 | 5.2 | 5.2 |
| 92 | Printing and publishing | 128,573 | 125,179 | — 3 | 685,242 | 717,070 | 12.5 | 11.8 | 6.4 | 6.0 |
| 99 | Chemical products | 1,145,750 | 1,269,024 | +11 | 1,909,355 | 2,080,239 | 18.4 | 17.9 | 10.5 | 10.3 |
| 23 | Paint and allied products | 85,868 | 84,791 | — 1 | 1,078,893 | 1,200,574 | 11.9 | 10.4 | 4.7 | 4.3 |
| 40 | Drugs and medicines | 350,659 | 372,042 | + 6 | 9,709,840 | 10,276,417 | 11.8 | 12.3 | 7.3 | 7.6 |
| 36 | Soap, cosmetics, etc. | 204,616 | 220,371 | + 8 | 1,189,589 | 1,315,678 | 17.2 | 16.7 | 6.2 | 6.1 |
| 122 | Petroleum prod. and refining | 3,073,270 | 3,298,476 | + 7 | 29,615,879 | 31,343,389 | 10.4 | 10.5 | 8.7 | 8.7 |
| 21 | Cement | 98,068 | 97,374 | — 1 | 865,774 | 939,071 | 11.3 | 10.4 | 11.2 | 12.5 |
| 15 | Glass products | 145,576 | 159,315 | + 9 | 1,310,015 | 1,365,887 | 11.1 | 11.7 | 7.1 | 7.2 |
| 51 | Other stone, clay products | 261,096 | 275,039 | + 5 | 2,436,469 | 2,570,090 | 10.7 | 10.7 | 7.6 | 7.4 |
| 78 | Iron and steel | 714,203 | 605,532 | —15 | 11,081,377 | 11,228,896 | 6.4 | 5.4 | 5.1 | 4.1 |
| 59 | Nonferrous metals | 349,628 | 385,575 | +10 | 5,165,886 | 5,329,470 | 6.8 | 7.2 | 5.8 | 6.2 |
| 53 | Hardware and tools | 85,067 | 99,843 | +17 | 674,816 | 719,679 | 12.6 | 13.9 | 6.7 | 7.0 |
| 80 | Other metal products | 145,264 | 186,545 | +28 | 1,122,848 | 1,130,344 | 4.6 | 6.3 | 2.4 | 3.0 |
| 50 | Building, heat., plumb. equip. | 51,845 | 71,088 | +37 | 1,976,485 | 2,050,183 | 7.3 | 9.1 | 3.2 | 3.9 |
| 54 | Farm, constr., mat.-hdlg. equip... | 172,885 | 242,912 | +41 | 2,966,337 | 3,004,752 | 5.8 | 8.1 | 3.4 | 4.4 |
| 33 | Office, computing equipment | 261,078 | 311,476 | +19 | 1,619,561 | 1,886,212 | 16.1 | 16.5 | 7.5 | 8.0 |
| 213 | Other machinery | 401,915 | 457,295 | +14 | 4,513,988 | 4,753,130 | 8.9 | 9.6 | 4.5 | 4.8 |
| 308 | Electrical equip. & electronics.... | 743,101 | 899,536 | +21 | 7,465,285 | 7,927,846 | 10.0 | 11.3 | 3.6 | 3.8 |
| 17 | Household appliances | 80,595 | 96,728 | +20 | 876,676 | 912,411 | 9.2 | 10.6 | 4.2 | 4.7 |
| 13 | Autos and trucks | 1,352,223 | 2,077,406 | +54 | 10,221,123 | 10,699,383 | 13.2 | 19.4 | 6.1 | 7.5 |
| 47 | Automotive parts | 89,954 | 143,206 | +59 | 1,313,242 | 1,346,011 | 6.8 | 10.6 | 3.3 | 4.4 |
| 13 | Railway equipment | 42,671 | 54,135 | +27 | 841,758 | 850,794 | 5.1 | 6.4 | 3.4 | 3.7 |
| 47 | Aircraft and space | 119,528 | 351,072 | +194 | 2,737,684 | 2,728,152 | 4.4 | 12.9 | 0.9 | 2.4 |
| 84 | Instruments, photo goods, etc. | 248,814 | 290,774 | +17 | 2,006,999 | 2,174,938 | 12.4 | 13.4 | 6.7 | 6.9 |
| 96 | Misc. manufacturing | 185,471 | 189,640 | + 2 | 1,596,246 | 1,731,296 | 11.6 | 11.0 | 4.7 | 4.4 |
| 2,316 | Total manufacturing | 12,683,756 | 14,680,957 | +16 | 127,704,263 | 134,145,009 | 9.9 | 10.9 | 5.2 | 5.5 |
| 18 | Metal mining - c | 28,373 | 32,690 | +15 | 314,019 | 324,047 | 9.0 | 10.1 | 8.8 | 9.9 |
| 23 | Coal mining - c | 66,060 | 72,545 | +10 | 937,011 | 968,790 | 7.1 | 7.5 | 7.0 | 7.1 |
| 17 | Other mining, quarrying - c | 43,432 | 45,721 | + 5 | 413,795 | 431,857 | 10.5 | 10.6 | 17.2 | 16.4 |
| 58 | Total mining - c | 137,865 | 150,956 | + 9 | 1,664,825 | 1,724,694 | 8.3 | 8.8 | 9.1 | 9.2 |
| 61 | Chain stores—food | 249,765 | 253,934 | + 2 | 2,048,428 | 2,193,428 | 12.2 | 11.6 | 1.2 | 1.2 |
| 72 | Chain stores—variety, etc. | 128,832 | 128,521 | ..† | 1,572,946 | 1,636,324 | 8.2 | 7.9 | 2.6 | 2.4 |
| 70 | Department and specialty | 229,947 | 243,941 | + 6 | 2,441,231 | 2,560,478 | 9.4 | 9.5 | 2.6 | 2.5 |
| 9 | Mail order | 250,035 | 271,121 | + 8 | 2,230,403 | 2,355,228 | 11.2 | 11.5 | 1.6 | 1.8 |
| 159 | Wholesale and misc. | 166,580 | 175,905 | + 6 | 1,716,174 | 1,911,738 | 9.7 | 9.2 | 1.9 | 1.8 |
| 371 | Total trade | 1,025,159 | 1,073,422 | + 5 | 10,009,182 | 10,657,196 | 10.2 | 10.1 | 1.9 | 1.8 |
| 103 | Class I railroads - d | 384,000 | 574,000 | +49 | 17,312,733 | 17,283,908 | 2.2 | 3.3 | 4.2 | 6.1 |
| 22 | Common carrier trucking | 20,274 | 33,709 | +66 | 194,685 | 208,708 | 10.4 | 16.2 | 2.0 | 3.1 |
| 8 | Shipping | 17,691 | 23,087 | +31 | 353,451 | 367,124 | 5.0 | 6.3 | 2.3 | 4.0 |
| 20 | Air transport | D-28,033 | 55,541 | ..‡ | 907,097 | 900,916 | ...‡ | 6.2 | 0.4 | 1.9 |
| 48 | Misc. transportation | 55,893 | 61,885 | +11 | 653,107 | 684,229 | 8.6 | 9.0 | 4.9 | 5.0 |
| 201 | Total transportation | 449,825 | 748,222 | +66 | 19,421,073 | 19,444,885 | 2.3 | 3.8 | 3.4 | 5.0 |
| 231 | Electric power, gas, etc. - d | 2,259,593 | 2,483,894 | +10 | 22,696,698 | 24,012,002 | 10.0 | 10.3 | 12.7 | 13.1 |
| 29 | Telephone and telegraph - d.... | 1,442,397 | 1,564,738 | + 8 | 14,552,336 | 16,467,555 | 9.9 | 9.5 | 13.8 | 14.0 |
| 260 | Total public utilities | 3,701,990 | 4,048,632 | + 9 | 37,249,034 | 40,479,557 | 9.9 | 10.0 | 13.1 | 13.5 |
| 56 | Amusements | 47,420 | 45,329 | — 4 | 562,936 | 610,482 | 8.4 | 7.4 | 4.1 | 3.7 |
| 32 | Restaurant and hotel | 16,910 | 16,196 | — 4 | 206,264 | 216,047 | 8.2 | 7.5 | 2.3 | 2.0 |
| 101 | Other business services | 107,345 | 122,390 | +14 | 806,662 | 900,672 | 13.3 | 13.6 | 4.2 | 4.3 |
| 28 | Construction | 40,180 | 56,038 | +39 | 462,023 | 492,324 | 8.7 | 11.4 | 3.8 | 3.9 |
| 217 | Total services | 211,855 | 239,953 | +13 | 2,037,885 | 2,219,525 | 10.4 | 10.8 | 3.9 | 3.8 |
| * | Commercial banks | 1,712,000 | 1,689,000 | — 1 | 17,398,000 | 18,410,000 | 9.8 | 9.2 | ... | ... |
| 54 | Fire and casualty insurance | 241,193 | 198,255 | —18 | 4,025,336 | 5,045,137 | 6.0 | 3.9 | ... | ... |
| 218 | Investment trusts - e | 702,988 | 781,388 | +11 | 22,271,990 | 28,854,020 | 3.2 | 2.7 | ... | ... |
| 82 | Sales finance | 306,565 | 306,705 | ..† | 2,360,927 | 2,569,549 | 13.0 | 11.9 | ... | ... |
| 54 | Real estate | 21,441 | 31,477 | +47 | 256,904 | 301,909 | 8.3 | 10.4 | ... | ... |
| 408 | Total finance | 2,984,187 | 3,006,825 | + 1 | 46,313,157 | 55,180,615 | 6.4 | 5.4 | ... | ... |
| 3,831 | Grand total | 21,194,637 | 23,948,967 | +13 | 244,399,419 | 263,851,481 | 8.7 | 9.1 | 5.5 | 5.7 |

a—Book net assets at the beginning of each year are based upon the excess of total balance sheet assets over liabilities; the amounts at which assets are carried on the books are far below present-day values. b—Profit margins computed for all companies publishing sales or gross income figures, which represent about nine tenths of total number of reporting companies, excluding the finance groups; includes income from investments and other sources as well as from sales. c—Net income is reported before depletion charges in some cases. d—Due to the large proportion of capital investment in the form of funded debt, rate of return on total property investment would be lower than that shown on net assets only. e—Figures in most cases exclude capital gains or losses on investments. *—Federal Reserve Board tabulation of all member banks; number of banks (6,050) not included in our totals; assets are annual averages. †—Increases or decreases of less than 0.5%. ‡ Not calculable. D—Deficit.

A year ago this bank published for the first time special tabulations of net income, depreciation, corporate income taxes, dividends, retained income and cash flow as reported to shareholders. The following table summarizes the pertinent data for the years 1961 and 1962. Because detailed information is not available for many companies, the sample for this survey is considerably smaller than for the regular tabulation.

# CORRECTED TABLE
## For page 40, April 1963 Issue
### FIRST NATIONAL CITY BANK
*Monthly Economic Letter*

## Net Income of Leading Corporations for the Years 1961 and 1962
(Dollar Figures in Thousands)

| No. of Cos. | Industrial Groups | Reported Net Income After Taxes 1961 | 1962 | Per Cent Change | Book Net Assets Jan. 1-a 1961 | 1962 | % Return on Net Assets-a 1961 | 1962 | % Margin on Sales-b 1961 | 1962 |
|---|---|---|---|---|---|---|---|---|---|---|
| 16 | Baking | $ 58,993 | $ 61,144 | + 4 | $ 608,533 | $ 624,113 | 9.7 | 9.8 | 2.7 | 2.7 |
| 12 | Dairy products | 104,026 | 109,367 | + 5 | 947,991 | 1,031,140 | 11.0 | 10.6 | 2.6 | 2.7 |
| 21 | Meat packing | 45,350 | 53,570 | +18 | 975,603 | 991,699 | 4.6 | 5.4 | 0.6 | 0.6 |
| 13 | Sugar | 30,020 | 35,308 | +18 | 453,445 | 448,819 | 6.6 | 7.9 | 3.0 | 3.4 |
| 91 | Other food products | 439,541 | 464,454 | + 6 | 3,423,275 | 3,647,434 | 12.8 | 12.7 | 4.3 | 4.3 |
| 17 | Soft drinks | 68,149 | 74,462 | + 9 | 435,884 | 467,920 | 15.6 | 15.9 | 6.8 | 6.9 |
| 17 | Brewing | 37,353 | 38,572 | + 3 | 395,007 | 416,838 | 9.5 | 9.3 | 4.1 | 4.1 |
| 14 | Distilling | 114,938 | 115,199 | ..† | 1,414,746 | 1,478,579 | 8.1 | 7.8 | 4.0 | 3.9 |
| 15 | Tobacco products | 277,441 | 281,891 | + 2 | 1,878,980 | 2,004,533 | 14.8 | 14.1 | 6.1 | 6.0 |
| 62 | Textile products | 128,450 | 167,458 | +30 | 2,231,152 | 2,286,735 | 5.8 | 7.3 | 2.7 | 3.1 |
| 79 | Clothing and apparel | 70,290 | 80,617 | +15 | 656,960 | 715,327 | 10.7 | 11.3 | 3.5 | 3.6 |
| 27 | Shoes, leather, etc. | 25,990 | 47,887 | +84 | 477,701 | 478,595 | 5.4 | 10.0 | 1.8 | 3.1 |
| 47 | Rubber and allied products | 249,992 | 245,451 | — 2 | 2,440,895 | 2,586,690 | 10.2 | 9.5 | 4.1 | 3.7 |
| 27 | Lumber and wood products | 76,961 | 90,905 | +18 | 1,165,019 | 1,198,986 | 6.6 | 7.6 | 5.3 | 5.3 |
| 34 | Furniture and fixtures | 24,382 | 24,795 | + 2 | 342,832 | 359,213 | 7.1 | 6.9 | 3.3 | 3.1 |
| 80 | Paper and allied products | 394,162 | 425,503 | + 8 | 4,874,873 | 5,126,476 | 8.1 | 8.3 | 5.2 | 5.2 |
| 92 | Printing and publishing | 128,573 | 125,179 | — 3 | 1,078,893 | 1,200,574 | 11.9 | 10.4 | 4.7 | 4.3 |
| 99 | Chemical products | 1,145,750 | 1,269,024 | +11 | 9,709,840 | 10,276,417 | 11.8 | 12.3 | 7.3 | 7.6 |
| 23 | Paint and allied products | 85,868 | 84,791 | — 1 | 685,242 | 717,070 | 12.5 | 11.8 | 6.4 | 6.0 |
| 40 | Drugs and medicines | 350,659 | 372,042 | + 6 | 1,909,355 | 2,080,239 | 18.4 | 17.9 | 10.5 | 10.3 |
| 36 | Soap, cosmetics, etc. | 204,616 | 220,371 | + 8 | 1,189,589 | 1,315,678 | 17.2 | 16.7 | 6.2 | 6.1 |
| 122 | Petroleum prod. and refining | 3,073,270 | 3,298,476 | + 7 | 29,615,579 | 31,343,389 | 10.4 | 10.5 | 8.7 | 8.7 |
| 21 | Cement | 98,068 | 97,374 | — 1 | 865,774 | 939,071 | 11.3 | 10.4 | 11.2 | 12.5 |
| 15 | Glass products | 145,576 | 159,315 | + 9 | 1,310,015 | 1,365,887 | 11.1 | 11.7 | 7.1 | 7.2 |
| 51 | Other stone, clay products | 261,096 | 275,039 | + 5 | 2,436,469 | 2,570,090 | 10.7 | 10.7 | 7.6 | 7.4 |
| 78 | Iron and steel | 714,203 | 605,532 | —15 | 11,081,377 | 11,228,896 | 6.4 | 5.4 | 5.1 | 4.1 |
| 59 | Nonferrous metals | 349,628 | 385,575 | +10 | 5,165,886 | 5,329,470 | 6.8 | 7.2 | 6.8 | 6.2 |
| 53 | Hardware and tools | 85,067 | 99,843 | +17 | 674,816 | 719,679 | 12.6 | 13.9 | 6.7 | 7.0 |
| 50 | Building, heat., plumb. equip. | 51,845 | 71,088 | +37 | 1,122,848 | 1,130,344 | 4.6 | 6.3 | 2.4 | 3.0 |
| 80 | Other metal products | 145,264 | 186,545 | +28 | 1,976,485 | 2,050,183 | 7.3 | 9.1 | 3.2 | 3.9 |
| 54 | Farm, constr., mat.-hdlg. equip. | 172,885 | 242,912 | +41 | 2,966,337 | 3,004,752 | 5.8 | 8.1 | 3.4 | 4.4 |
| 33 | Office, computing equipment | 261,078 | 311,476 | +19 | 1,619,561 | 1,886,212 | 16.1 | 16.5 | 7.5 | 8.0 |
| 213 | Other machinery | 401,915 | 457,295 | +14 | 4,513,988 | 4,753,130 | 8.9 | 9.6 | 4.5 | 4.8 |
| 308 | Electrical equip. & electronics | 743,101 | 899,536 | +21 | 7,465,285 | 7,927,846 | 10.0 | 11.3 | 3.6 | 3.8 |
| 17 | Household appliances | 80,595 | 96,728 | +20 | 876,676 | 912,411 | 9.2 | 10.6 | 4.2 | 4.7 |
| 13 | Autos and trucks | 1,352,223 | 2,077,406 | +54 | 10,221,123 | 10,699,383 | 13.2 | 19.4 | 6.1 | 7.5 |
| 47 | Automotive parts | 89,954 | 143,206 | +59 | 1,313,242 | 1,346,011 | 6.8 | 10.6 | 3.3 | 4.4 |
| 13 | Railway equipment | 42,671 | 54,135 | +27 | 841,758 | 850,794 | 5.1 | 6.4 | 3.4 | 3.7 |
| 47 | Aircraft and space | 119,528 | 351,072 | +194 | 2,737,684 | 2,728,152 | 4.4 | 12.9 | 0.2 | 2.4 |
| 84 | Instruments, photo goods, etc. | 248,814 | 290,774 | +17 | 2,006,999 | 2,174,938 | 12.4 | 13.4 | 6.7 | 6.9 |
| 96 | Misc. manufacturing | 185,471 | 189,640 | + 2 | 1,596,246 | 1,731,296 | 11.6 | 11.0 | 4.7 | 4.4 |
| 2,316 | Total manufacturing | 12,683,756 | 14,680,957 | +16 | 127,704,263 | 134,145,009 | 9.9 | 10.9 | 5.2 | 5.5 |
| 18 | Metal mining - c | 28,373 | 32,690 | +15 | 314,019 | 324,047 | 9.0 | 10.1 | 8.8 | 9.9 |
| 23 | Coal mining - c | 66,060 | 72,545 | +10 | 937,011 | 968,790 | 7.1 | 7.5 | 7.0 | 7.1 |
| 17 | Other mining, quarrying - c | 43,432 | 45,721 | + 5 | 413,795 | 431,857 | 10.5 | 10.6 | 17.2 | 16.4 |
| 58 | Total mining - c | 137,865 | 150,956 | + 9 | 1,664,825 | 1,724,694 | 8.3 | 8.8 | 9.1 | 9.2 |
| 61 | Chain stores—food | 249,765 | 253,934 | + 2 | 2,048,428 | 2,193,428 | 12.2 | 11.6 | 1.2 | 1.2 |
| 72 | Chain stores—variety, etc. | 128,832 | 128,521 | ..† | 1,572,946 | 1,636,324 | 8.2 | 7.9 | 2.6 | 2.4 |
| 70 | Department and specialty | 229,947 | 243,941 | + 6 | 2,441,231 | 2,560,478 | 9.4 | 9.5 | 2.6 | 2.5 |
| 9 | Mail order | 250,035 | 271,121 | + 8 | 2,230,403 | 2,355,228 | 11.2 | 11.5 | 1.6 | 1.8 |
| 159 | Wholesale and misc. | 166,580 | 175,905 | + 6 | 1,716,174 | 1,911,738 | 9.7 | 9.2 | 1.9 | 1.8 |
| 371 | Total trade | 1,025,159 | 1,073,422 | + 5 | 10,009,182 | 10,657,196 | 10.2 | 10.1 | 1.9 | 1.8 |
| 103 | Class I railroads - d | 384,000 | 574,000 | +49 | 17,312,733 | 17,283,908 | 2.2 | 3.3 | 4.2 | 6.1 |
| 22 | Common carrier trucking | 20,274 | 33,709 | +66 | 194,685 | 208,708 | 10.4 | 16.2 | 2.0 | 3.1 |
| 8 | Shipping | 17,691 | 23,087 | +31 | 353,451 | 367,124 | 5.0 | 6.3 | 2.3 | 4.0 |
| 20 | Air transport | D-28,033 | 55,541 | ..‡ | 907,097 | 900,916 | ...‡ | 6.2 | 0.4 | 1.9 |
| 48 | Misc. transportation | 55,893 | 61,885 | +11 | 653,107 | 684,229 | 8.6 | 9.0 | 4.9 | 5.0 |
| 201 | Total transportation | 449,825 | 748,222 | +66 | 19,421,073 | 19,444,885 | 2.3 | 3.8 | 3.4 | 5.0 |
| 231 | Electric power, gas, etc. - d | 2,259,593 | 2,483,894 | +10 | 22,696,698 | 24,012,002 | 10.0 | 10.3 | 12.7 | 13.1 |
| 29 | Telephone and telegraph - d | 1,442,397 | 1,564,738 | + 8 | 14,552,336 | 16,467,555 | 9.9 | 9.5 | 13.8 | 14.0 |
| 260 | Total public utilities | 3,701,990 | 4,048,632 | + 9 | 37,249,034 | 40,479,557 | 9.9 | 10.0 | 13.1 | 13.5 |
| 56 | Amusements | 47,420 | 45,329 | — 4 | 562,936 | 610,482 | 8.4 | 7.4 | 4.1 | 3.7 |
| 32 | Restaurant and hotel | 16,910 | 16,196 | — 4 | 206,264 | 216,047 | 8.2 | 7.5 | 2.3 | 2.0 |
| 101 | Other business services | 107,345 | 122,390 | +14 | 806,662 | 900,672 | 13.3 | 13.6 | 4.2 | 4.3 |
| 28 | Construction | 40,180 | 56,038 | +39 | 462,023 | 492,324 | 8.7 | 11.4 | 3.8 | 3.9 |
| 217 | Total services | 211,855 | 239,953 | +13 | 2,037,885 | 2,219,525 | 10.4 | 10.8 | 3.9 | 3.8 |
| * | Commercial banks | 1,712,000 | 1,689,000 | — 1 | 17,398,000 | 18,410,000 | 9.8 | 9.2 | ... | ... |
| 54 | Fire and casualty insurance | 241,193 | 198,255 | —18 | 4,025,336 | 5,045,137 | 6.0 | 3.9 | ... | ... |
| 218 | Investment trusts - e | 702,988 | 781,388 | +11 | 22,271,990 | 28,854,020 | 3.2 | 2.7 | ... | ... |
| 82 | Sales finance | 306,565 | 306,705 | ..† | 2,360,927 | 2,569,549 | 13.0 | 11.9 | ... | ... |
| 54 | Real estate | 21,441 | 31,477 | +47 | 256,904 | 301,909 | 8.3 | 10.4 | ... | ... |
| 408 | Total finance | 2,984,187 | 3,006,825 | + 1 | 46,313,157 | 55,180,615 | 6.4 | 5.4 | ... | ... |
| 3,831 | Grand total | 21,194,637 | 23,948,967 | +13 | 244,399,419 | 263,851,481 | 8.7 | 9.1 | 5.5 | 5.7 |

a—Book net assets at the beginning of each year are based upon the excess of total balance sheet assets over liabilities; the amounts at which assets are carried on the books are far below present-day values. b—Profit margins computed for all companies publishing sales or gross income figures, which represent about nine tenths of total number of reporting companies, excluding the finance groups; includes income from investments and other sources as well as from sales. c—Net income is reported before depletion charges in some cases. d—Due to the large proportion of capital investment in the form of funded debt, rate of return on total property investment would be lower than that shown on net assets only. e—Figures in most cases exclude capital gains or losses on investments. *—Federal Reserve Board tabulation of all member banks; number of banks (6,050) not included in our totals; assets are annual averages. †—Increases or decreases of less than 0.5%. ‡ Not calculable. D—Deficit.

| Summary of Results for 1,933 Nonfinancial Corporations in 1961 and 1962 (In Millions of Dollars) | | | |
|---|---|---|---|
| | 1961 | 1962 | Per Cent Change |
| Income before tax ...:...... | $24,655 | $28,334 | +15 |
| Corporate income tax ...... | 11,142 | 12,634 | +13 |
| Income after tax .......... | 13,513 | 15,700 | +16 |
| Dividends ................. | 8,544 | 9,074 | +6 |
| Retained income ........... | 4,969 | 6,626 | +33 |
| Depreciation .............. | 10,922 | 11,893 | +9 |
| Cash flow ................. | 15,892 | 18,519 | +17 |

Changes in Net Income, Dividends, and Cash Flow for 1,933 Nonfinancial Corporations, 1961-62

| No. of Cos. | Industry Group | Per Cent Change | | | | |
|---|---|---|---|---|---|---|
| | | Net Inc. | Divi- dends | Ret'd Inc. | Depre- ciation | Cash Flow |
| 89 | Food products .... | + 6 | + 5 | + 8 | + 7 | + 8 |
| 26 | Beverages ........ | + 2 | + 3 | 0 | + 4 | + 2 |
| 10 | Tobacco products.. | + 2 | + 8 | − 7 | +15 | + 2 |
| 39 | Textile products .. | +27 | + 2 | +60 | +18 | +31 |
| 35 | Clothing, apparel . | +24 | − 6 | +51 | +12 | +31 |
| 14 | Shoes, leather, etc.. | + * | + 1 | † | + 4 | + * |
| 31 | Rubber & allied... | − 2 | + 4 | − 7 | + 9 | + 2 |
| 11 | Lumber & allied .. | +10 | + 1 | +53 | +12 | +17 |
| 21 | Furniture ........ | − 6 | − 1 | −12 | +10 | 0 |
| 51 | Paper & allied..... | + 5 | + 3 | + 8 | + 8 | + 8 |
| 45 | Printing, publish... | −14 | + 9 | −34 | + 7 | −13 |
| 76 | Chemicals, paint .. | +10 | + 2 | +30 | + 7 | +14 |
| 29 | Drugs, soap, etc.... | + 6 | + 7 | + 5 | +13 | + 8 |
| 74 | Petrol. prod. & ref. | + 7 | +13 | + 2 | + 7 | + 5 |
| 63 | Cement, glass, etc. | + 4 | + 2 | + 8 | + 6 | + 7 |
| 52 | Iron and steel .... | −12 | − 8 | −35 | +27 | +19 |
| 36 | Nonferrous metals. | +15 | + 2 | +46 | + 1 | +12 |
| 101 | Fabricated metals. | +28 | + 3 | +88 | + 4 | +27 |
| 206 | Machinery ........ | +21 | + 5 | +40 | +12 | +21 |
| 141 | Elec. eq., electronics | +25 | + 4 | +68 | +13 | +32 |
| 36 | Automobiles & pts. | +52 | +18 | + * | + 3 | +43 |
| 39 | Aerospace & rwy. eq. | + * | + 5 | † | + 4 | + * |
| 90 | Other mfg. ....... | + 5 | + 9 | + 1 | + 7 | + 4 |
| 1315 | Total mfg. ....... | +18 | + 7 | +35 | + 9 | +18 |
| 26 | Total mining ..... | + 6 | + 7 | + 4 | + 4 | + 4 |
| 153 | Total trade ....... | + 2 | + 4 | − 1 | +10 | + 5 |
| 153 | Total transptn. .... | +47 | 0 | + * | + 8 | +28 |
| 192 | Total pub. utilities | + 9 | + 7 | +15 | + 9 | +11 |
| 94 | Total services .... | + 8 | + 8 | + 8 | +11 | +10 |
| 1933 | Total nonfinancial. | +16 | + 6 | +33 | + 9 | +17 |

* Increase of more than 100 per cent. † Change from negative to positive figure.

The next table presents the major financial items related to cash flow for reporting corporations by industry groups. As was the case a year ago, the over-all change in cash flow was virtually the same as the change in net earnings. Some deviation from this pattern, however, may be observed in individual industries, notably in iron and steel, where depreciation charges were increased considerably by the adoption of shorter equipment lives.

Altogether, depreciation totals were up 9 per cent compared with an increase of 5 per cent in 1961. It should be noted, however, that this tabulation does not include additional depreciation taken by companies for tax purposes only.

## *Measuring Employment and Unemployment*

The unemployment rate has come to be regarded as a measure of the nation's economic health. When this rate, seasonally adjusted, rises much above 4 per cent of the civilian labor force, complaints are raised about the ailing state of the economy, and the nation's political leaders start thinking of ways to stimulate activity.

We have been in just such a situation since 1957. President Kennedy is hopeful that the stimulation of tax cuts will correct what he calls "persistent slack," evidenced by unemployment at or above 5 per cent of the labor force for more than five years. The latest figures, for February, show that, after seasonal adjustment, 6.1 per cent of the civilian labor force was unemployed. On March 11, the President sent to Congress a comprehensive report on the nation's manpower, describing unemployment as the country's "number one economic problem."

At the same time, doubts continue to be expressed about the reliability of the official unemployment figures. Some people feel that present definitions and methods exaggerate the level of unemployment; others think it is understated. Both sides agree that better data are needed and also better understanding of the data.

In recognition of these doubts, President Kennedy in November 1961 appointed a six-man Committee to Appraise Employment and Unem-ployment Statistics, headed by Professor Robert A. Gordon of the University of California, to come up with a verdict. After almost a year, the Committee last fall submitted its report, *Measuring Employment and Unemployment.*

In its letter of transmittal, the Committee assured the President that the United States "has the most comprehensive system of statistics on employment and unemployment of any country in the world," and expressed confidence in the "scientific integrity and objectivity" of the agencies collecting these statistics. The body of the report discusses shortcomings of present methods and offers suggestions for improvement. The Committee particularly stresses needs for greater accuracy and detail.

### *"The Most Important Single Statistic"*

In newspaper headlines and political oratory, *the* unemployment rate is the seasonally adjusted percentage of unemployed in the civilian labor force, as defined by the Bureau of Labor Statistics. It is calculated on the basis of a nationwide survey of roughly 35,000 households, conducted around the middle of each month by the Census Bureau. As the Gordon Committee notes, this figure has such political impact that it has been called "the most important single statistic published by the Federal Government." The Committee, however, warns against attaching too much significance to this one figure: "there is no single definition of labor force or of unemployment which is obviously *the* correct one."

An appropriate definition depends largely on what kind of figure is wanted—whether it is to be used as a measure of underutilization of manpower, as a business indicator, as an index of personal hardships imposed by lack of jobs, or as a weathervane of political discontent. In fact, the monthly labor force survey does generate an interesting variety of supplementary data that throw light on many of the shadowy areas of the unemployment problem. But they are usually neglected because they are published too late to be "news."

Among these alternative concepts, shown in the accompanying chart, are: the unemployment rate for married men, which affords a better indicator of social hardships; the rate for experienced workers, which reflects the extent of layoffs; and the rate for teenagers, which reveals this group's role in lifting the over-all rate.

The Gordon Committee endorses the regular, over-all definition of unemployment, shown in detail in the accompanying box, as "in general, soundly conceived," but it also calls for intensive research "looking toward a sharpening of the unemployment concept."

There can be no doubt that a lot of sharpening

## Unemployment Officially Defined

The following is the official definition of unemployment used by the Bureau of the Census and the Bureau of Labor Statistics (as shown on page 49 of the Gordon Report):

Unemployed persons include those who did not work at all during the survey week and were looking for work. Those who had made efforts to find jobs within the preceding 60-day period—such as by registering at a public or private employment agency, writing letters of application, canvassing for work, etc.—and who, during the survey week, were awaiting the results of these efforts are also regarded as looking for work. Also included as unemployed are those who did not work at all during the survey week and—

a. Were waiting to be called back to a job from which they had been laid off; or

b. Were waiting to report to a new wage or salary job scheduled to start within the following 30 days (and were not in school during the survey week); or

c. Would have been looking for work except that they were temporarily ill or believed no work was available in their line of work or in the community.

A person is recorded as unemployed under (c) only when he volunteers such information; the interviewer does not ask questions on these points.

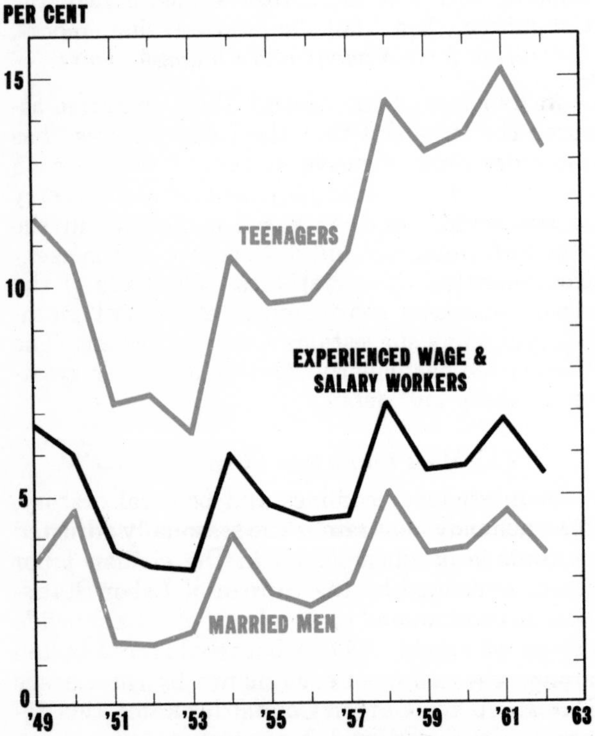

is needed. The reader may judge for himself how arbitrary the definition is by trying his hand at classifying the hypothetical examples found in the accompanying quiz. When applied to actual cases, the present definition can and does result in people being classified as *unemployed* or "not in the labor force," even though they actually do have jobs, are not looking for any other work, and are more or less satisfied with their situations.

There are many things about employment and unemployment data that may seem odd to the statistically uninitiated. Employment, for example, is not synonymous with working. People are classified as employed as long as they have jobs they could be performing; actually, they may be out on strike, sick, on vacation, or kept home by bad weather. As another oddity, some of these statistically employed persons may be collecting unemployment insurance.

There are other persons who have jobs but nevertheless are counted as *unemployed*: people not at work because of temporary layoff or with a new job starting within 30 days. The effect of this one definitional practice has been to boost total unemployment by 250,000 to 300,000 persons, and to shove the average unemployment rate up by about 0.4 of a point.

**PER CENT**

TEENAGERS

EXPERIENCED WAGE & SALARY WORKERS

MARRIED MEN

'49  '51  '53  '55  '57  '59  '61  '63

**Alternative Measures of Unemployment**
(Unemployment as per cent of civilian labor force in each category.)

## Working Wives and Teenagers

Further confusion arises from the concept of including part-time and casual workers—such as teenagers and wives with working husbands—along with chief breadwinners. The social impact of unemployment is entirely different on these groups.

The official definition of the labor force comprises all those 14 years and over outside of institutions (hospitals, jails, etc.) who either had jobs or said they were looking for work. In 1961, the labor force included 1.1 million 14- and 15-year-old youngsters; in July of that year the number reached a seasonal peak of 1.8 million. Opportunities for employment of teenagers are very limited, as a matter of public policy through child labor and minimum wage laws.

A high school student is officially counted as unemployed if he is looking for an odd job during vacation. If he finds work for as little as one hour in the week covered by the labor force survey, his "job" counts just as much as that of an executive in business or government working 60 hours a week. The same is true of many housewives who seek work to supplement the family income, but often want to work for only a few hours a week. Jobs are not always available for the particular hours that these people are available and they may be choosy about the type of work they will accept; often, their "unemployment" may be more of a disappointment than an acute hardship. A special survey taken in February 1961 showed that nearly a million persons, half of them teenagers, worked only 1 to 4 hours a week.

In none of these cases—youngsters, casual members of the labor force, or persons who work part-time—is there much hardship or underutilization of resources. The Committee believes that the numbers involved are not large enough to justify changing the classifications, since a change would impair the historical continuity of the figures. It does, however, urge that separate figures be published for those working less than 5 hours a week and that unemployment rates be shown for 14- to 17-year-olds separately.

## Improvements in Survey Methods

On the other hand, the Committee shows much greater concern about finding out whether people are seriously searching for jobs or only say they are. The present procedure, the Committee points out, does not go far enough in testing whether a person is truly looking for a job.

---

### Who's What in the Labor Force

Official definitions of employment and unemployment may lead to curious results. The reader is invited to designate the labor force status of the following persons:

| | Employed | Unemployed | Not in Labor Force |
|---|---|---|---|
| 1. Mr. A, a West Virginia coal miner, has neither worked nor looked for work in over a year, since, as he tells the Census interviewer, there is no work in his line available in the community. | ☐ | ☐ | ☐ |
| 2. Mr. B has been on strike for more than 8 weeks and under New York State law has begun to collect unemployment insurance. | ☐ | ☐ | ☐ |
| 3. Three school teachers are traveling together during the summer. | | | |
| a. Miss C has a contract to return to her old teaching job in three weeks. | ☐ | ☐ | ☐ |
| b. Miss D has a contract for a new teaching job starting in three weeks. | ☐ | ☐ | ☐ |
| c. Miss E has a contract for a new teaching job starting in five weeks. | ☐ | ☐ | ☐ |
| 4. Mr. F is starting a newspaper delivery service in two weeks and has hired two teenagers, who will help him at that time. | | | |
| a. Mr. F. | ☐ | ☐ | ☐ |
| b. Tom G, who is still attending high school. | ☐ | ☐ | ☐ |
| c. Dick H, who graduated last semester. | ☐ | ☐ | ☐ |
| 5. Mr. I was laid off several months ago and is spending most of his time job hunting, although he earned a few dollars doing odd jobs last week. | ☐ | ☐ | ☐ |
| 6. Mrs. J lost her regular job. While looking for a new job, she is helping 3 hours a day without pay in her husband's store. | ☐ | ☐ | ☐ |
| 7. Miss K, a teenager, is registered with a baby-sitting service, but had no assignments last week. | ☐ | ☐ | ☐ |

This is how these people would have been classified according to the official definitions: 1. unemployed; 2. employed; 3a. employed; 3b. unemployed; 3c. not in labor force; 4a. employed; 4b. not in labor force; 4c. unemployed; 5. employed; 6. employed; 7. unemployed.

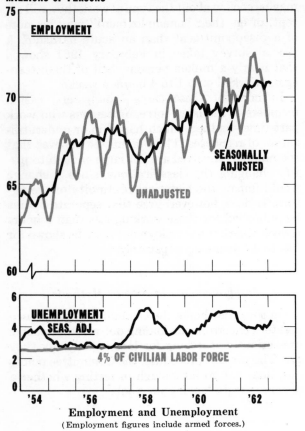

EMPLOYMENT

SEASONALLY
ADJUSTED

UNADJUSTED

UNEMPLOYMENT
SEAS. ADJ.

4% OF CIVILIAN LABOR FORCE

'54    '56    '58    '60    '62

**Employment and Unemployment**
(Employment figures include armed forces.)

Elsewhere in the report, the Gordon Committee recommends additional measures to improve the technical reliability of the survey, primarily by expanding the present sample from 35,000 households to as much as ten times that many.

The Committee also finds room for improvement in the methods used to adjust the data for seasonal variation. As the accompanying chart shows, the seasonal swings in employment are wide. Failures of the method used to remove seasonal changes accurately create meaningless fluctuations in the seasonally adjusted percentages.

One suggestion which the Committee does not discuss is expansion of the employment concept to include members of the armed forces, as has been done in the chart. The present practice is a hangover from World War II when the size of the armed services was not published and the concern was enlargement of civilian employment to absorb men released from military service after the war. Today, employment in the armed services is a normal part of life. If the unemployment rate were computed as a percentage of the total labor force, rather than the civilian labor force alone, the effect would be to lower the rate by 0.3 or 0.4 points.

Though the statistics collected by the monthly labor force survey are the most important and widely publicized, the Federal Government publishes a great deal of other data on employment conditions, including payroll figures submitted by employers and statistics of unemployment insurance claims. The Committee notes unexplained inconsistencies among the different series, but praises their usefulness and urges strong efforts to improve them.

The Committee calls for additional statistics on the labor market, to meet growing needs. It particularly stresses the desirability of new figures on unfilled jobs to help in the matching of workers and jobs. Together with improved occupational statistics, which the Committee also recommends, such figures would guide vocational counseling and job retraining programs.

### Questions for Further Study

All through the Great Depression of the Thirties when unemployment reached unprecedented totals, the nation was forced to grapple with this immense problem with only a hazy idea of how many people were actually out of work. We are far better off today with an array of statistics measuring employment and unemployment. Though finding a number of shortcomings and a pressing need for improvement, the Gordon Committee generally upholds the accuracy of our system of measurements.

These investigators, however, restricted their study to the *concepts* and *measurement* of employment and unemployment. Broader issues raised about the figures were not considered. Yet ordinary observation suggests many questions about the meaning of the relatively high rate of unemployment shown by the figures. Has the increasing generosity of welfare programs made people more choosy about accepting jobs or reluctant to admit to a government interviewer that they actually have been working? Do bigger unemployment compensation checks and longer benefit periods encourage laid-off workers to rest before looking for a new job? Are higher minimum wage laws making it harder for employers to offer work to teenagers and other unskilled persons?

### Toward "Full" Employment

On the positive side of the question, employment has been setting new records, surpassing 70 million—if the armed services are included—in 1962. Nevertheless, numbers of people listed as seeking work create the unemployment percentage so widely cited in the press, at home and abroad. Senator Paul H. Douglas in 1952 calculated normal unemployment in the United States at 6 per cent. The Administration had set 4 per cent as its initial target and the Secretary of Labor has suggested that we should aim for an even lower rate. Walter Reuther, according to *Business Week*, recently defined "full" employment as 2 to 2½ per cent unemployment.

President Kennedy has described the achievement of full employment as "the most pressing internal challenge before the nation today." The OECD has urged the United States to seek full employment as part of the announced goal of achieving an average 50 per cent expansion in gross national product for its members during the decade of the Sixties. Wherever the goals for full employment may be set, the experience in this country is that unemployment figures below 4 or 5 per cent have been associated with price and wage inflation. Even with 6 per cent unemployment we have a number of unions insisting on higher wages which put pressures on the employer to reduce work forces.

No one finds fault with efforts to help family breadwinners who want work and try diligently but unsuccessfully to find it. But no government or private program can eliminate unemployment completely—except, as behind the Iron Curtain, by defining it out of existence. As Senator A. Willis Robertson told the Senate on March 7:

> To be sure, I am not unmindful of the problem of unemployment. I am concerned to see it solved, although I don't think that boys who drop out of high school, housewives who have never had and do not want full employment, and certain others who have become firmly wedded to rocking chair money, should be included with the chronically unemployed such as we have in the coal mining fields of southwest Virginia and elsewhere in the nation.

## The Pot and the Kettle

For more than a quarter century, this country has muddled through its farm problem while paying scant attention to how its policies square with free market principles or affect nations abroad. Now the chickens are coming home to roost—and not only in the figurative sense.

In one of the first actions under its common agricultural policy affecting prices of competitive imports, the European Economic Community last July raised import duties on chicken from 4½ cents a pound to 12½ cents. As a result, EEC takings of U.S. poultry meat, which had climbed to over $50 million in the year ended June 30, 1962, have dropped precipitously. The significance of this action extends far beyond the matter of chickens.

The EEC is the largest purchaser of U.S. farm products—$1.1 billion in recent years, out of the $3.4 billion total of our agricultural sales for dollars, i.e., not counting the $1.6 billion shipped under various aid programs. Understandably, decisions on import policies by such a big trading partner are matters of great concern. If barriers are raised high, particularly for wheat and feed grains, the gate may be closed against as much as a third of our recent farm exports to the EEC.

Such an action would have many consequences. It would tend to raise food prices in Europe. And it would set back this country's efforts to help relieve as much of its balance-of-payments deficit as possible through enlarged export trade. Moreover, reduced dollar sales of U.S. farm products would add to our surplus stocks and further boost federal spending in support of agriculture —budgeted at $6.7 billion this fiscal year—at a time when Congress is trying to find ways to cut spending to make way for tax reductions. Most serious of all, European restrictions could set in motion a new wave of protectionism just as trade talks with the EEC are getting started under the 1962 Trade Expansion Act. Lowering

### Status of Major U. S. Farm Exports to the EEC

| Commodity Group | Fiscal 1962 (In Millions) | Prospects |
|---|---|---|
| Feed grains | $271.2 | Endangered; depends on level of internal target prices |
| Cotton | 162.2 | Good; import duty free |
| Soybeans | 147.1 | Good; import duty free |
| Wheat and flour | 121.3 | Endangered; depends on level of internal target prices |
| Tobacco | 104.5 | Endangered; increased ad valorem tariff |
| Fruits and vegetables | 80.7 | Generally good; may be affected by grade standards |
| Poultry and eggs | 66.7 | Already down; import levies boosted on poultry meat |
| Other commodities | 230.3 | Generally good |
| **Total value** | **$1,184.0** | |

Sources: Dept. of Agriculture and Dept. of Commerce.

trade barriers has played a key role in the present prosperity of the free world.

### Merits of Free Competitive Enterprise

This new threat to our export trade arises out of the common agricultural policy, adopted on January 14, 1962, whereby the EEC will insulate producers within from the effects of outside competition. The member nations have intervened for years in farm product markets. This national protection will now be gradually replaced by a uniform system. Exactly how much protection would be given farmers in the EEC will depend upon decisions still to be made on price support levels. Anticipating the danger to our farm exports, Agriculture Secretary Orville L. Freeman and other U.S. Government officials began drawing attention to the underlying issues even before the common farm policy was adopted.

In a speech at Brussels on September 6, 1961, Secretary Freeman emphasized the belief that "what gives us superiority is our system of competitive free enterprise which brings out the best efforts and the best rewards":

> Our approach toward international trade is quite simple. Basically we believe in the efficacy of the commercial marketing mechanism as the best means of providing consumers with goods and services. Where the commercial marketing mechanism has problems in rendering this service, it is our desire to help strengthen it so that it can function adequately.

\* \* \*

> Although the EEC agricultural proposals seek to remove barriers in agricultural trade between members, we who are not members of the fraternity can only look on them as restrictive if they disrupt the pattern of our agricultural trading relations with the area. The United States is doing its best to pursue a liberal policy of agricultural trade, in consonance with the spirit of GATT. We ask no more than access to markets under fair and reasonable competition as between imports and domestic production.

Since then, Secretary Freeman and other U.S. officials have continued to shuttle across the Atlantic in an attempt to preserve access for American farm exports. The decision on chicken last July therefore came as a shock and seemed a harbinger of a restrictionist trend of events.

Yet, it should come as no surprise that Secretary Freeman's reasoned arguments against restrictions have failed to impress knowledgeable Europeans. They are more observant of what we practice than what we preach. The unhappy fact is that the EEC's new farm policy has all too many resemblances to our own, raising prices for the benefit of local producers at the expense of local consumers and overseas producers. It is a case of the pot calling the kettle black.

### The Common Agricultural Policy

As here, the basic aim of the EEC's common agricultural policy is to support agricultural prices in order to protect farm income. For a number of products exported by the United States and other nations—including cotton, soybeans, hides and skins, and some fruits and vegetables—imports are permitted to enter freely or with low fixed duties.

But for those products that are produced in volume on European farms, the protection will be significant. For these—including wheat, feed grains, rice, poultry, beef, pork and dairy products—the EEC has planned price-support machinery based on variable import levies. Internal target prices will be established and maintained by levying import duties calculated as the difference between the lowest world prices at European ports and the target price (plus a small additional charge to insure a further domestic advantage). Duties are variable from day to day, but if the price of an item still falls much below the target price, government authorities would buy up surplus production for disposal. The program will be phased to achieve price uniformity by the end

of 1969. Meanwhile, variable duties on trade within the EEC will be maintained by each country.

The centerpiece of the complex structure is the price of wheat, which will largely determine relative prices of feed grains; the latter, in turn, will influence livestock and meat prices. Decisions on the eventual target price for wheat may be put off, but interim prices for the crop year beginning July 1, 1963, now being considered, are expected to give a good indication of the eventual target level. As a practical matter, the question comes down to whether wheat will be priced close to the present French support level of $2.15 per bushel or the German level of more than $3 per bushel.

A price close to the German level would encourage French farmers to expand their production by planting additional acreage to wheat—perhaps as much as 6 million more acres. France alone might then be in a position to supply all of the EEC's additional needs now imported, thus shutting off imports of American wheat, except for high-quality types. U.S. exports of feed grains, larger than exports of wheat and expected to climb substantially in future years, could also be hurt by high target prices, set in a fixed relationship to wheat. In all, exports amounting to as much as $400 million a year would be directly affected.

This is why Mr. Freeman is so concerned. Speaking in St. Paul last December, he pointed out the economic principles involved:

> The internal target prices or support prices to be established for grains by the Community are crucial. The level at which these prices are set will signal the direction which agricultural policies of the Community will take. If these price targets are established at unreasonably high levels, then uneconomic production within the Community will be substituted for imports. Consumer prices for animal products within the Community will be unnecessarily increased and imports of wheat, feed grains, dairy, and livestock products will wither away.
> It is absolutely essential, therefore, that these price targets be established at moderate levels, in order to both assure the United States and other agricultural exporting nations continued access to EEC markets and to prevent the distortion in the allocations of resources in Western Europe. Higher price target levels also will mean high consumer prices.

### Similar Issue at Home

Few Americans would disagree with Mr. Freeman in his endorsement of free competition or his view that both the EEC and the exporting nations would benefit from moderate grain price levels in the Community. What is good advice for the EEC is equally good for the United States.

But we ourselves are embarked upon policies to hold up wheat prices. A referendum will be conducted among wheat growers on May 21, as required under the Food and Agriculture Act of 1962, to vote on high price supports for the 1964 crop. If two thirds of voting farmers approve, growers will need marketing certificates in order to sell fixed quotas of wheat at an average support of $2 per bushel. Growers will be restricted in acreages planted but given generous bonus payments for diverting land from wheat. A "no" vote would still leave restrictions on acreage in force, but with wheat supports at about $1.30 a bushel.

Given the lopsided nature of the choice, it seems doubtful that farmers will ask for $1.30 when the Agriculture Department wants to give them $2. But the American Farm Bureau Federation, the nation's biggest farm organization, which described the Administration farm bill last year as an attempt at "naked coercion," is urging wheat farmers to reject the Administration plan. Opposing it, Farm Bureau President Charles B. Shuman does not see the choice as lying between $2 wheat or $1 wheat, as Secretary Freeman has maintained, but between government regimentation and greater freedom for the farmer. By voting down the plan, Mr. Shuman thinks that the way could be cleared for better legislation that would lead to less regulation and freer markets.

Writing in the Farm Bureau publication, *Nation's Agriculture*, Mr. Shuman has called the wheat program "the tightest, most restrictive control device ever proposed for any farm crop":

> Every farmer in America has a stake in the outcome of this referendum. If the certificate plan is not defeated, the door will be opened for the extension of similar controls and certificates or licenses to the producers of feed grain, livestock, poultry, dairy products, cotton, fruits and vegetables . . . .
> What is the alternative to this miserable mess of compulsory controls, red tape, and the army of USDA payrollers who will be snooping around every farm? Here, then, is an opportunity for farmers to convince Congress that they want less control, less CCC dumping to break markets and more opportunity to produce for consumers, not storage bins.

### U.S. Trade Restrictions

In short, what we are doing to suppress price competition and regiment production sets a poor example of the policies we would like Europe—in her interests as well as ours—to pursue. On wheat, to continue that example, we have an annual quota permitting only 800,000 bushels to enter the country for human consumption. Quotas are also applied to cotton, sugar, peanuts and certain dairy products. On the other hand, we give free entry to such noncompetitive imports as coffee, cocoa beans, crude rubber, bananas, silk and tea. These account for about half of our farm imports. Another third is subject to moderate tariffs: feed grains, beef, lamb, pork, vegetable oils, cattle, tobacco, apparel wool, canned meats, and fruits and vegetables.

Moreover, the President is authorized under Section 22 of the Agricultural Adjustment Act to impose quotas or additional fees on imports which interfere with our price-support programs.

Secretary Freeman has defended U.S. farm import policy as being relatively liberal compared with practices in other countries. We need protection from imports mainly to avoid giving the benefit of our price supports to overseas producers. Meanwhile, we injure foreign producers by subsidies on agricultural exports, colloquially known as export "dumping."

For example, we shipped abroad 716 million bushels of wheat (and flour equivalent) valued at $1.3 billion in the 1961-62 crop year. About 70 per cent of this was either donated or "sold" for local currencies which cannot be converted into dollars. The remaining 30 per cent sold for hard currencies—mainly to Western Europe and Japan—required an export subsidy of about 55 cents a bushel. E. E. Kelm, president of the grain exporting firm of Cargill, Inc., has said that, without the government subsidy, "not one bushel of U.S. wheat would be sold abroad."

Thus, the wheat situation *vis-a-vis* the EEC boils down to this: the United States supports its own wheat at $2 a bushel; it wants to sell to the EEC at $1.45; the EEC in turn wants to impose import levies of anywhere from around 70 cents to $1.55 or more to raise import prices to their target level of somewhere between $2.15 and $3 a bushel or thereabouts. It is quite a mess. So far as U.S. wheat does continue to move to Europe under the EEC common agricultural policy, American taxpayers will be turning over money under the heading of export subsidies which will be realized by European treasuries under the label of tariff duties.

### Practicing What We Preach

It is a rare paradox that we—and the EEC—should go to such lengths, raising the cost of food to our peoples and spawning bureaucracies to suppress the economies of international division of labor in agricultural production. The EEC's protectionist farm policy is a mirror of our own: it forces us to see ourselves as others see us. The most wholesome outcome of our troubles with the Common Market would be to awaken us to the inconsistency of our farm policies with our avowed principles of free markets and individual enterprise and consideration for the welfare of people. But whatever others may do, we need to mend our ways and set a proper example, remembering that the essential purpose of agriculture is not arbitrarily to raise incomes for producers but to raise crops for human consumption.

*"They only dive for First National City Travelers Checks*
*— they're better than money."*

Why should the divers—or you—settle for less than FNCB Travelers Checks? They're better than money because you can get an on-the-spot refund if they're lost or stolen. You'll get a prompt refund through any of FNCB's global network of thousands of refund agents. They are spendable anywhere—here and abroad—but only by you. And they are backed by First National City, best-known name in world-wide banking. Ask for them by name at your bank.

**Fastest refund in case of loss or theft—** Checks missing? Anywhere in the U.S. except Alaska and Hawaii, simply phone WESTERN UNION OPERATOR 25 for nearest refund location. For information concerning refund points in other countries, Alaska and Hawaii, ask at principal hotels.

# FIRST NATIONAL CITY BANK
# TRAVELERS CHECKS

Member Federal Deposit Insurance Corporation

# Monthly Economic Letter

## General Business Conditions

Business has moved up in recent weeks, breaking away from the plateau in production and trade which stretched from mid-1962 through the early months of this year. To be sure, part of the advance represents the bunching of business deferred from past months because of strikes or uncommonly cold weather. Some of the activity —building of protective inventories against overhanging strike threats—is borrowing from the future. Nevertheless, much of the improvement is clear gain.

Not only are many signposts of economic activity once more pointing upward, but confidence has also rallied. Most observers in business and government have raised their sights on the outlook for 1963. Businessmen, encouraged by the Administration's understanding of the need for better profits as an essential support to increased production and employment, have been adding to their capital investment plans for 1963, and now

expect to push beyond $40 billion for the first time.

An essential part of this upgrading of expectations has been the emergence of better feeling between business and government. The business community was especially heartened by President Kennedy's willingness to let the forces of supply and demand determine whether selective price increases for steel products would stick. Sentiment has been further helped by the prospect of income tax rate reductions. As evidence of the hopes raised among investors, the Dow-Jones industrial stock price average by late April had risen within 2½ per cent of the record high set in December 1961. Underlying all this is a steady flow of business statistics which have, in most cases, turned out better than expected.

### Favorable Business Developments

According to preliminary estimates by the Council of Economic Advisers, the gross national product reached a seasonally adjusted annual rate of $572 billion in the first quarter, up no less than $8.5 billion over the fourth quarter of 1962. The widespread worry over a recession starting last fall or winter proved to be a false alarm.

Practically all the major indicators of the nation's economic health gave plus readings in March, and preliminary April figures were also favorable. Department stores reported an excellent Easter season, and retail sales generally maintained a substantial 7 per cent gain over a year earlier. Auto dealers continued to move cars at a near-record pace. For this year through April 20, sales were 11 per cent ahead of the corresponding 1962 period and within 2 per cent of the peak sales year, 1955.

Industrial production has been picking up. As measured by the Federal Reserve index (seasonally adjusted, 1957-59=100), output broke out of its narrow eight-month range of 118.9 to 119.8 and rose to 120.4 in March. The index appears to have advanced somewhat further in April. The inflow of orders for durable goods continued strong during March, and backlogs again increased.

Employment (seasonally adjusted and including the armed forces) exceeded 71 million persons for the first time, and the unemployment rate receded from 6.1 per cent of the civilian labor force in February to 5.6 per cent in March. However, this reduced level of unemployment—equal to the average rate for 1962—is still considered excessive and it remains a powerful factor in the Administration's tax cut proposals.

### The 1 Per Cent Steel Price Rise

The steel industry—and indeed all American industry—has been encouraged by the President's understanding attitude toward the recent steel price increases. Price adjustments on selected items in strong demand were initiated by some of the smaller companies in early April, followed by major producers to a more limited extent. In a couple of cases, prices were cut. In the end, increases amounted to $4 to $7 per ton on various types of sheet and strip, accounting for a minor share of total steel shipments. This is equivalent to an increase of roughly 1 per cent in the average price of all steel products.

The hue and cry raised over such modest adjustments is understandable only against the

**$ BILLIONS**

OTHER
PUBLIC UTILITIES*
MANUFACTURING

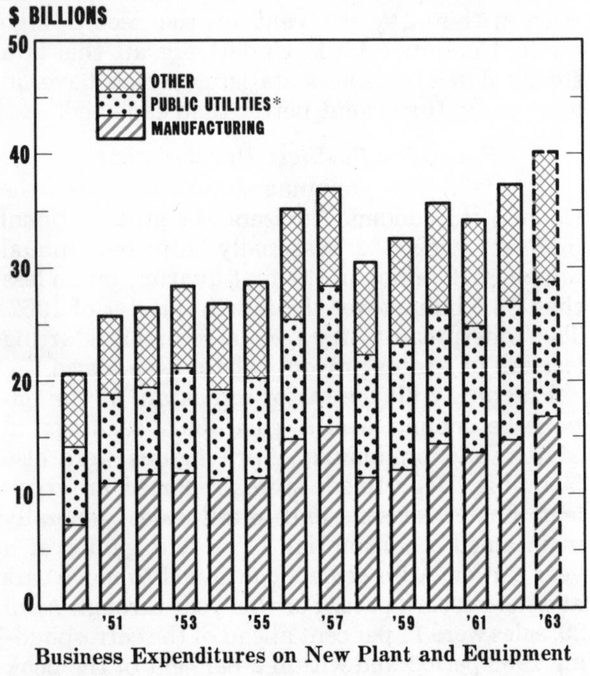

**Business Expenditures on New Plant and Equipment**

* Includes communication and transportation.
Source: 1950-62, U.S. Department of Commerce and Securities and Exchange Commission; 1963 (anticipated), McGraw-Hill Department of Economics.

background of political controversy which has plagued the steel industry for years. In a speech to the American Society of Newspaper Editors, as reported in *The New York Times*, the President gave the steel industry due credit for acting with restraint and noted that the 1 per cent price increase really no more than offsets the price erosion since 1959. Mr. Kennedy cautioned both the steel union and steel users against employing this price rise as an excuse to send wages and prices spiraling, pointing out that "price stability . . . is the best thing for the steel industry and wage stability is the best thing for the union."

The steel mills are active, operating at the highest rate in over three years. In the Pittsburgh area, some furnaces not in use since April 1960 are being put back into service. In April, mills were pouring ingots at a rate equivalent to 130 million tons a year. Trade circles expect a further production gain for May.

No one anticipates that steel output will approach a total for the year of 130 million tons, or even the 117 million tons turned out in the record year, 1955. Nevertheless, 1963 bids fair to produce a total comfortably exceeding 100 million tons for the first time since 1957. Part of the improvement in steel reflects inventory accumulation among steel-consuming industries, apprehensive over the possibility that the steel workers will reopen the wage contract entered into a year ago and strike for higher wages. Even though steel consumption is running at the best rate in several years, some letdown in activity is in the cards for the second half.

### Increases in Capital Spending

Many businessmen have been reviewing and expanding their capital expenditure plans for 1963. According to the latest survey, taken in March and April by the McGraw-Hill Department of Economics, outlays for plant and equipment are scheduled to exceed $40 billion in 1963—a rise of 7.4 per cent over the $37.3 billion spent for this purpose in 1962 and 8.4 per cent above the previous high in 1957 of $37.0 billion. Evidently, businessmen boosted their investment plans about a billion dollars in the two months following the January-February survey by the Department of Commerce-Securities and Exchange Commission. This had come up with a figure of $39.1 billion.

It took a long time to get plant and equipment spending above the old peak set in 1957. As shown in the accompanying chart, manufacturers plan to spend $16.1 billion in 1963, a rise of 9.5 per cent over 1962, but scarcely more than was spent in 1957. Among the individual industries planning sizable increases in investment over

1962 are autos (23 per cent), steel (27 per cent), fabricated metals (29 per cent) and nonferrous metals (34 per cent). Less than one third of the 1963 outlays is scheduled to go into expansion of capacity; the balance will provide for modernization and replacement of present facilities of which 22 per cent is reported as technologically outmoded. Participants in the survey indicated their investment planning is geared more closely to long-term growth prospects than to current sales or utilization of capacity.

From what is already known of plant and equipment expenditures in the first half of 1963, it is clear that a marked expansion in capital spending will be required during the second half to meet the goals set for the year as a whole. Present indications are that the fourth quarter rate will be about 10 per cent higher than it is now in the second quarter. Here, then, is an expansionary force which can help offset any softening that may occur later this year in the current high rates of steel and automobile production.

## *First Quarter Corporate Earnings*

In the face of a severe winter and a disruptive dock strike, business profits, after allowing for normal seasonal changes, appear to have retreated slightly from the advanced level reached in the fourth quarter. Nevertheless, the first quarter performance was sufficiently encouraging to support hopes that profits for the year may achieve some increase over 1962.

This bank's tabulation for 1,026 nonfinancial corporations shows aggregate net income of $3.7 billion, representing an increase of 4 per cent from first quarter 1962 but a decline of 12 per cent from the fourth quarter. In manufacturing alone, 789 companies reported combined profits of $2.8 billion, up 4 per cent from the year-earlier quarter but down 13 per cent from the December quarter.

The profit pattern in the initial quarter bore the imprint of storms and frigid temperatures in

January and February that boosted earnings in some industries and penalized others. The oil companies, and electric power and gas utilities, experienced decisive improvement in sales and earnings. On the other hand, weather conditions hurt profits for producers of cement, farm chemicals, glass and cans. Also cutting a wide swath was the East and Gulf Coast waterfront strike, which reduced export business for thousands of firms.

Aside from these temporary influences, the diversity in the earnings picture also reflected more basic differences in business trends. The brightest part of the earnings spectrum was dominated by manufacturers of consumer durables. While auto producers were selling cars and trucks at a near-record rate, makers of other consumer hard goods—including color television receivers,

### Net Income of Leading Corporations for the First Quarter
(Dollar Figures in Thousands)

| No. of Cos. | Industry Groups | Reported Net Income | | | Per Cent Change from | |
| | | First Qtr. 1962 | Fourth Qtr. 1962 | First Qtr. 1963 | First Qtr. 1962 | Fourth Qtr. 1962 |
|---|---|---|---|---|---|---|
| 30 | Food products | $ 55,201 | $ 69,661 | $ 56,328 | + 2% | —19% |
| 17 | Beverages | 19,788 | 33,337 | 18,619 | — 6 | —44 |
| 8 | Tobacco products | 60,945 | 76,787 | 59,190 | — 3 | —23 |
| 40 | Textiles & apparel | 29,244 | 33,575 | 29,725 | + 2 | —11 |
| 19 | Rubber & allied products | 20,791 | 26,180 | 20,730 | —..* | —21 |
| 32 | Paper & allied products | 52,435 | 62,027 | 51,030 | — 3 | —18 |
| 21 | Printing & publishing | 3,402 | 14,048 | 1,457 | —57 | —90 |
| 59 | Chemicals, paint, etc. | 259,149 | 282,161 | 264,204 | + 2 | — 6 |
| 38 | Drugs, soap, cosmetics | 135,329 | 141,561 | 145,237 | + 7 | + 3 |
| 40 | Petroleum prod. & refining | 730,695 | 819,149 | 835,458 | +14 | + 2 |
| 40 | Cement, glass, and stone | 56,879 | 89,393 | 47,922 | —16 | —46 |
| 42 | Iron and steel | 203,933 | 142,961 | 135,661 | —33 | — 5 |
| 24 | Nonferrous metals | 58,727 | 57,073 | 45,967 | —22 | —19 |
| 56 | Fabricated metal products | 60,887 | 69,084 | 61,799 | + 1 | —11 |
| 103 | Machinery | 145,907 | 170,984 | 146,206 | +..* | —14 |
| 79 | Electrical equip. & electronics | 132,063 | 184,777 | 133,821 | + 1 | —28 |
| 32 | Automobiles & parts | 529,257 | 725,565 | 598,111 | +13 | —18 |
| 32 | Aerospace & railway equipment | 65,708 | 86,618 | 65,439 | —..* | —24 |
| 77 | Other manufacturing | 96,829 | 133,187 | 97,835 | + 1 | —27 |
| 789 | Total manufacturing | $2,717,169 | $3,218,128 | $2,814,739 | + 4% | —13% |
| 22 | Mining & quarrying | 32,187 | 39,891 | 30,541 | — 5 | —23 |
| 48 | Trade (retail and wholesale) | 37,629 | 53,357 | 38,258 | + 2 | —28 |
| 38 | Service & amusement | 21,773 | 27,340 | 20,194 | — 7 | —26 |
| 42 | Railroads | 60,133 | 188,663 | 59,823 | — 1 | —68 |
| 13 | Common carrier trucking | 3,131 | 6,505 | 2,574 | —18 | —60 |
| 67 | Electric power, gas, etc. | 341,014 | 291,170 | 365,111 | + 7 | +25 |
| 7 | Telephone & telegraph | 362,852 | 387,524 | 380,280 | + 5 | — 2 |
| 1,026 | Grand total | $3,575,888 | $4,212,578 | $3,711,520 | + 4% | —12% |

* Increase or decrease of less than 0.5%.

high-fidelity sets and appliances—also enjoyed brisk sales and better earnings. Companies in the capital goods area, however, generally marked time in the January-March period, after chalking up good year-to-year gains during 1962. Though some markets have shown signs of strengthening since then, soft prices in the initial quarter continued to limit earnings in such fields as chemicals, plastics, aluminum and paper.

The net result of these divergent influences was that while profits were somewhat higher in the aggregate than in the year-earlier quarter, profit margins narrowed perceptibly. Among manufacturing companies, the average margin on sales in the March quarter came to 5.9 cents per sales dollar, compared with 6.0 cents in first quarter 1962 and 6.5 cents in the fourth quarter. And while 54 per cent of these companies managed to show increases in profits from a year earlier, only 37 per cent bettered their fourth quarter results. The seasonally adjusted percentage of companies showing increased profits from the preceding quarter is regarded as a leading indicator of business trends; in the first quarter, the adjusted figure came to 50 per cent, compared with 56 per cent in the fourth quarter.

### Mixed Trends in Manufacturing

In contrast with the initial quarter of 1962, when all the manufacturing groups had year-to-year increases, first quarter results this time show some groups losing ground while others continue to advance. On the up side, the most notable performances were turned in by the auto and petroleum industries. Detroit in the first quarter not only surpassed its fast 1962 pace in auto sales, but enjoyed a record rate of truck sales. The petroleum industry meanwhile benefited from improved gasoline prices as well as strong demand for heating oils; international companies also had good earnings overseas, where demand is expanding more rapidly than here.

Profits in the steel industry, on the other hand, not only fell sharply below the year-earlier quarter, when strike-hedge stockpiling was at its peak, but also declined from the fourth quarter. Individual performances were somewhat mixed; helped by high auto output, midwestern mills generally showed better results than producers elsewhere.

Chemical companies continued to suffer from price weaknesses, a problem compounded by the dock strike, which curtailed export sales. The industry as a group, however, earned slightly more than a year ago, as production and sales remained at advanced levels. Signs of some firming in prices were noted in the paper group, but earnings were slightly lower than in first quarter 1962. In aluminum, however, prices had eroded so far that dollar billings and earnings dropped from a year earlier even though physical shipments were higher.

In the broad electrical equipment and electronics group, improvement in consumer electronics sales was offset by slack in domestic shipments of electrical equipment, though overseas sales of generating equipment remained strong. Among machinery producers, farm equipment and machine tool makers generally scored year-to-year gains, while results varied among makers of office machinery and construction equipment. Can makers were hurt by the Florida freeze, which cut citrus juice production.

Year-to-year comparisons were somewhat less favorable in most consumer soft goods lines than in previous quarters, but this was partly owing to the fact that considerable improvement had occurred in 1962. Earnings declined in tobacco and beverages, but further gains were shown in foods and in the drug, soap and cosmetics group. Earnings in textiles and apparel were also moderately higher.

## The Alleged Shortage of Money

Even while the gross national product and employment are rising to new peaks, some people continue to express concern that the growth of the economy is being strangled by shortage of money. In the Congressional Joint Economic Committee's annual appraisal of the President's *Economic Report*, the majority members charged the Federal Reserve with providing too little money, not only now but ever since 1954. They noted that the money supply—narrowly defined*—had shrunk from 35.9 per cent of the gross national product in that year to 26.4 per cent in 1962. On the theory that the money supply should maintain some defined relation to the GNP, they recommended:

> . . . that the monetary authorities follow a policy of assuring that the money supply expands in line with the rising needs of an expanding economy. . . . As the volume of transactions of goods and services grows, something like a similar expansion in the media of exchange is necessary. . . .

> If an expansion in available [bank] reserves is not forthcoming, either the volume of transactions must be curtailed or the existing money supply called upon to do extra duty. . . .

> The upward trend in the turnover of demand deposits, most rapid in years of monetary restraint, is thus an indication that the public has not been supplied with sufficient amounts of new money. . . .

Federal Reserve officials are fully aware that

___
* Defined statistically as currency outside banks and checking accounts at commercial banks, minus interbank deposits, cash items in process of collection and U.S. Treasury deposits.

needs for money and credit grow with the economy, but it is very hard to say how much money is needed at any given time. For one thing, there is disagreement about the proper figures to use. Secondly, the rate of money use or turnover—labeled "velocity" by economists—fluctuates. When business is booming and people generally are actively borrowing and spending, there is a speed-up in money turnover, or velocity, which permits a given money supply to handle increased expenditures. The general approach followed by the Federal Reserve has been to increase the availability of credit and encourage expansion of the money supply in periods of business recession, and to hold back in periods of boom.

Chairman William McC. Martin of the Federal Reserve Board expressed the view last winter that the "domestic liquidity of our banks and our economy in general is now so high that still further monetary stimulus would do little if any good—and might do actual harm. . . ." The *Annual Report* of the President's Council of Economic Advisers agreed that "monetary policy has remained favorable to economic expansion." Treasury Secretary Douglas Dillon told the Joint Economic Committee that "easy money and ample availability of credit has been a major factor supporting the economy throughout this period of expansion." President Kennedy, speaking to the Economic Club of New York, said it was difficult for him to see how money could have been kept easier last year without causing a "hemorrhage" in the balance of payments.

### Difficulties of Definition

Central bankers have generally been suspicious of any rigid formula which would require the money supply to be increased by some fixed percentage each year. Allan Sproul, in 1956, stated the problem from his experience as President of the Federal Reserve Bank of New York:

> There are those who would discard or discount the evidence of the figures of bank credit if it does not jibe with certain formulae concerning the optimum relationship between the "money supply" and the growth of the economy. . . .

> I must confess that I have little confidence in these mechanical formulae. . . . There are inherent difficulties in defining the "money supply," in measuring it, and in allowing for its changing distribution and for the changing intensity of its use, which rob it of much of its short term validity as a guide to credit policy.

Many of these "inherent difficulties" were pointed up this winter in the hearings before the Joint Economic Committee.

Chairman Martin described the conventional or narrow measure of money supply as a "very poor one" that "considerably" understates the actual degree of monetary expansion. People and industry, he indicated, have accumulated large amounts of "money" not included in the definition. He expressed the opinion that the great bulk of the recent growth in time deposits is really a basic portion of the money supply.

A number of the Congressmen accepted the opinion of another member of the Federal Reserve Board, George W. Mitchell, that "monetary policy was inhibited throughout much of the year by balance-of-payments considerations and was less stimulative than was appropriate to the domestic situation." But Governor Mitchell, too, felt that the money supply statistics have understated monetary expansion:

> . . . there is no doubt that the advance in bank interest rates induced some individuals and business corporations to shift from demand deposits to interest-earning time deposits at commercial banks. . . . To the extent that such conversions occurred, our comparative statistics on money supply fail to take into account the increased substitution of time for demand deposits.

Governor Mitchell delved into monetary theory and described the growth in time and savings accounts at commercial banks as made up of various components. He concluded:

> It is unfortunate that we are unable to measure and compare these various components of the buildup in time deposits. All we can say is that the growth of *total* bank credit and deposits exaggerates the degree of monetary stimulus in 1962, while the growth of money supply understates the contribution of monetary policy to economic expansion.

A sizable part of the rise in time and savings deposits, he explained, reflects decisions of people and industry to use banks, among other financial institutions, to lend or invest on their behalf instead of making loans or investments themselves:

> . . . individuals acquired a considerably smaller volume of State and local government bonds and corporate stock in 1962 than in earlier years, even though their total savings increased. It is reasonable to think that as individuals reduced their purchases of securities they put the funds into time and savings deposits. . . .

> Similarly, corporations acquired a substantial volume of newly available negotiable certificates of deposit at commercial banks in 1962. These funds, too, would presumably have gone directly into Treasury bills and other short-term securities if they had not gone into commercial bank time accounts.

To the extent that this occurred, he said, "the resulting increase in total bank deposits and total bank assets should not be regarded as constituting monetary expansion or as contributing to total credit expansion."

To the student of monetary theory, the analysis becomes quite fascinating. It comes down in part to a question of defining money. The conventional narrow definition—checking account deposits, paper money and coins—includes only noninterest-bearing money. But besides this, there are interest-bearing liquid assets that people consider as money. And these go beyond time and savings deposits at commercial banks. They include deposits in mutual savings banks, savings and loan shares, short-term U.S. Government securities, and U.S. savings bonds, not to mention paper sold in the open market by finance companies and commercial houses. The interest-bearing money does not turn over anywhere nearly so fast as the noninterest-bearing variety. Nevertheless, these other liquid resources provide a sense of security and normally can be availed of to be spent at any time.

In the light of broadened concepts of what individuals, corporations, governments and central banks construe as "money," increased attention is being given to totals of liquid assets as opposed to totals of money supply narrowly defined.

### Money Turnover

Whether we take money in the narrow sense, or include other liquid assets as well, its velocity or rate of use can and does fluctuate a good deal. The Joint Economic Committee expressed velocity in the form of percentages of money supply to GNP, although it is more common to do it the other way around and calculate the ratio of GNP to money supply. We got close to $4 of GNP for

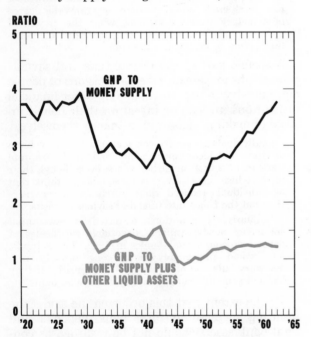

**RATIO**

GNP TO MONEY SUPPLY

GNP TO MONEY SUPPLY PLUS OTHER LIQUID ASSETS

'20  '25  '30  '35  '40  '45  '50  '55  '60  '65

**Ratio of Gross National Product to Money Supply and Other Liquid Assets**

Money supply figures—demand deposits adjusted and currency outside banks—from 1947 are annual averages. GNP is on a calendar year basis. All other data are June 30 figures.

Other liquid assets include the nonbank public's holdings of time and savings deposits at commercial and mutual savings banks, postal savings deposits, share accounts at savings and loan associations and credit unions, U.S. savings bonds and notes, and U.S. marketable securities maturing within one year (partly estimated before 1941).

$1 of narrowly defined money in 1929, $3 during the Great Depression of the Thirties, and only $2 at the end of World War II. Thereafter, velocity began to climb and is now back to the general level that prevailed in the Twenties.

This record is of limited help in judging what a normal velocity figure might be for the present day. The speed-up in velocity in the late Twenties was a product of the speculative fever and rising interest rates of that time. The ensuing fall in the rate of money use in the Depression, in turn, reflected the collapse of prices and interest rates and general economic demoralization. There was a rise in money supply incident to financing World War II, while spending was held back by rationing and shortages. When the war ended, and the brakes on civilian production and consumption were released, money turnover naturally accelerated.

Over the years since then, we have been growing up to the wartime increase in money supply. Part of this process has been the recovery of interest rates to more normal figures from the abnormally low levels of depression and wartime, thereby once again making it "expensive" for people to hold money idle. The idea now seems plausible that we will need a somewhat more rapid increase in money supply in the years ahead than we have had since 1945.

Yet old norms are of doubtful validity. For one thing, people have experienced inflation and sense that, in a world that no longer accepts deflation, any drift of prices is bound to be upwards. This tends to hasten spending decisions and hence velocity.

Furthermore, today's money and liquid assets are quite different from those of 30 years ago. Checking deposits, in particular, have become a much less attractive way of holding one's money. For example, commercial banks used to pay interest on checking deposits. When this was forbidden in 1933, there was a fairly considerable permanent switch of funds from demand deposits to interest-bearing time deposits and marketable investments. Government savings bonds, introduced in 1935, are cashable for the most part on demand and are widely held not only as an investment but as a store of buying power. The growth of charge accounts and instalment credit has enabled people to do their buying with much less concern about the immediate balance in their checking accounts.

### Corporate Cash at Work

Corporations, and their banks, have made a science of economizing on cash holdings. The possibilities for putting cash to work have been vastly improved by the speed of modern communications and transportation. Wire transfers of funds and securities, and close forecasting of cash receipts and expenditures, have enabled corporations to free much of their working balances for investment in interest-bearing "money."

Demand deposit balances are still held to cover current payments, compensate banks for services performed and support credit lines. But extra money, reserved for future needs, is put out at interest in short-term investments which are consolidated with cash in evaluating a company's liquidity position.

Corporations buy short-dated notes of sales finance companies and other business borrowers in the commercial paper market. They lend money temporarily to government security dealers, in a form analogous to a collateralized interest-bearing deposit. Since 1961, major banks, which long resisted offering interest for corporate time deposits, have entered the market with offerings of negotiable time certificates of deposit. The buyer pays for these by making a deposit for a specified length of time, but he gets a certificate that he can sell to some other firm in the open market, should he want his money back sooner.

The most common outlets for short-term funds, however—not only for domestic corporations but also for foreign governments and central banks—are U.S. Treasury bills and other short-term U.S. Government securities. An active trading market in Treasury bills enables business firms to buy or sell these instruments by means of a telephone call, at no risk of significant capital loss.

The growth of all forms of interest-bearing money has been particularly rapid in the last two years. Though business in general was improving, corporations did not step up their investment in plant, equipment and inventories as rapidly as in previous upswings, and so had more funds to put temporarily into the short-term market. Also important has been the Federal Reserve's policy of keeping short-term interest rates at levels better aligned than before to foreign short-term money rates—this, of course, has enticed domestic short-term money, too. In the two preceding periods of easy money, Treasury bill rates stayed below 2 per cent and were sometimes below 1 per cent. In 1961, they were always above 2 per cent, and in 1962 they averaged a little over 2¾ per cent.

While narrowly defined money was growing by less than $7 billion during 1961 and 1962, a gain of 5 per cent, the nonbank public's holdings of the principal types of interest-bearing liquid assets expanded by no less than $53 billion, or 20 per cent. Measured in terms of narrowly defined money, the rate of turnover rose. Measured in terms of money including other liquid assets, it fell.

### Liquid Assets and Monetary Policy

There is, in this changing world, no precise way of saying exactly how much money, or how much liquid assets, is enough. The monetary authorities have no option but to play it by ear and make credit more or less readily available depending upon the prevailing economic conditions. If spending and credit usage accelerate and bring rising cost and price pressures, it becomes clear that brakes must be applied in order to avoid the unhappy sequence of boom-bust. On the other hand, when, as in the recent past, there has existed some slack of production capacity in an atmosphere of price stability, it has been possible to encourage ready availability of credit as an aid to expansion. It is, indeed, a source of reassurance that the calculated turnover of narrowly defined money has remained relatively high. For this means that people are confidently putting their savings to productive use.

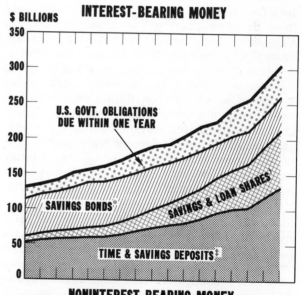

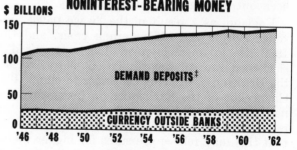

Growth in Nonbank Holdings of Interest-Bearing and Noninterest-Bearing Money

(June 30 dates)

\* Includes U.S. savings notes in the years when these were outstanding. † Includes share accounts of credit unions, which on June 30, 1962 amounted to $6.0 billion. ‡ Excluding U.S. Government deposits and deducting cash items in process of collection.

# Wage Inflation in Europe

After a decade of spectacular progress with only moderate pressures on costs and prices, Western Europe has been hit by an outbreak of wage-price spiraling that is proving difficult to arrest. While gains in labor productivity have shown some tendency to slacken, wage increases have gotten bigger. As a result, unit costs of production have risen. Prices have also risen, but equivalent advances have often been denied by international competitive conditions. Hence, as one might gather from the relative depression of stock prices in Amsterdam, Zurich, Frankfurt and Milan, "profit squeeze" has entered the European vocabulary. While economic growth runs on, and employment remains high, there are apprehensions that inflation may explode the boom. Shrinking profit margins weaken incentives for making new investments needed to sustain the increase in productivity and the per capita growth of output.

The speeding of price increases creates general social uneasiness and is particularly untimely from the standpoint of the need to build up European capital markets. Short-term funds are generally in good supply in Europe. The same is not true of long-term funds. The job of restoring confidence in the value of money, undermined by rampages of inflation during and after two world wars, has never been completed. This is evidenced in limited market demands for long-term bonds. The profit squeeze has removed some of the luster from common stocks as inflation hedges but gold, continually absorbed into private holdings, retains its attraction as a store of value.

Germany, the Netherlands, France and Italy, along with Japan, have realized the biggest gains in productivity in recent years and hence have been best able to afford exceptional increases in wage levels. Yet, from the recent performance of prices, it is apparent that wage increases have been outrunning gains in productivity.

England, as a result of the "wage pause" invoked during the 1961 sterling crisis, and the 1962 rise in unemployment, has experienced a slackened rate of wage inflation. Nevertheless, the British cost of living continues to climb. The Chancellor of the Exchequer, in presenting the new British budget a month ago, proposed tax reductions for lower-income groups in the hope that this may relieve pressures for higher wages while a new investment allowance scheme spurs modernization of plant and equipment and helps take up slack in employment. It is recognized that achievement in Britain of more rapid economic growth and an improved record of price stability will require better gains in productivity as well as a slower rate of increase in money wages.

Figures on wages, cost of living and productivity, to be sure, have no fixed mathematical interrelationships. The rise in European cost-of-living indexes last year was influenced by the effect on food prices of bad weather during the winter of 1961-62, higher price supports for agricultural commodities, and decontrols of rents, increased freight rates, etc. But, as an OECD* report on *Policies for Price Stability* notes, prices of other goods and services have also been moving up. Most European economies are unusually liquid; restraints on money, credit and government spending have not been brought into play effectively to impose limits on wage-price spiraling.

The Department of Economic and Financial Affairs of the European Economic Community (EEC) Commission in Brussels, reporting toward the end of April on trends in wages, productivity and labor costs in industry, expressed hope for some flattening out of the upward trend of wages in Europe:

> In 1963 the development of labor productivity is expected to be again a little more favorable in Italy, the Netherlands and the Federal Republic of Germany. In these countries the upward wage-cost trend might well weaken, the more so as it is reasonable to expect some flattening out of the upward trend of wages. It is still too early to say whether such an improvement can be counted on in the other member countries as well.

## A Tough Problem

That the problem is persisting is apparent in news dispatches from Europe. In France, early last month, 200,000 employes of the nationalized coal mines went back to work after a 35-day strike and a settlement that reportedly gives increases of 6½ per cent immediately, 8 per cent by October 1 and at least 12½ per cent by April 1, 1964; these increases are designed in part to fill a gap in wages between state-owned and private industries. Demands for a fourth week of paid vacation will be adjudicated later. In the wake of the coal strike, the government reimposed certain credit restrictions. Toward the end of April, it reestablished controls over the prices of a number of industrial goods in common use; these represent a temporary compromise with the principle of freedom which, since the financial and economic reforms four and a half years ago, has been one of the main pillars of France's extraordinary progress.

The problem—as the table shows—is by no means confined to France. Struggling to protect the value of its currency and its export trade,

---

* The Organization for Economic Cooperation and Development includes 18 member nations in Europe plus the United States and Canada.

| Percentage Increases in Cost of Living and Wages | | | | | |
| --- | --- | --- | --- | --- | --- |
| | Cost of Living* | | | Wages† | |
| | '59-60 | '60-61 | '61-62 | '59-60 | '60-61 | '61-62 |
| Germany | 1.5% | 2.5% | 3.5% | 11.0% | 10.7% | 11.6% |
| Denmark | 1.1 | 3.4 | 6.9 | 6.9 | 12.4 | 10.9‡ |
| France | 4.2 | 2.4 | 5.2 | 7.2 | 7.7 | 8.6 |
| Netherlands | 2.2 | 1.3 | 3.3 | 9.8 | 5.4 | 8.5 |
| Italy | 2.8 | 2.9 | 5.8 | 5.0 | 6.9 | 8.3 |
| Belgium | 0.3 | 1.0 | 1.4 | 3.9 | 2.8 | 8.3 |
| Austria | 1.8 | 3.6 | 4.4 | 9.3 | 8.5 | 6.5 |
| Sweden | 3.9 | 2.4 | 4.7 | 6.1 | 9.0 | 6.4‡ |
| Switzerland | 1.4 | 1.9 | 4.3 | 2.9 | 4.8 | 5.7 |
| United Kingdom | 1.0 | 3.4 | 4.2 | 8.6 | 6.4 | 3.7‡ |
| United States | 1.5 | 1.1 | 1.2 | 3.2 | 2.7 | 3.0 |
| Canada | 1.2 | 0.9 | 1.2 | 3.5 | 2.8 | 2.7 |

\* Cost of living in Belgium and Denmark excludes rent.
† In manufacturing, except for Sweden, which includes mining; Denmark, which includes construction and services; and Switzerland, which includes construction. The percentage increases are based on average hourly earnings, except for Austria, where monthly earnings are used, and for France, Switzerland and the Netherlands, where wage rates are used. For Germany, including family allowances; for Italy, including payments in kind; U.S. figures pertain to production workers; Switzerland includes cost-of-living allowances.
‡ Based on the first three quarters of 1962; the U.K. figures relate to October.

Sources: UN *Monthly Bulletin of Statistics* and *Statistical Yearbook*; OECD *General Statistics*; IMF *International Financial Statistics*; for the United Kingdom, U.N. figures are updated by using the *British Labour Gazette* wage index.

Note: Countries are arranged in the order of percentage increases in wages in 1962.

Denmark last March prohibited strikes for two years and established strict regulatory controls over wages, prices, gross profits and dividends.

In Germany, a strike affecting part of the metal-working and engineering industry was answered by a lockout involving 500,000 workers. The dispute concerns labor demands for an 8 per cent wage increase and the employers' offer of a 3½ per cent rise, corresponding to a recommendation submitted last March by the Government of the Federal Republic to Parliament in its first Annual Economic Report. Germany, it is true, has had exceptional gains in productivity, but the steady rise in wages, at an annual rate of about 11 per cent in the past three years, has been even larger; as a result, profit margins have been reduced and the price advance has steepened.

In fact, rates of productivity gain are slowing in a number of the industrialized countries, as stands out from EEC data. Exceptional gains were easiest during the phase of reconstruction in which a rapid catching up to the newest techniques was accomplished.

The OECD, headquartered in Paris, has been studying means to accomplish its goal for the decade of the Sixties of a 50 per cent growth in the real gross national product of its 20 member countries taken together. Its Economic Policy Committee has had expert groups at work preparing reports on *Policies for Economic Growth* and the closely interrelated subject of *Policies for Price Stability*. The document on

*Economic Growth* lays stress on expansion of demand through deficit financing, with particular emphasis on the United States. The report on *Price Stability* notes that, while prices have been remarkably stable in North America, "the problem of bringing to a halt the rise in costs and prices has become more acute in Europe." Vice President Robert Marjolin of the EEC Commission warned the Common Market Assembly a month ago that:

The essential problem this year is the rise of prices in Europe. A brake absolutely must be put on this rise in prices to prevent us being faced with the alternatives either of seeing an anti-social movement develop or a slow-up in expansion whose maintenance is indispensable.

### Foreign Wages in U.S. Perspective

Upward adjustments of wages and prices in industrial countries that have strong international trading positions do help to rectify imbalances in international payments. The much greater rate of wage increase in these countries has shaved in some degree the serious competitive disadvantage in terms of labor costs at which American industry operates.

The chart brings out the reduction in international wage differentials that has occurred since 1950. Wages for the United States represent 100 on the scale. Foreign wages are converted at prevailing exchange rates; a decline for France prior to 1959 was thus explained by

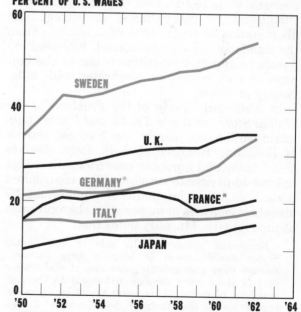

PER CENT OF U. S. WAGES

**Movement of Manufacturing Wages in Selected Foreign Countries Relative to the U.S.**

(U.S. dollar equivalents of average hourly earnings in manufacturing, expressed as a percentage of hourly earnings in the U. S.)

\* Affected by changes in currency values.

Note: The series for wages used in the chart are described in the footnotes to the table above.

the depreciation of the franc, while the steepened rise for Germany in 1961 was accounted for in part by the upvaluation of the mark.

For Canada, not shown in the chart, wages expressed in U.S. dollars are about one fourth lower than here. Canadian wages declined in relationship to those in the United States over the past two years as the Canadian dollar came down from around U.S. $1.03 in 1960 to a parity of 92½¢ effective May 2, 1962.

By and large, the gap between U.S. and foreign wages has been narrowing over the past decade, slowly at first but of late to a more marked degree. Not reflected in the chart are fringe benefits and social security charges which generally add appreciably more to basic wage costs in Europe than here.

### Policies for the United States

In a speech last month, Alfred Hayes, President of the Federal Reserve Bank of New York, pointed out that, "with respect to increasing our exports and our favorable trade balance, the level of our costs and prices is crucial." The sharp rises in European wage rates and attendant price increases have helped us to some extent, he said, but "it would be foolishly complacent to count on Europe to continue indefinitely this involuntary help." We still have our $2 billion-plus annual balance-of-payments deficits and will have to depend for fundamental improvement upon retrenchment of U.S. government outlays overseas, close restraint on wage advances here, stimulation of cost-reducing investment and liberalization of trade restrictions abroad. From the standpoint of nations abroad, increased exposure to import competition is one of the best ways to cool economies overheated with inflationary pressures.

In a scholarly study of the *Problems of the United States as World Trader and Banker* published earlier this year by the National Bureau of Economic Research, Hal B. Lary observes that Continental European countries with sizable balance-of-payments surpluses have contributed toward restoring international equilibrium by accepting increases in money wages beyond gains of productivity. Mr. Lary notes that:

> Reciprocal action on the side of the United States would consist of keeping wage increases smaller than productivity gains and of distributing part of these gains through reductions in the general level of prices. This result would be of special importance in manufactures, both because of their role in international competition and because of the more rapid increase in productivity in manufacturing than in most other sectors. So far, however, official policy expressions do not seem to aspire to more than price stability.

In a succession of recent speeches, Per Jacobs-son, Managing Director of the International Monetary Fund, has had some trenchant comments to offer. Delivering the Arthur K. Salomon Lecture at New York University in February he said:

> Let me . . . state here and now that moderation in cost increases is the right policy, both in order to stimulate growth internally and to improve the balance-of-payments position. One of the difficulties of the United States after the war was that wage costs were relatively high in relation to wage costs in Western Europe.
>
> Once war damage was repaired, the main surge of pent-up demand had been satisfied and some currencies not so well placed had been devalued, this differential became very important. Therefore, an equilibrium in exchange relations under the conditions prevailing since 1957 could be restored only by moderation in wage increases in the United States and sharper increases in the European countries, and that is what has been happening. . . .
>
> It is perhaps not yet possible to say that on a cost basis an equilibrium has been reached, but the adjustment has certainly gone a long way towards achieving such an equilibrium.

Dr. Jacobsson has supported the point of view of Federal Reserve Board Chairman Martin that we can, by appropriate policies, reduce unemployment and improve the balance-of-payments position at the same time. While deprecating the idea of permanently unbalanced budgets as "the emanation of permanently unbalanced minds," he advocates a tax cut as necessary even though it must lead to an increase in the budget deficit, and favors "a sufficiency of credit" to accommodate economic expansion. But for expansionist fiscal and monetary policies to work, wage stability must be maintained. Otherwise, the result is simply a blow-off of inflationary steam.

### A Neglected Aspect of Keynes

Dr. Jacobsson calls attention to a neglected aspect of the teachings of the celebrated British economist, J. M. Keynes. While an advocate of expansionist fiscal and monetary policies in periods of high unemployment, Keynes—as Dr. Jacobsson reminds us—made it clear that:

> . . . the number of unemployed would not be significantly reduced if there were an increase in money wages. In other words, an expansion of credit would permit employment of more workers if the price of labor remained constant, i.e., if money wages were not allowed to rise.
>
> . . .
>
> Clearly it will not do to pick out of the Keynesian recommendations those which to some may seem palatable, such as deficit spending, and neglect those which are not so widely attractive, such as the maintenance of stable money wages, and still expect success to follow according to the Keynesian prescription.

In practice it is no doubt difficult to obtain a freezing of wages; the goal is, therefore, often set to keep the wage rises within the increase in productivity, which will ensure stable prices. Such an approach may be compatible with higher output, but it will not lead to the same reduction in unemployment as would be achieved by the maintenance of stable wages, or wage increases less than the increase in productivity.

This touches thorny questions of the real or alleged freedom of collective bargaining and raises a specter of price as well as wage controls. Officially inspired "guide lines" for wage negotiations, Dr. Jacobsson states, should not be regarded as something opposed to the workings of the market system:

> In my opinion one of [the] main purposes would be to facilitate adjustments conforming to the requirements of the market, that cannot any longer be easily brought about by the unaided forces of the market itself.

In other words, while prices of commodities are sensitive to conditions of supply and demand in the market, the same is not true in this day and age of employment costs, which are contractually arranged to go up more or less every year. The most positive and permanent losses in the internal value of money occur when wage levels increase extravagantly. Demands naturally arise to enlarge money supplies to make the new wage levels viable. Balance-of-payments problems follow as imports rise, exports fall and capital moves out to safer havens. To avoid this unhappy sequence, and to improve the opportunity for orderly growth in an environment of liberal trading policies, it would be particularly useful if countries in deficit positions could learn to accept a wage pause as a natural consequence of balance-of-payments deficits.

In the United States, we have our guideposts to noninflationary wage settlements, laid out in the 1962 *Annual Report* of the President's Council of Economic Advisers and briefly restated in the Council's report this year. Even though flagrantly violated in some cases, the guideposts are important for the recognition they give to the implications of wage settlements on employment opportunities, price behavior and balances of payments. The 1963 *Economic Report* notes that prices here "have been essentially stable for 5 years." On the other hand, as Mr. Lary observes:

> It may be that the relative improvement in our cost and price position vis-à-vis Europe over the past three or four years is no more than can be explained by the unsatisfactory levels of employment and corporate profits in the United States during this time.

### Policies for Europe

In Europe, the problem of cost inflation is being discussed under the politically dispassionate heading of "incomes policy." The OECD Working Party's report on *Policies for Price Stability* describes the expert bodies or commissions set up by member countries to deal with the problem. The report states that:

> It is still too early to make any detailed assessment of the merits of the alternative approaches being explored; and, indeed, what is appropriate for one country may not be most suitable for another.

> The Working Party does, however, feel that there is one general conclusion of considerable importance which emerges from its work. Governments are becoming increasingly convinced from their own circumstances of the need to evolve some form of a national incomes policy to supplement the means by which they seek to achieve their fundamental objectives of full employment, rapid growth, price stability, and balance of payments equilibrium.

> At the same time they are committed to the maintenance and smooth functioning of free economic institutions and the maximum degree of freedom for wage and price determination. It follows that in our kind of societies a successful incomes policy must derive its ultimate sanction from the understanding and co-operation of all those concerned.

One clear point made by the Working Party is that governments must set a proper example in their own wage and salary scales. This is something we have not learned to do in the United States. Moreover, the power of resistance of employers is weakened by such things as payments of unemployment compensation to people out on strike and increases in minimum wages that tend to raise the whole wage structure as employers and employes seek to maintain appropriate differentials based on skills and experience.

An earlier report by a group of economists for OEEC, published two years ago,* had dealt with the problem of rising prices in a penetrating way. It found that wage-push inflation must be firmly resisted if past economic performance is to be improved upon.

It must be understood that working people, among others, have a vital stake in price stability. As is being increasingly recognized at home and abroad, moderation in the rate of wage increases can lead to higher employment and faster economic growth. The OEEC experts pointed out that:

> As against these tangible and significant benefits to our working population and to the nation, there is nothing significant that excessive wage increases have to offer. Particular labor groups may gain a small differential over other workers for a time, though the evidence shows that this is not long lasting. It is our belief that any gains in real income which labor as a whole might make at the expense of profits, or vice-versa, are insignificant compared with the gains which can be realized by both parties through the maintenance of fuller average employment and more steady economic growth.

---

* Discussed in the September 1961 issue of this *Letter*. The OEEC was the predecessor of OECD.

# Caribbean Coverage!

**How First National City Helps Stir "Trade" Winds in the Tropics.** As they explore the Caribbean area, businessmen are finding new markets, new sources of supply . . . and old friends at First National City. We have 11 full-fledged branches in Puerto Rico alone, and our branch coverage extends throughout the West Indies, the Bahamas and South America. △ You will discover the people staffing these offices intimately familiar with the economic opportunities of their areas. △ If you're making a survey of the Caribbean scene, pick up a pilot at  any of the Citibank branches there. He'll steer you right, save you time. You can save even more time by starting your planning with First National City right here at home. Our Overseas Business Development Department has on tap first-hand information on trade conditions everywhere in the free world. In short, what we have to offer is *total banking*. △ Send for our fresh-off-the-press economic study—"Puerto Rico". **FIRST NATIONAL CITY BANK**

399 PARK AVENUE, NEW YORK 22, N.Y. • MEMBER FEDERAL DEPOSIT INSURANCE CORPORATION

PRINTED IN U.S.A.

*Local Citibanker looks over Jamaica bauxite mine with stateside aluminum executive.*

*Nassau, Bahamas, branch office building of FNCB ...combining island tradition with modern business.*

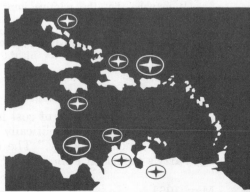

*Caribbean part of First National City's world-wide network which includes 92 offices in 32 overseas countries.*

# Monthly Economic Letter

## General Business Conditions

Business activity has continued to push ahead on a broad front in recent weeks. Strengthened new order flows and accumulated backlogs of unfilled orders have inspired confidence that activity will be sustained.

April and May were months of lively improvement in business. Industrial production stepped up decisively in April and appears to have moved into new high ground in May. New orders for durable goods advanced 4 per cent in April and broke a record that had stood for nearly seven years. Housing starts were up 7 per cent, giving reassurance that faltering figures for the first quarter were not indicative of a general decline in residential building activity. Over-all employment (including the armed forces) expanded to 71.6 million persons in April, and personal income attained a record annual rate of $456 billion. Growth in numbers of persons seeking work, nevertheless, left the calculated unemployment rate about unchanged at 5.7 per cent.

The year-to-year gain in retail sales, which had run up to 7 per cent in the first quarter, narrowed to 2 per cent in April and May. Passenger car sales have leveled off at a monthly rate of around 700,000 cars, about matching the peak months of the record year 1955 and also the initial selling month for the 1963 models—October 1962. It already seems quite evident that the 1963 model cars will set a new sales record, with the calendar year's performance depending on the initial reception of the 1964 designs.

### Elements of Uncertainty

There is recognition that some business is being borrowed from the second half of the year, and that some fresh stimulation may be required later to improve upon present performance. Another area of concern is the possibility that unions, seeking to take advantage of better business, may make demands that could disrupt prosperity with a wave of strikes. At the same time, business leaders are anxiously waiting to see the shape of the tax bill that will emerge from the deliberations of the House Ways and Means Committee. This will affect decisions management must make with respect to new investments.

The balance-of-payments problem persists though there is a feeling that it will be licked if we can keep the lid on U.S. wage costs, retrench federal spending with special emphasis on outlays overseas, and gain reductions in foreign barriers to our exports. The tough bargaining at the GATT meetings reminds us not only that business today is highly competitive all around the world but also that the competitive power of American products is well respected in Europe.

This year's temperate approach to wage negotiations in the steel industry may spare the economy the prolonged and frantic wave of stockpiling, and subsequent letdown, which too often in the past have upset the steady momentum of business. A real breakthrough of business confidence into new altitudes of expectations is within reach if, with reasonable peace on the labor front, tax reductions dedicated to stimulation of enterprise and investment are enacted.

Meanwhile, the wheat farmers' rejection of the Administration plan for high price supports plus tough marketing controls came as a heartening sign that Americans are willing to pay a price for greater economic freedom.

### Broad Increase in Production

The recent rise in industrial activity has been broad, though somewhat lopsided. The Federal Reserve index of industrial production (seasonally adjusted, 1957-59=100) increased to 122.4 in April, compared with 120.6 in March and up 2½ per cent from the average of 119.4 maintained during the July-February plateau phase. Virtually every major industry showed an increase over the first quarter.

From January to April, steel output accounted for two fifths of the increase in the over-all production index, and other durable goods for nearly one fourth. Steel production, which in each of the last 5 years has fallen short of 100 million tons, seems headed for an annual total of at least 105 million tons. Production in April and May reached an annual rate of more than 130 million tons, under the influence of increased consumption by the automobile and

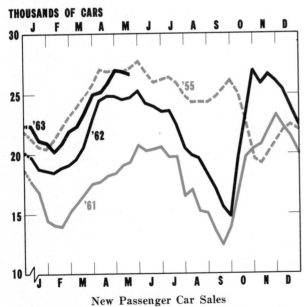

THOUSANDS OF CARS

'55

'63

'62

'61

New Passenger Car Sales

Daily average sales of domestic cars for preceding 30 days, plotted on 10th, 20th, and final day of month.

Source: *Ward's Automotive Reports.*

other industries and widespread efforts to build inventories in anticipation of possible labor difficulties. Although the presidents of two important steel companies agreed at recent meetings of the American Iron and Steel Institute that efforts of customers to accumulate inventories had been partially frustrated by unexpectedly high consumption rates, it is natural to expect a sharp letdown in steel mill operations during the summer.

Anxieties of steel customers over the adequacy of their stocks were relieved on May 1 when the steelworkers union did not elect to reopen its contract on that date, the earliest permitted. Both union president David McDonald and United States Steel chairman Roger Blough expressed hopes that a formal reopening can be avoided through use of the industry's Joint Human Relations Committee, set up after the bitter and prolonged 1959 strike.

The impression of industry leaders that growth of stocks has been moderate finds support in estimates by the U.S. Bureau of the Census that the steel inventory build-up in the first quarter of 1963 was less than a million tons, compared with 3.3 million tons in the first quarter last year, when stockpiling in fear of a strike at midyear was in full swing. In the current quarter, trade sources figure that stocks are growing at a rate of perhaps a million tons a month.

A large part of this increased use of steel has come from the automobile industry. *Ward's Automotive Reports* indicates that successive increases in production schedules have boosted prospective total assemblies of '63 model cars to 7,267,000 by the end of the model year in August. The old record was 7,131,000 set in the '55 model year. In the '62 model year, 6,687,000 cars were produced.

### Consumer Credit Expanding

Some questions have been raised about the sustainability of the growth of consumer credit which has accompanied the renewed expansion in business and, in particular, the high rate of auto sales. During the first quarter of this year, instalment indebtedness on automobile paper was rising at a seasonally adjusted rate of $2.8 billion a year, compared with $3.7 billion in 1955, when liberalized credit terms were a principal feature of the auto sales boom. This year, however, more goods other than autos are being bought on time. As a result, the increase in total consumer instalment credit outstanding in the first quarter reached a rate of $5.4 billion a year. This is about equivalent to the increase during 1955, but short of the biggest annual rise, $5.6 billion, which occurred in 1959.

While sales on the instalment plan were never

greater than now, the rate of repayments is also larger than ever before. It is the ratio of repayments to disposable personal income that economists watch as a guide for judging whether people may be getting a bit overloaded with instalment purchase obligations.

This ratio of instalment repayments to disposable personal income rose for a decade after World War II as people were equipping themselves with new cars and appliances, reaching a peak of 13.1 per cent in the first quarter of 1958. After a decline during the balance of 1958, the ratio moved up to 13.3 per cent in the first quarter of 1961, the bottom of our most recent business recession. After receding to 13.0 in the next six

months, the ratio has crept upward slowly to 13.6 per cent of disposable income in the first quarter of 1963.

There is certainly no fixed limit on the amount of instalment credit which consumers may commit themselves to repaying. There is a long-term trend toward financing an increasing share of purchases on credit, and the fact that individuals are willing to enlarge their forward commitments is evidence of optimism over the outlook and their ability to meet future payments. The current period of business expansion can be prolonged if people do not go overboard borrowing to spend and if instalment lenders avoid unsound extension of credit terms.

## Tax Reduction vs. Expenditure Increase

The President's fiscal program holds the center of the stage in Congress this year. The House Ways and Means Committee, after taking time out to deal with the public debt limit, has resumed work on the tax bill. The President had proposed cuts in income tax rates—plus a complex of technical changes—calculated to give up revenues at a rate of $10 billion a year. Meanwhile, the Appropriations Committees of both Houses have been busy dealing with spending authorizations, sometimes adding to the President's proposals for increases totaling around $5 billion, but more often trimming down.

There is no question about possibilities for cutting expenditure. The U. S. Chamber of Commerce has itemized 117 ways to effect cuts totaling $9.1 billion. But no one should equate publicized cuts in appropriations with reductions in expenditures. To regain the power of the purse, Congress would need to prune drastically unexpended balances of authorizations enacted in prior years. It is the Executive branch which has control over immediate spending decisions.

In putting the emphasis on tax reduction, the President offered the provocative observation:

> No doubt a massive increase in federal spending could also create jobs and growth, but in today's setting, private consumers, employers, and investors should be given a full opportunity first.

The Administration would seem to be proposing something like $2 of tax reduction for every dollar of expenditure increase. But this sort of comparison is misleading. Social security taxes were raised effective January 1, 1963, and the personal income tax cuts would be phased out over three years. The corporate tax reductions would not become fully effective until way off in 1969. In fact, with help from growth of taxable incomes, the budget contemplates continuing increases in revenue despite tax rate reductions.

Moreover, the proposed increase in spending strikes many observers as quite massive. The inclusive cash budget puts spending for fiscal '64 at $122.5 billion, up $5.7 billion from fiscal '63. This exceeds the average annual increase of $5.3 billion in federal cash outlays over the seven years, 1956-62.

### Habitual Underestimation of Expenditure

Significantly, in every one of these years the original budgets underestimated actual spending by anywhere from $0.5 billion to $8.1 billion. If the average underestimate—$4.4 billion—is added to the fiscal '64 cash outlay figure set down

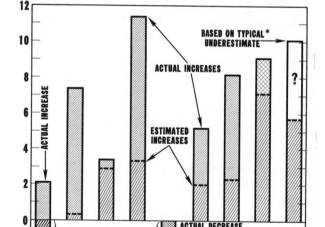

Annual Changes in Federal Cash Spending
Fiscal Years Ended June 30

\* $4.4 billion average for 1956-62.
Note: Tops of solid areas measure actual year-to-year changes. Tops of shaded areas measure changes that would have occurred if expenditures had not been underestimated.

in the budget, expenditures will reach $126.9 billion or a fat increase $10.1 billion over the January estimate for fiscal '63.

The business community, eager as it is to accept the "full opportunity first" to show what it can do to "create jobs and growth," is not only concerned over the perpetuation of deficits but also over the inconsistency of scheduling big increases in federal spending at a time when the emphasis of policy is supposed to be shifting from the public to the private sector.

### Lessons of History

The futilities of massive increases in government spending to achieve prosperity are documented by history. When governments fail to discipline their spending, the result is price inflation, balance-of-payments difficulties, and demands for all kinds of regulatory patch plasters to try to cover over the irresistible forces that have been unleashed.

These unhappy sequels have not followed our tax reductions. Prices did rise after the first tax cuts following World War II but this was a consequence of the freeing of markets from wartime controls; the budget swung heavily to the surplus side as the armed forces were demobilized and procurement contracts canceled. The 1948 and 1954 tax cuts were followed by gently receding prices; 1949 and 1955, indeed, have been the only years in the last 23 in which the cost-of-living index has shown any decline in the United States. But these tax cuts—unlike those presently proposed—were preceded or accompanied by retrenchments in federal spending.

Further income tax rate reduction—corporate as well as individual—has been discussed and promised perennially for ten years. But the spending lobbies have always won out and unchanged income tax rates have effectively become higher rates as rising incomes and prices have pushed people up into higher tax brackets. Taxes levied on individuals are taking the highest percentage of personal income in all our history, and we are still stuck with a 52 per cent corporate income tax rate—contrasted with 38 per cent before Korea.

The failures of massive increases in government spending to produce high-level prosperity during the Great Depression are well known. Now we have had two more recent experiences: the $11 billion increase in fiscal '59 and the increase of $9 billion estimated for fiscal '63 which ends this month. Neither of these massive increases in spending succeeded in lifting economic activity to the heights of which we are capable. They simply left trails of red ink, in the budget and also in the balance of payments.

It is small wonder that so many citizens are demanding a real shift of emphasis, a genuine pause in the growth of federal spending to make sizable income tax reductions prudently possible. If the public debt must be increased, let the borrowing buy things of lasting value—invigoration of individual effort and enterprise, encouragement of the base of business activity to a point where a budgetary balance can be restored, and dissipation of anxieties over the future worth of the dollar earned and saved.

### Control of Expenditure

As Henry Ford II said at the annual meeting of the Ford Motor Company, May 23:

> Cutting tax rates means accepting a larger deficit for a time. But if we do not control government expenditures, we will not long be able to maintain tax rates low enough to stimulate growth. In a government, as in a private company, there is only one effective way to control expenditures: you have to set an absolute dollar limit.

For lack of better methods, Congress has been trying to use the public debt limit, which sets a ceiling on the amount of money the Treasury may borrow, as a way of putting a limit on expenditure. This has not worked effectively, as evidenced by the fact that the "temporary" debt limit is presently being raised to $307 billion against a permanent level of $285 billion. Moreover, contracts entered into must be fulfilled. Expenditures cannot as a practical matter be tailored to the ebbs and flows of revenues.

What is most urgently needed is over-all control of expenditure. In 1946, the Legislative Reorganization Act provided for a Joint Legislative Budget Committee, to be composed of the full membership of the Committees of Ways and Means and Appropriations of the House, and the Committees on Finance and Appropriations of the Senate, with the object of establishing an annual expenditure limit. For a variety of practical reasons, the Legislative Budget, as envisioned, has never been put into use.

Reflecting on this experience, the New York Chamber of Commerce favors incorporation of all appropriations legislation in a single bill to get away from the present situation where 12 to 14 regular appropriation bills, as well as supplemental bills, add up to more than the Federal Government can afford to spend.

The Chamber urges that the President and Congress jointly create a Commission on Federal Fiscal Procedures leading to recommendations in 1964 for achieving more responsible coordination between expenditures and revenues, and a better control of federal outlays. There is scarcely any more urgent task.

# The Wheat Referendum

In this day when there is so much concern over the welfare of people, one might suppose that our government would encourage lower prices and greater supplies of the basic essentials of life. Instead, paradoxically, we go to great trouble and expense to raise food prices and suppress supplies. Though malnutrition is far more serious in many other countries, President Kennedy once asserted that 17 million Americans go to bed hungry every night. Yet, as a result of official price support activities and despite a widening variety of giveaway programs, we have accumulated enormous food reserves in storage. Government bins hold enough wheat to provide two dozen loaves of bread to each member of the human race. And bread is the proverbial staff of life.

Against this broad background, May 21 goes down as an historic day. U.S. wheat farmers, voting in a national referendum, rejected the Administration's plan for high price supports and tighter controls on the 1964 crop designed to reduce output. Approval by a two-thirds majority was necessary for acceptance of the plan. In a record vote, 547,151 (48 per cent) favored the plan; 597,776 (52 per cent) were opposed. In 12 previous referenda, American wheat farmers had voted to accept acreage restrictions in order to get the benefit of high price supports. This time, to offset the abundant yields efficient farmers have learned to realize on their allotted acreages, the proposal was to set marketing quotas in terms of bushels for the 1964 crop as well as to offer financial inducements to divert allotted acreage to specified other uses.

President Kennedy, following the defeat of the control plan, declared that: "We accept this judgment and it is my sincere hope that this will prove to be a wise choice for wheat farmers and the country." Although the Administration's program has been defeated, allotments of 49.5 million acres remain in effect and producers complying will be eligible for price support at about $1.25 per bushel on their 1964 crop. The only penalty for overplanting wheat acreage allotments will be loss of price support. There will be no marketing quotas and no diversion payments.

The reaction in world markets for wheat in the days following the vote was mild and gave no sign of the chaos that Secretary of Agriculture Orville L. Freeman had predicted would follow if the plan were defeated. The price of No. 2 hard, ordinary wheat at Kansas City declined from $2.20 per bushel on May 20 to $2.16 on May 27, no more than might be expected seasonally at this time. Of course, wheat now being traded reflects the basic 1963-crop price support of $1.82 per bushel, national farm average, equivalent to $1.95 during July at Kansas City.

Whether the Congress will enact another, less onerous, scheme before adjournment remains in doubt. In any case, the prospect is that, given reasonably good growing conditions, the price of wheat in the 1964-65 crop year will be lower. The rise in the price of bread may be checked and a sizable amount chopped out of the swollen budget of the Department of Agriculture. High-cost producers of the grain will turn their efforts to other activities. The game of buying farm land to get the benefit of acreage allotments may become less interesting.

The referendum result constituted a resounding victory for the American Farm Bureau Federation, the nation's biggest farm organization, which has long advocated "less government in agriculture" as a first step toward solving the farm problem. On the other hand, the verdict was a big disappointment for other leading organizations, including the National Farmers Union and the National Grange.

Strong language was used in the course of the wheat election campaign. Secretary Freeman predicted that defeat of the plan would knock the price down to $1 per bushel. On the other hand, it is clear that great numbers of American farmers have become restive over the widening bureaucratic controls.

The sentiment of many thoughtful farmers was well expressed by *The Daily Pantagraph* of Bloomington, Illinois, which urged a "no" vote in the referendum:

> Farmers have been devoting more and more of their time cultivating Congress rather than the land. This hasn't been very rewarding. It hasn't solved the problems of agriculture. It hasn't captured any new markets for our great agricultural production potential.

> It is time for farmers to decide they don't want to cultivate this Congressional crop, but rather to decide to do what they know best—concentrate on producing what the market will absorb at a profit to the grower. If given a free hand they can do this.

> There would be casualties in such a program. But there will be greater casualties under an agriculture managed from Washington. The small farmer is likely to get caught in a squeeze either way. He stands a better chance of survival under a system which permits him to expand if he has the necessary management skill. Management from Washington as proposed in the wheat referendum would freeze him at unprofitable production levels. He could not survive.

# Annual Report on the 100 Largest

American business has come a long way over the past 100 years in the reporting of its activities. In 1866, a railroad company listed on the New York Stock Exchange, when asked to contribute a financial report, replied that it "makes no reports and publishes no statements—and has done nothing of the sort for the past five years." In fact, written reports were hardly necessary at the time as most companies, mills and stores were largely local enterprises with few stockholders; a small room would often suffice for the most important meetings. Beginning in 1868, Henry V. Poor was able to gather together sufficient information to publish his annual *Manual of*

*the Railroads of the United States.* It was not until 1900 that publication began of John Moody's *Manual of Industrial and Miscellaneous Securities.* Such publications, expanded over the years as corporate statistics have become more plentiful, and shareholders more numerous, have developed into standard reference works for the investor.

Today, American business has come to realize that the more knowledgeable investors become, the more likely they will confidently continue to provide needed capital. Most large corporations go to considerable effort and expense in preparing attractive and informative annual reports. One company, American Telephone & Telegraph, goes so far as to make its annual report available in Braille and on phonograph records to its blind stockholders.

These corporate annual reports are the basis for our tabulation of the 100 largest U.S. non-financial corporations for 1962 as measured by total revenues. Such revenues consist primarily of sales receipts but also include proceeds from interest, dividends, rentals, royalties and other sources.

Each of the 100, on a consolidated reporting basis, passed management's acid test for the year by writing its earnings story in black ink. Sixty seven of them have paid dividends for at least the past 25 years. Eleven have paid cash dividends each year since before the turn of the century.

Indicative of the competitive nature of our free enterprise system is the changing membership of the list of 100 largest. Since our last comparable tabulation, which covered 1958, there have been nine changes. Added have been a department store chain, an aerospace firm, two processors of food, and one company each in autos, rubber and tires, glass, nonferrous metals, and adhesives and abrasives. They displace two railroads, two food processors, and one company each in heavy industrial equipment, nonferrous metals, glass, steel and petroleum. In 1958, a company had to show revenues of $536 million to place in the top 100; in 1962, it required $657 million.

Together, the 100 largest had revenues of $178.2 billion in 1962. Manufacturing companies predominate, accounting for 76 entries with combined revenues of $137.4 billion. A vast diversity of products is represented—from can openers to nuclear reactors. Completing the list of 100 are 18 retail and wholesale trade companies with revenues totaling $27.7 billion, 3 public utilities ($10.6 billion) and 3 railroad systems ($2.5 billion).

## Total Revenues, 100 Largest U.S. Nonfinancial Corporations, as Reported for Year 1962

(In Millions of Dollars)

### Manufacturing

| | |
|---|---|
| Allied Chemical | $ 873 |
| Aluminum Co. of Amer. | 950 |
| American Can | 1,181 |
| American Cyanamid | 665 |
| American Motors | 1,065 |
| American Tobacco | 657 |
| Anaconda | 695 |
| Armco Steel | 939 |
| Armour | 1,862 |
| Bendix | 797 |
| Bethlehem Steel | 2,097 |
| Boeing | 1,771 |
| Borden | 1,056 |
| Borg-Warner | 661 |
| Burlington Industries | 1,013 |
| Caterpillar Tractor | 827 |
| Chrysler | 2,390 |
| Cities Service | 1,104 |
| Colgate-Palmolive | 674 |
| Continental Can | 1,186 |
| Continental Oil | 872 |
| Corn Products | 807 |
| Douglas Aircraft | 757 |
| Dow Chemical | 946 |
| E. I. duPont | 2,601 |
| Eastman Kodak | 1,087 |
| Firestone | 1,285 |
| Ford Motor | 8,099 |
| General Dynamics | 1,901 |
| General Electric | 4,843 |
| General Foods | 1,216 |
| General Motors | 14,852 |
| Gen. Tel. & Electronics | 1,328 |
| General Tire | 968 |
| B. F. Goodrich | 816 |
| Goodyear | 1,600 |
| Gulf Oil | 2,869 |
| Inland Steel | 768 |
| Intl. Business Machines | 1,977 |
| International Harvester | 1,853 |
| International Paper | 1,107 |
| Intl. Tel. & Tel. | 1,111 |
| Jones & Laughlin Steel | 795 |
| Lockheed Aircraft | 1,755 |
| Martin-Marietta | 1,202 |
| Minn. Mining & Mfg. | 692 |
| Monsanto Chemical | 1,075 |
| National Dairy | 1,827 |
| National Steel | 753 |
| North Amer. Aviation | 1,635 |
| Olin Mathieson Chem. | 744 |
| Phillips Petroleum | 1,261 |
| Pittsburgh Plate Glass | 665 |

### Manufacturing (cont'd.)

| | |
|---|---|
| Procter & Gamble | $1,632 |
| Radio Corp. of America | 1,752 |
| Ralston Purina | 686 |
| Republic Steel | 1,066 |
| R. J. Reynolds Tobacco | 901 |
| Shell Oil | 1,970 |
| Sinclair Oil | 1,198 |
| Socony Mobil Oil | 4,014 |
| Sperry Rand | 1,187* |
| Standard Oil of Calif. | 2,313 |
| Standard Oil (Ind.) | 2,177 |
| Standard Oil (N. J.) | 9,786 |
| Sun Oil | 804 |
| Swift | 2,498 |
| Texaco | 3,465 |
| Tidewater Oil | 657 |
| Union Carbide | 1,658 |
| United Aircraft | 1,166 |
| U. S. Rubber | 1,010 |
| U. S. Steel | 3,501 |
| Western Electric | 2,776 |
| Westinghouse Electric | 1,979 |
| Wilson | 712 |

### Trade

| | |
|---|---|
| Acme Markets | 1,082 |
| Allied Stores | 771 |
| Anderson, Clayton | 751 |
| Federated Dept. Stores | 897 |
| First National Stores | 711* |
| Food Fair | 925† |
| W. T. Grant | 687 |
| Great A. & P. Tea | 5,312 |
| Kroger | 1,948 |
| McKesson & Robbins | 756 |
| May's Dept. Stores | 711 |
| Montgomery Ward | 1,425 |
| National Tea | 979 |
| J. C. Penney | 1,704 |
| Safeway Stores | 2,510 |
| Sears, Roebuck | 4,642 |
| Winn-Dixie Stores | 778 |
| F. W. Woolworth | 1,139 |

### Public Utilities

| | |
|---|---|
| American Tel. & Tel. | 9,148 |
| Con. Edison Co. of N.Y. | 725 |
| Pacific Gas & Electric | 732 |

### Railroads

| | |
|---|---|
| New York Central | 720 |
| Pennsylvania | 906 |
| Southern Pacific | 847 |

\* Fiscal year ending March 31, 1962.

† Fiscal year ending April 30, 1962.

### A Huge Investment

It takes a lot of money to buy the plants, machines and tools that enable the American worker to outproduce any other in the rest of the world. To develop $178.2 billion of revenues last year, the 100 largest employed some 6½ million Americans and assets of $168.8 billion. Net property covering land, buildings and equipment was carried at $92.3 billion (after deducting accumulated depreciation and depletion charges of $68.4 billion). The remainder consisted mainly of current assets—receivables, inventories, marketable securities and cash.

About one of every nine employes in the nation works for the 100 largest. These companies, on the average, have invested $26,000 of capital for each employe. The largest investment per worker was in the petroleum industry with an average of $73,000 per worker, followed by public utilities ($53,000) and transportation ($47,000).

Equally impressive is the extent of ownership in these companies. Their shareholder rolls aggregated 13.2 million names, a rise of 3.0 million since 1958 that represents a resounding vote of confidence from the public. Of course, there is some duplication in these figures—the same person may hold stock in more than one of the 100 largest. On the other hand, many names are nominees, trustees or financial institutions acting for large numbers of individuals.

Thirty eight of the companies had more than 100,000 owners at the end of 1962, with American Telephone & Telegraph (2.2 million) and General Motors (1.1 million) heading the list. By a rare coincidence, these two companies, which are also the front runners in dividend payments, each paid $863 million in cash dividends last year. Only 8 of the 100 largest had fewer than 20,000 stockholders, and 66 companies had more shareholders than employes. The work of transferring the stocks of large companies as they are traded in the market, of keeping track of the new owners, and of sending them their dividend checks, meeting notices, proxies and other information has mounted to fantastic proportions. Automated procedures have helped to cope with the blizzard of paper work, but even so the modern machines used by paying agents have a tough time keeping up.

### Slicing Up the Sales Dollar

Revenues of 58 of the companies topped a billion dollars each in 1962. But while over-all receipts of the 100 largest were climbing towards $180 billion in 1962, total costs were not trailing far behind. Net income was $11.3 billion, only about 6 cents on the sales dollar. The following table accounts for the other 94 cents.

| Disposition of Receipts by the 100 Largest Nonfinancial Corporations in 1962 | Total (millions) | % of Receipts |
|---|---|---|
| Total receipts from sales, revenues, etc.*.. | $178,243 | 100.0 |
| Costs: | | |
| Cost of goods and services purchased from others, etc. ................. | 96,697 | 54.3 |
| Wages, salaries, and employe benefits† | 44,425 | 24.9 |
| Provision for depreciation and depletion | 8,569 | 4.8 |
| Interest paid ........................ | 1,283 | 0.7 |
| Federal income tax ................. | 7,752 | 4.3 |
| Other federal, state, local & foreign taxes* ......................... | 8,171 | 4.6 |
| Total cost of operations ............. | $166,897 | 93.6 |
| Net income .......................... | 11,346 | 6.4 |
| Dividends paid ...................... | 6,467 | 3.6 |
| Retained in business ................... | $ 4,879 | 2.7 |

* Exclusive of various sales and excise taxes collected from customers (petroleum, $4,661 million; motor vehicles, $1,867 million; tobacco, $1,216 million; telephones, $730 million; tires, $380 million; other, $77 million).
† Partly estimated.

The cost of goods and services purchased from others, the largest category of expense, amounted to $96.7 billion, or 54 cents on the dollar. Wages, salaries and employe benefits came to approximately $44.4 billion. This was 25 cents on the sales dollar, and represents an average $6,800 per employe.

Provision for depreciation and depletion of properties came to 5 cents per dollar of receipts, while interest on borrowed money took less than 1 cent on the dollar.

The federal income tax bill for these 100 companies, about $7.8 billion, was equal to about one third of the total for all corporations in 1962. Income taxes payable by the 100 largest were one fifth more than the dividends these firms felt warranted in distributing to their owners. Total tax payments of $15.9 billion by these companies took 9 cents of every sales dollar.

With Federal Government budget expenditures nearly equal in amount to the combined personal incomes in our two most populous states, California and New York, the need for a smoothly functioning business community capable of helping carry the tax load is clear. Tax bills exceeding a billion dollars (including excise, import, operating and foreign taxes) were paid by Standard Oil (N. J.), $3.3 billion; General Motors, $3.1 billion; A.T.&T., $2.8 billion; Socony Mobil, $1.2 billion; and Ford, $1.1 billion. Business firms, as involuntary collection agents for withholding, sales and excise taxes, play the role of unofficial—and unpaid—revenue officers. Indeed, they have to hire and carry on their own payrolls uncounted thousands of people to keep the records.

### *Financing for the Future*

Today, more than a million corporations of all sizes provide over half the jobs on the country's payrolls and produce approximately 55 per cent of the gross national product. The challenge of carrying forward complex research and development projects requires accurate long-range planning and development by these corporations. Oftentimes, financial resources must be invested for years in experimental work before salable products are developed. DuPont, which spent $60 million in 1962 on basic research alone, keeping 1,300 scientists on the job, is representative of the many companies that have succeeded in staying among the 100 largest over a long stretch of years through continued development of new products.

Enterprising spirit such as this rests on the underpinnings of the capital and creativity provided by individuals who are willing to assume responsibility and risk. Instead of increasing the incentives to engage in such socially productive activity, our present tax structure penalizes those who make the effort. Liberalized depreciation rules and the investment tax credit enacted by Congress last year have helped. But they do not correct the basic inequity—income taxes that have made government the majority shareholder in corporate profits. Cutting the corporate income tax rate is an urgent necessity for invigorating the flow of investment for progress, just as cutting personal income tax rates is an urgent necessity for recharging the batteries of individual effort and opportunities for risk capital formation.

## *Federal Credit Programs*

In order to make room for income tax rate reductions, and to keep the federal deficit within tolerable limits, the Congressional Appropriations Committees have been busy trying to figure out where Federal Government outlays may be pared. Many citizen groups have offered proposals to cut billions off the proposed fiscal '64 spending figure, blown up to $122.5 billion —30 per cent higher than fiscal '60.

One fruitful way to curtail federal spending is

to cut back on federal lending activities. The President, in submitting his budget, held down the size of his projected increase in expenditures by proposing that the Export-Import Bank sell off more of its seasoned loans to private lenders, domestic as well as foreign, and that the Federal National Mortgage Association sell to private lenders more of the government-insured mortgages it now holds.

Notwithstanding these plans, loans outstanding under federal credit programs were scheduled in the budget to rise to $30.9 billion at the end of fiscal '64, up from $29.5 billion estimated for the end of the current fiscal year, $26.8 billion last year and $18.5 billion only five years ago. Furthermore, loan commitments, which pave the way for future disbursements and are the best indicators of forthcoming trends in federal lending, are headed upward. New direct lending commitments of $8.7 billion budgeted for fiscal '64 are $2.2 billion, or one third, higher than actual commitments in 1962. There is plenty of room here for cutting back.

Although some cutbacks in these figures have reportedly been made since the budget was issued, much more can be accomplished if all government departments and agencies administering loans and loan-guarantee and insurance programs (including related grant programs) heed the President's suggestion that they be guided by principles outlined in the recent report of the President's Committee on Federal Credit Programs. The Committee was headed by Treasury Secretary Douglas Dillon and included Budget Director David E. Bell, Council of Economic Advisers Chairman Walter W. Heller and Federal Reserve Board Chairman William McC. Martin, Jr. It is one of three interagency groups (the other two being the so-called Heller

**$ BILLIONS**

Outstandings and Commitments Under
Major Federal Credit Programs
(Fiscal Years 1950-1964)

Note: Includes international lending programs, but excludes Commodity Credit Corporation, whose outstandings for 1964 are estimated at $751 million.
Source: Bureau of the Budget.

Committee on Financial Institutions and the Labor Secretary's Committee on Private Pension and Welfare Programs) set up to appraise certain recommendations by the privately sponsored Commission on Money and Credit and to look broadly toward improvement of the financial system.

### Government Lending Activities

The Federal Government's role as borrower overshadows, of course, its role as lender. Yet the government is also a lender on a large scale. Indeed, lending activities account for a sizable chunk of the present $300 billion federal debt. Furthermore, apart from the $29.5 billion of direct loans outstanding on the books of federal agencies, about $82 billion of loans made by private lenders, notably in housing, have been insured or guaranteed by the government.

The business of lending money, on the whole, has not been profitable to the government. By measurements of private lenders, losses have been high on credit to businesses, particularly new ones, unable to obtain financing on "reasonable" terms from private sources. It is a pretty fair

assumption that loans which banks and insurance companies turn down as too risky for the safety of their shareholders, depositors and policyholders are also risky from the standpoint of the U.S. taxpayer.

Some of the best loans which U.S. Government agencies make are those which are barely submarginal and where the offer of some guarantee, for a fixed fee, is enough to make a loan "bankable." Apart from the Export-Import Bank, which has earned the reputation of a businesslike lender, and recent repayments of post-World War II loans to certain European countries, the general experience of the U.S. Government in foreign lending has been costly to the taxpayer.

Sometimes the loans are not really loans but grants repayable on easy terms. The Agency for International Development has been making 40-year loans at no interest at all. Only a service charge of ¾ of 1 per cent to cover administrative costs is levied. We have examples at home as well as abroad of loans made at lower costs than the government itself must pay. This practice of offering an element of subsidy to borrowers penalizes creditworthy borrowers who rely on private sources and naturally attracts

## Major Federal Credit Programs

| Federal Credit Program | Rates (%) | Maturity (years) | Loans Outstanding end fiscal 1963 ($ million)* | Disbursements fiscal 1963 ($ million)* | Disbursements fiscal 1964 ($ million)* |
|---|---|---|---|---|---|
| **Department of Agriculture:** | | | | | |
| Commodity Credit Corporation | 3½—4 | 6 mos.—4 | 1,471 | 3,030 | 2,088 |
| Rural Electrification Administration | 2 | 10—35 | 3,720 | 330 | 410 |
| Farmers Home Administration | 3—5 | 1—50 | 1,572 | 740 | 807 |
| **Department of Commerce:** | | | | | |
| Area Redevelopment Administration | 3½—4 | 25—40 | 29 | 28 | 98 |
| Maritime Administration | † | † | 110 | .. | .. |
| **Department of Health, Education and Welfare:** | | | | | |
| Office of Education | 3—4⅛ | 10—20 | 294 | 89 | 147 |
| **Department of the Interior:** | | | | | |
| Bureau of Reclamation | 0—3⅞ | 50 | 74 | 22 | 14 |
| **Department of State:** | | | | | |
| Loans to United Nations | 2 | 25 | 141 | 100 | .. |
| Agency for International Development | ¾—5¾ | 10—40 | 6,202 | 1,416 | 1,551 |
| **Treasury Department:** | | | | | |
| Loans to District of Columbia | 3⅞ | 30—40 | 122 | 53 | 31 |
| 1946 Loan to United Kingdom | 2 | 50 | 3,205 | .. | .. |
| **Housing and Home Finance Agency:** | | | | | |
| Community Facilities Administration | 0—3¾ | 20—50 | 1,821 | 509 | 468 |
| Urban Renewal Administration | 3⅞ | 3 mos. | 153 | 109 | 115 |
| Federal National Mortgage Association | 3¼—6 | 10—40 | 3,377 | 343 | 401 |
| Federal Housing Administration | 5¼ | 30—40 | 650 | 267 | 196 |
| Public Housing Administration | 3—4⅛ | Demand | 91 | 269 | 289 |
| Veterans Administration | 5¼ | 30 | 1,935 | 401 | 388 |
| Export-Import Bank of Washington | 4—6 | 1—25 | 3,466 | 490 | 670 |
| Interstate Commerce Commission | † | † | 15 | .. | .. |
| Small Business Administration | 3—5½ | 5—25 | 894 | 369 | 445 |
| Expansion of Defense Production | † | † | 137 | 17 | 10 |
| Total | .. | .. | 29,479 | 8,582 | 8,128 |

Note: Interest rates and maturities are minimums and maximums for different programs and are not intended in every case to suggest a range. * Budget estimates and projections. † No loans made or projected in fiscal 1963 or 1964.
Source: Bureau of the Budget.

long waiting lists for federal funds. Subsidized lending tends also to become political lending. It is better policy, and better economics, to charge market rates on loans. It is also fairer to taxpayers who have enough of a burden carrying the existing public debt.

Some loans made by the Federal Government and its credit agencies are loans in name only. The prime example is the Commodity Credit Corporation, which goes through a rigmarole of lending money to farmers when it is actually buying their crops. The money is lent against crops locked in storage, which the farmer may redeem and repay his loan. But the government usually ends up as sole owner of the crops and with no further claim upon the borrower.

The Committee on Federal Credit Programs did not deal with all types of federal lending. It omitted from consideration all international programs, CCC price-support and storage-facility loans, and other smaller items such as loans remaining from credit programs that are now defunct. Appropriately, the report also excludes the loan and investment activities of the Federal Reserve Banks; these do not involve burdens upon the federal budget.

The principal concern of the report is with the activities of numerous federal agencies that have been set up partly or wholly for the purpose of lending to domestic borrowers funds supplied by the U. S. Treasury. Among these agencies are the Rural Electrification Administration, which lends to electric power cooperatives; Farmers Home Administration, whose loans are used for farm operating expenses, crop production, farm ownership and improvement, and recently for the purchase of rural residences; and the Small Business Administration, which makes a variety of loans to small firms. The accompanying table provides a more complete picture of federal lending programs, though it does not include all the agencies involved.

### The Dillon Committee Recommendations

By drawing on repayments of old loans to make new ones, many of these credit programs have become self-perpetuating. Moreover, because the agencies involved dispense low-interest loans for local projects, they have many friends in Congress. Indeed, the Dillon Committee pointed out that some federal agencies appear reluctant to turn off the spigot, filling all applications on a first-come, first-served basis until their funds run out. Then they go back to Congress for more money, or they build up backlogs of unfilled applications. In these circumstances, it is easy to see why politically popular lending programs grow and grow.

This situation led the Credit Programs Committee to recommend that the agencies ad-

ministering these programs try harder to develop credit standards (and ask for supporting legislation, if necessary) to help them do a more efficient job in allocating their large, but nonetheless limited, funds among would-be borrowers with virtually insatiable appetites.

Some other recommendations by the Committee aim at reducing the costs of, and tightening budgetary control over, credit programs. They include these points:

• Government credit programs should, in principle, supplement or stimulate private lending rather than substitute for it.

• Credit programs filling needs that arise solely out of gaps in the private credit system should normally be self-supporting, i.e., cover all costs of the programs.

• Legislation authorizing new credit programs, or major expansions of present ones, should avoid rigid or relatively inflexible interest rate ceilings or floors. Even where rates charged are set below those in private markets, the lending agency should be permitted to vary the rate charged new borrowers, at least as much as market rates and current Treasury borrowing costs vary.

• Budget presentations of government credit programs should include enough detail about each major program to permit Congress and the Treasury to determine its financing requirements as well as its economic impact.

• Subsidies to recipients of federal credit programs arising from low interest rate loans should be measured and reported.

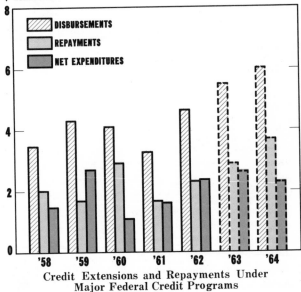

**$ BILLIONS**

Credit Extensions and Repayments Under
Major Federal Credit Programs
(Fiscal Years 1958-1964)

Note: Includes international lending programs, but excludes Commodity Credit Corporation for which disbursements of $2 billion are projected for fiscal 1964. Net expenditures are a result of disbursements exceeding repayments.

Source: Bureau of the Budget.

## The Subsidy Element

To help government lending agencies determine when a rate of interest represents a subsidy, the Committee provided this guideline: If the rate is not at least as high as the prevailing cost of borrowing by government on securities of comparable maturity, plus an allowance for administrative costs and a margin for defaults, a subsidy exists.

But even when the federal lending program covers all costs the Committee recognizes that the users of government credit enjoy an advantage over persons forced to borrow in the market place:

> The amount of such additional advantage is difficult to measure, but it clearly exists. Because of his more limited resources, even the competitive and efficient private lender has to build up reserves to cover not merely the losses normally anticipated, but also the threat of abnormally high losses. This will be reflected in his charge for risk. The Government, on the other hand, can rely upon its taxing power to take care of such contingencies. Moreover, because of its taxing power, the Government enjoys a high credit rating, which enables it to borrow at a substantially lower cost than any private lender.

At present, many federal lending programs fail even the first test and are, in effect, lending money the Treasury has to borrow, without so much as recovering the interest the government has had to pay. Indeed, most present lending programs seem designed and intended to subsidize special borrower groups.

### Competition with Private Industry

Senator A. Willis Robertson, speaking on the floor of the Senate in March, called attention to the fact that the budget for fiscal '64 proposes funds for loan programs which are not needed and which compete with private lenders. Specifically, he referred to the request by the Rural Electrification Administration for $495 million of new loan funds for electric and telephone plants in 1964. "Yet today," he said, "98 per cent of the nation's farms now have electric power. And five out of every six of the new member customers of REA-financed electric cooperatives in recent years have been industrial, commercial and nonfarm residential consumers." He added that if this agency held to its proper purposes, a sizable reduction in its spending could be achieved.

The REA was created by President Roosevelt on May 11, 1935 under the authority of the Emergency Relief Appropriations Act of that year. About 11 per cent of the country's farms were electrified at that time. Since then, legislation has given permanence to the agency and broadened its scope. With access to the Federal Treasury, and with authority to make loans at only 2 per cent per annum to finance electric cooperatives which pay no federal income tax, the REA has become the object of sharp criticism by the nation's investor-owned taxpaying electric utility industry. How far the REA has wandered from its original function is suggested by recent complaints that REA loans have been used to finance such projects as snow-making equipment for a ski resort, a housing development and electric equipment for a lumber mill and a race track. The increasing aggressiveness of the REA is swelling the ranks of its critics and opponents in Congress and among business groups.

The REA is not the only federal credit agency to come under attack. Criticisms have also been recently leveled against the Farmers Home Administration, which, like the REA, is under the Department of Agriculture.

### 33-Year 4% Loans

Not long ago Miles L. Colean, a consultant in the mortgage field, and Raymond J. Saulnier, Chairman of the President's Council of Economic Advisers from 1957 to 1960, produced a study citing cases in which Farmers Home Administration loans have directly competed with private credit. This program was originally established in 1937 to assist farm tenants to buy farms of their own. Successive amendments, however, have broadened the agency's role beyond farms. Starting in 1961, the agency was allowed to make direct loans for housing in communities not in excess of 2,500 population, which could be suburban areas. In 1962, this authority was further expanded to permit financing construction of rental units, including apartments, for elderly persons. Now the agency is making 33-year loans at 4 per cent to finance rural residences for persons who have nothing to do with farming.

To obtain a Farmers Home Administration loan a borrower must give evidence that he could not obtain credit on reasonable terms from private sources. As the Colean-Saulnier report commented, it is difficult for government credit not to supplant private "when the terms offered are, by virtue of governmental subsidization in one form or another, below anything that can be met by private lending institutions, or where the basis for extending credit is need rather than the ordinary criteria of the market." For private lenders, as well as the Federal Government, the cost of money now exceeds 4 per cent. A private financial institution would court bankruptcy lending on such terms as those offered by the Farmers Home Administration. The Federal Government is spared this hazard by its ability to levy taxes to make up the subsidy.

**FIRST NATIONAL CITY BANK**

13-country, 27,500 mile test trip of
Mr. & Mrs. S. Joseph Gore demonstrates that

# First National City Travelers Checks are "Better Than Money"*

To make an unprecedented and objective "test in use" of First National City Bank Travelers Checks, Mr. and Mrs. S. Joseph Gore of Florissant, Missouri were selected at random. Their instructions were simple: to tour, using FNCB Travelers Checks exclusively— for hotels, meals, souvenir shopping... indeed for all major travel purposes.

They were required to test these three important features: (1) the nationwide and world-wide availability of FNCB Travelers Checks; (2) the unique FNCB refund service (in case of loss, Western Union Operator 25 service directs travelers to thousands of refund points in the U.S.—and there are

thousands more overseas!) and (3) the full acceptability of FNCB Travelers Checks everywhere around the globe.

Each of these outstanding advantages was proved conclusively for the Gores in test after test after test... in country after country. In their own

words, "If there is one thing we have learned from 27,500 fascinating miles of testing, it is this—there is no safer, more convenient, more acceptable way to carry money than First National City Travelers Checks. It's true, they are 'Better Than Money'."

Member Federal Deposit Insurance Corporation

*"Better Than Money" is the service mark of First National City Travelers Checks

PRINTED IN U.S.A.

# Monthly Economic Letter

## General Business Conditions

Summertime brings a temporary, but none the less radical, transformation of the economy. In the weeks ahead, millions of people will be going off on vacation. While retaining their incomes and jobs, and remaining employed for purposes of Labor Department statistics, they will be enjoying the pleasures of paid "unemployment." Many plants will shut down for plant-wide holidays as the pace of industry slackens. Retail trade in the cities will drop into its summer doldrums.

Nevertheless, there are compensating increases of activity. Work reaches a high pitch in construction and agriculture. Gasoline consumption attains its annual peak. Nowhere is the acceleration of business greater than among recreational areas and summer camps. It is safe to predict that more than 2½ million teenagers and college students will be absorbed into the labor force between May and July to help out at resorts, in construction, on the farms, and in other activ-

ities that expand with summertime. While the level of unemployment may remain undesirably high, total employment, including members of the armed forces, seems likely to pass 73 million for the first time.

The question being asked is whether, after the vacation season, industrial activity can improve upon the first half year's performance. It is clear that some stimuli which had been helping activity will weaken. In two important lines, steel and automobiles, production is receding from crests that are unlikely to be duplicated in the second half.

Fortunately, increased business lies in prospect for other areas. Business outlays on new plant and equipment—which have been lagging—are scheduled to rise during the second half and will no doubt expand more affirmatively if corporate tax reductions are enacted. Individuals are borrowing and spending more freely than was the case last year, and it is a foregone conclusion that retail trade as a whole will show a significant gain over the second half of 1962.

### Record Industrial Production

Industrial production capped a four-month advance in May with a rise to 123.8 in the Federal Reserve index (seasonally adjusted, 1957-59 = 100) from 122.5 in April and 119.2 in January. This represented a decisive break-out from the plateau which stretched from July 1962 through January. Over this period, the index remained in the remarkably narrow range of 119.0 to 119.7. In the months ahead, as steel operations contract and the automobile industry enters the model change-over period, other lines of industrial activity will need to move ahead to hold the ground gained.

Preliminary production figures available for

June suggest the beginning of a new plateau. Order backlogs, particularly orders booked for machinery and equipment, are believed by most observers to insure sustained levels of industrial activity. Businessmen are planning expenditures on new plant and equipment of $39.2 billion for 1963, according to the Commerce Department-SEC survey published in early June. To attain this rate, outlays in the second half will have to be 8 per cent higher than those presently estimated for the first half. Disappointingly, in both fourth quarter 1962 and first quarter 1963, capital expenditures fell short of anticipated levels. In part, spending may have been lower than anticipated because of the unusually severe winter, but this performance nevertheless serves as a warning that capital spending plans can be deferred or canceled as well as expanded.

The extent to which ups and downs in durable goods activity have been concentrated in the steel industry is illustrated in the chart below. New orders for steel jumped 58 per cent from December to April, reflecting the efforts of steel-consuming industries to rebuild stocks, hedging against the possibility of a strike, as well as to cover increased consumption. Backlogs of unfilled orders expanded 46 per cent. In May, well before the new labor agreement was announced, new orders had already fallen 10 per cent. Further sizable declines can be expected for June and July, but part of the fall-off is seasonal. The roller-coaster behavior of steel order backlogs, related to strikes or fear of strikes, was not so pronounced this year as on previous occasions in 1959 and early 1962.

Durable goods other than iron and steel have shown continuing progress. New orders are up 9 per cent in the first five months of 1963, and unfilled orders have risen about 5 per cent. Inventories, which would include accumulation of protective steel stocks, rose only 2 per cent through April 30.

The new weekly figures of the Department of Commerce on total retail sales, which ran 8 per cent ahead of the corresponding period of 1962 during the first quarter, have subsequently shown somewhat narrower gains over last year's performance. The increase for the four weeks ended June 22 was 5 per cent. Much of the first half gain is explained by a decisive pickup of spending on durable goods, particularly for autos. It is now plain that output and sales of 1963 model passenger cars will set a new record, surpassing the 7.1 million '55 models.

### The Steel Agreement

The amicable agreement in the steel industry to modify the present wage contract and extend it to 1965 is a constructive step. It eliminates fears that a protracted steel strike might break the rhythm of prosperity—as happened in 1959—and should assure an extra year or two of labor peace in this key industry.

The cost of the contract changes—an estimated average 15 cents an hour over the life of the contract—is figured to be no more than 2 per cent a year, within the limits of the average annual increase of productivity per man-hour in the private economy since World War II. Instead of a raise in wages, the United Steelworkers gained benefits through a sabbatical leave plan. This plan, long sought by USW President David J. McDonald, and won last year from the can companies, is designed to spread work and make

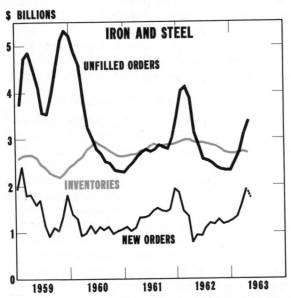

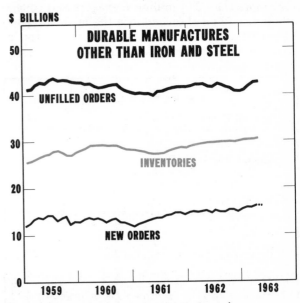

**Orders and Inventories in Iron and Steel and in Other Durable Goods Industries**
(New orders and inventories seasonally adjusted; unfilled orders unadjusted; May data partly estimated.)

room for additional employes. Half the workers in each company—those with the longest service —will get a 13-week vacation every five years, while the other half will have their vacations lengthened according to a formula. Also included were a new plan for settling certain kinds of local disputes and additional insurance benefits.

The financial cost to the steel industry is not small. Yet it is modest against the background of mounting employment costs under previous contracts and will help preserve the competitive power of the industry in world markets. It is to be hoped that the example of moderation will be copied in other industries.

## *Capital Market in Review*

The American financial markets are the largest in the world. They are international markets in the sense that foreign banks, governments and corporations come here both to invest and to raise money. It is safe to say that shares listed on the New York Stock Exchange are held by citizens of every country that allows people freedom to invest here. Foreign participation is even greater in the money market—the market for Treasury bills and other short-term instruments used by people at home and abroad as depositories for interest-bearing cash.

But the financial leadership of the United States is nowhere stronger than in the area of the capital market and particularly the market for long-term loans in forms of mortgages and bonds. This reflects a faith, absent in so many other countries, in the enduring value of money. We have had experience with price inflation, but far less than in most other countries. The reconstruction of capital markets overseas, even in Europe, has been painfully slow. People look back to what has happened to the purchasing power of their currencies over the last 20 or 30 years when they think about committing funds 20 or 30 years into the future. The limited capacity of foreign capital markets is a source of some embarrassment to the United States with its balance-of-payments deficit. For creditworthy borrowers, there is a greater availability of funds here—and at relatively low rates and much lower flotation costs—than in all the rest of the world put together.

The vital job of the capital market is to assemble the savings of millions of individuals and channel them to users—consumers, businesses, governments—that are willing and able to pay for capital to finance projects that could not be undertaken without the help of other people's money. The Federal Reserve Board calculates that net funds raised by nonfinancial sectors of the economy in 1962 reached a record-breaking $58 billion, of which $36 billion was represented by long-term securities and mortgages. The public's savings, mainly channeled through financial institutions, made available $24 billion for increase in mortgage indebtedness, supplying around 56 per cent of the $43 billion expended on private construction in 1962. Public utility

and other corporations raised about $5½ billion (net of retirements) through sales of stocks and bonds, and state and local governments obtained a similar net amount through issuance of new securities. Foreigners came to the New York market in 1962 to raise approximately $1 billion net.

Beyond this, our financial markets handle many billions of refinancing transactions and trades among investors in seasoned securities. Underwriters, brokers and dealers perform the function of bringing together buyers and sellers of securities. These middlemen earn their living through commissions, as in the stock exchange, or through spreads between the prices at which they buy and sell, as in the over-the-counter markets. The skilled professionals on the firing line must be highly alert and well-informed—for there is scarcely any important development anywhere that does not affect some market values.

### *Principal Financial Intermediaries*

Although individuals make diversified investments on their own, or through trust departments of banks and through mutual funds, the biggest markets for interest-bearing securities are found among a group of six financial intermediaries: commercial banks; life insurance companies; savings and loan associations; mutual savings banks; trusteed pension funds; and fire, casualty and marine insurance companies. Their relative sizes and the general breakdown of their loans and investments are portrayed in the chart on the following page.

Many of these institutions specialize in the ways they put money to work. Pension funds invest mainly in corporate stocks and bonds. Savings banks, and savings and loan associations to an even greater extent, have most of their money in real estate mortgages. Life insurance companies divide their resources mainly between corporate bonds and mortgages. The most diversified lenders are the commercial banks, whose loans and investments range from day loans to security dealers at one end of the spectrum to long-term mortgages for homeowners at the other. The vital roles performed by commercial banks are as financiers of industry, domestic and foreign trade, and federal, state and local governments.

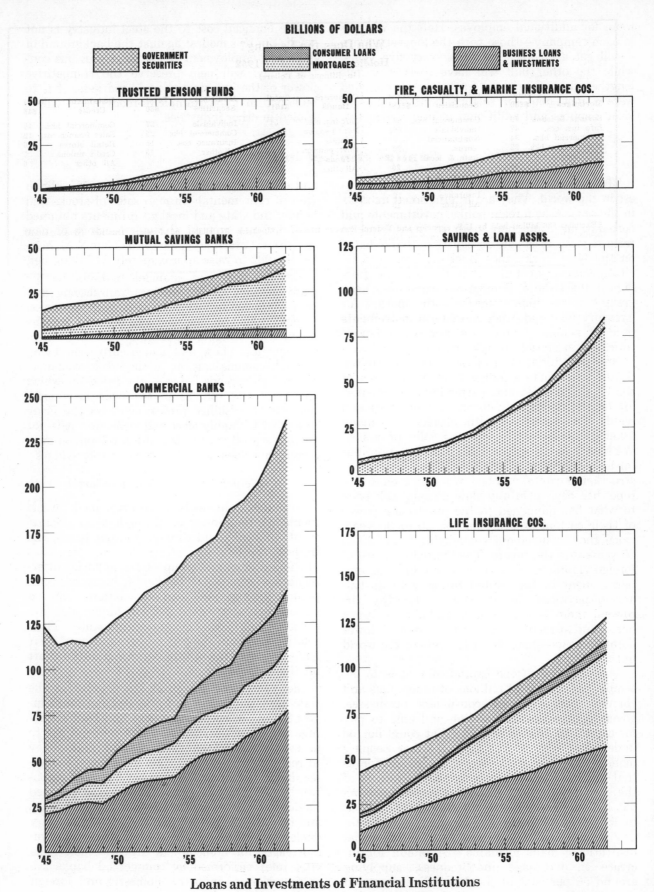

**Loans and Investments of Financial Institutions**

(Year-end holdings, 1962 partly estimated.)

## Who Does the Lending?
### Holdings at the End of 1962
#### (In Billions of Dollars)

| Mortgages | Total $250 | U.S. Govt. Securities | Total $218* | Corporate Bonds | Total $101† | Municipal Securities | Total $80 | Instalment Credit | Total $48 |
|---|---|---|---|---|---|---|---|---|---|
| Savings & loans | 79 | Commercial bks. | 66 | Life ins. cos. | 54 | Individuals | 27 | Commercial bks. | 19 |
| Life ins. cos. | 47 | Individuals | 66‡ | Pvt. pension funds | 17 | Commercial bks. | 25 | Sales finance cos. | 12 |
| Commercial bks. | 34 | Nonfinancial corps. | 20 | Govt. pension funds | 11 | Insurance cos. | 15 | Retail stores | 6 |
| Mut. savings bks. | 32 | State & local govts. | 20 | All other | 19 | All other | 13 | Credit unions | 5 |
| U.S. agencies | 12 | Foreign & international | 15 | | | | | All other | 6 |
| All other | 46 | Insurance cos. | 12 | | | | | | |
| | | All other | 19 | | | | | | |

*Excludes $86 billion held by U.S. agencies and Federal Reserve Banks.     †Includes $7 billion of foreign (mainly governmental) bonds.  ‡Includes $47 billion of U.S. savings bonds.

Source: Federal Reserve Board and Securities and Exchange Commission.

During the 1950's bonds became hard to sell on several successive occasions—1953, 1957 and 1959—as interest rates moved upward, step-like, searching for a level at which supplies and demands of long-term funds could come into balance. The outstanding characteristic of the capital market of the early 1960's, in contrast, has been the plentiful supply of loan funds developed out of intensive promotional efforts of savings institutions. Rates have not been so cheap as in phases of easy money during the 1950's but the flow of funds into new lending has maintained a very high level.

The failure of interest rates paid by borrowers to decline more is attributable to three main factors:

• First, there are the heavy interest costs shouldered by financial institutions to attract funds; rates paid on savings deposits are the highest in a generation.

• Second, increased amounts of funds have been taken up by the enlarged federal deficit and the growing absorption of money by the mortgage market and states and municipalities; demand for long-term credit and equity money by business remains sluggish, a financial counterpart of the lagging rate of plant and equipment spending and the inadequacy under the tax laws of profit incentive to investment.

• Third, there has been the chronic balance-of-payments deficit. This has forced the Treasury and the Federal Reserve, while pursuing an over-all policy of credit ease to encourage domestic economic expansion, to sustain short-term interest rates and hence the attractiveness to foreigners of accumulating U.S. dollar investments in lieu of gold. Even so, the interest rates that have prevailed in our easily accessible and highly efficient money and capital markets have attracted more foreign borrowings than our balance of payments, already burdened by heavy governmental outlays abroad, can accommodate comfortably. Many experts feel that somewhat higher interest rates are needed in the United States to help relieve the balance-of-payments problem.

### Competitive Forces

Of particular importance these past few years has been the determination on the part of commercial banks to regain ground lost in recent years in the mortgage and other long-term credit markets. This means, among other things, competing more aggressively for savings and time deposits. The door to more effective competition was opened wider by federal banking authorities at the beginning of 1962, when they raised the legal maximum interest rate that banks may pay on such deposits, a step recently described by Federal Reserve Board Vice Chairman C. Canby Balderston as "one of the most important monetary actions that the Board has taken in recent times." The greater stability of savings and time deposits as compared with checking accounts—and the pressure to earn the revenue needed to pay depositors the higher rates—has propelled banks into the capital market on a much larger scale than before.

Money market observers sense that the Federal Reserve has recently moved toward somewhat less easy money. In the past, such steps have at times caused sizable swings in bond prices. The moderate, almost nonchalant, response of the capital market on this occasion suggests a general expectation that long-term funds will continue to flow in abundance. The U.S. Treasury has been taking advantage of the opportunity to put at least some modest amounts of public debt into the form of long-term bonds.

The U.S. capital market is a bastion of strength to the entire free world. Abroad, the need is to develop similar markets so that disproportionate dependence upon our market can be reduced. Here, the need is to find a combination of fiscal and monetary policies which will direct a larger portion of savings into business investment while, at the same time, restraining the inflationary pressures that can undermine the capacity of the capital market to keep growing for the benefit of all borrowers and all people.

## Grants and Loans, Hard and Soft

Since World War II, foreign aid financed by U.S. taxpayers has exceeded $100 billion. Two thirds of this amount has been spent on economic aid, either outright grants or loans. Today, with the persistent excess of expenditures abroad beyond our receipts, the need to re-evaluate overseas programs is imperative. It is timely to take a look back over the road we have traveled.

In the early postwar years, U.S. aid was extended in the form of loans—most notably the $3,750 million 2 per cent, 50-year British loan of 1946—and contributions for immediate relief and rehabilitation of war-damaged areas. In 1948, when the European Recovery Program (Marshall Plan) was launched, the emphasis shifted to grants designed to wind up after four years and justified on the ground that they would get Europe on its feet, spare burdens of servicing foreign debts, and help restore the international monetary system by repairing dollar shortage.

In 1949, when the United States embarked upon technical assistance to less-developed nations (President Truman's Point Four Program), the Administration did not advocate government grants. It was widely assumed that private capital, together with loans available on commercial terms from the Export-Import Bank and the World Bank, would do the job. The outbreak of the Korean War, and the increasingly evident need to check Russian and Chinese imperialism, led to a succession of new military and economic aid programs. Nevertheless, up to 1957, the Export-Import Bank continued as the principal U.S. agency for financing selected investment projects abroad and also—sometimes jointly with the International Monetary Fund or private financial institutions—for helping tide developing nations over recurrent balance-of-payments crises.

### Getting Away from Grants

The acceptance of grant programs in the early years of postwar reconstruction is explainable by unhappy memories of government loans during and after World War I that did not prove to be collectible. It was felt that if loans were not collectible it would be preferable to make outright grants.

On a continuing basis, grants are objectionable to taxpayers. Loans sound better and seem more businesslike. Loan procedures can exert a discipline on the borrower and impose an economic test that a project can pay for itself with interest on the funds required. This is a test constantly applied in our own country, from the decision of an individual to build or buy a house to the decision of a corporation to put up a new plant or introduce a new product line.

Thus, the trend has been to get away from "giveaways." But many of the loans under aid programs are loans in name only. The word "soft loans" has been invented to characterize loans repayable in inconvertible foreign currencies or extended at rates of interest below the cost of money to the lender. Doing business on such terms would bankrupt a private financial institution.

The first important use of soft loans by the U.S. Government began in 1954, under Public Law 480. To give aid in the tangible form of surplus agricultural commodities, the government began to dispose of surplus wheat, feed grains, cotton and soybean oil in exchange for foreign currencies inconvertible into dollars. In 1957, Congress created the Development Loan Fund to extend loans in dollars repayable, in whole or in part, in the borrower's own currency. The Fund was abolished in 1961 after having made some 200 loans to 50 countries totaling approximately

### U. S. Foreign Aid, 1946-62
(In Millions of Dollars)

| Fiscal Years | Economic Aid* Grants† | Loans ‡ | Total | Military Aid ¶ | Total |
|---|---|---|---|---|---|
| 1946-48 | $ 6,331 | $ 7,724 | $14,055 | $ 481 | $14,536 |
| 1949-52 | 16,223 | 3,127 | 19,351 | 2,839 | 22,190 |
| 1953 | 2,159 | 454 | 2,613 | 4,272 | 6,885 |
| 1954 | 2,268 | 152 | 2,419 | 3,412 | 5,831 |
| 1955 | 2,013 | 674 | 2,686 | 2,509 | 5,195 |
| 1956 | 1,885 | 735 | 2,620 | 2,979 | 5,598 |
| 1957 | 2,017 | 1,270 | 3,287 | 2,134 | 5,421 |
| 1958 | 1,728 | 1,239 | 2,967 | 2,404 | 5,371 |
| 1959 | 1,730 | 1,845 | 3,574 | 2,160 | 5,735 |
| 1960 | 1,955 | 1,417 | 3,372 | 1,845 | 5,217 |
| 1961 | 2,202 | 2,224 | 4,426 | 1,454 | 5,880 |
| 1962 | 2,248 | 2,836 | 5,084 | 1,526 | 6,611 |
| Total | $42,760 | $23,695 | $66,455 | $30,678 | $97,133 |

* Data are on an obligation or loan authorization basis. † Includes grants by the Agency for International Development and its predecessors, P.L. 480 programs (sales of surplus farm products for local currencies, etc.) and capital subscriptions to the World Bank, the International Development Association, the International Finance Corporation and the Inter-American Development Bank. ‡ Includes loans by the Agency for International Development and its predecessors, Export-Import Bank long-term loans and the $3,750 million loan of 1946 to the United Kingdom. ¶ Primarily grants of military equipment, supplies and services; annual data are net deliveries, while the 1946-62 total represents amounts programmed rather than the sum of deliveries (the difference between the cumulative total and the sum for the fiscal years being the value of goods programmed but not yet delivered).

Source: Agency for International Development, *U.S. Foreign Assistance, July 1, 1945- June 30, 1962*, April 1963.

$2 billion, four fifths of which were repayable in the borrowers' currencies. The rapid accumulation of inconvertible foreign currencies under this program, as well as from sales of surplus agricultural commodities, proved an embarrassment, a possible source of friction over ultimate disposition.

## A Hodgepodge of Terms

In 1961, the Development Loan Fund and other aid agencies were replaced by the Agency for International Development (AID), which adopted a new variety of soft loan—loans repayable in dollars but without interest (except for a ¾ per cent annual service charge) and extending over 40 years with repayments beginning after 10 years. Since it costs the U.S. Treasury more than 4 per cent to borrow long-term funds, this arrangement involves interest rate subsidies extending 40 years into the future. Since there are elements of both grant and loan, some wags use the term "groan" for the crossbreed.

The dollar-repayable, long-term loans at no interest were originally devised for the International Development Association (IDA), a World Bank affiliate, which began operations at the end of 1960. The U.S. contribution to IDA was $320 million out of total convertible currency contributions of $763 million. These funds have been largely committed and further contributions are now under consideration.

The World Bank itself meanwhile has continued financing development projects on a businesslike basis. The interest rate it charges fluctuates in accordance with changes in the cost of money in world capital markets.

The Inter-American Development Bank, which like IDA began business in 1960, has three loan windows. At one, loans are extended on terms similar to those of the Export-Import Bank or the World Bank. At the second, loans are made at lower rates and longer maturities repayable in currencies loaned or, sometimes, in the borrowers' own currencies. At the third window—handling a trust fund managed for the U.S. Government under the Alliance for Progress—loans are made for so-called social overhead projects at still lower rates and longer maturities, repayable in the borrowers' currencies.

Other countries using government funds to lend in support of economic development overseas adopt a wide variety of practices although none are more generous than the terms offered by our AID. France extends loans with token rates of interest and very long repayment periods to countries with which it has had long historical associations. Other European nations, Canada and Japan provide loans to less-developed countries either on market terms or on softer terms

### Typical Terms and Conditions of Development Loans by U.S. and International Financial Institutions

| | Int. rate*  (%) | Repayment Currency | Terms Maturity† (years) | Authorized in 1962 ($ mil.) |
|---|---|---|---|---|
| **United States** | | | | |
| Export-Import Bank‡ | 5¾ | Dollars | 5–26 | 676 |
| Agency for Int'l Development Loans to: | | | | |
| Governments | ¾ | Dollars | 40 ⎫ | ⎱ 1,069 |
| Pvt. borrowers | 5¾ | § | § ⎭ | ⎰ |
| **International** | | | | |
| World Bank | 5½ | Dollars ‖ | 15–20 | 646 |
| Int'l Dev. Assn. | ¾ | Dollars ‖ | 50 | 187 |
| Int'l Fin. Corp. ¶ | 7–7½ | Dollars ‖ | 7–13 | 23 |
| Inter-Am. Dev. Bk. Loans to govts from: | | | | |
| Ord. capital | 5¾ | Dollars ‖ | 8–20 | 60 |
| Fund for Sp. Op. | 4 | Dollars # | 10–30 | 41 |
| Social Progress Trust Fund | 2–3½ | Borrower's currency | 20–30 | 205 |
| Loans to private borrowers from: | | | | |
| Ord. capital | 5¾ | Dollars ‖ | 8–15 | 24 |

* Includes charges and commissions: AID and IDA, ¾%; World Bank 1% on loans from ordinary capital, ¾% on loans from the Social Progress Trust Fund. In addition, the following commitment fees are charged on undisbursed balances of loans: World Bank ¾%; IFC 1%; IDB ¾% on loans from ordinary capital. † Includes grace periods: AID and IDA, up to 10 years; IDB, varying periods for different categories of loans. ‡ Loans for specific development projects. § Private borrowers make repayments, in local currency and within relatively short time, to their own government, which in turn is to repay AID in dollars up to 40 years with an annual service charge of ¾%. ‖ Or currencies loaned. ¶ Beginning with 1961, when IFC was authorized to purchase stocks directly, the pattern of investment has normally consisted of a straight loan at fixed interest and acquisition of stock. # In several cases, repayment has been authorized in the currency of the borrower.

Source: Derived from annual reports, financial statements, etc.

without, however, going so far as AID or IDA. The United Kingdom Government makes loans prudently at rates which at least cover its own borrowing costs. Typical terms for British aid are 25 years with repayments beginning in the eighth year; interest rates (including a ¼ per cent management charge) range from 4⅛ per cent for a one-year loan to 6 per cent for 15-30 year loans.

### Objections to Soft Loans

Quite evidently, there has been a good deal of difference of opinion among Western nations as to terms on which aid should be offered for development purposes. An OECD report on *Development Assistance Efforts and Policies*, published last year, reviews the objections raised by European governments against soft loans, especially with regard to interest rates.

The objections to soft loans reported by the OECD are worth pondering on this side of the Atlantic. The United Kingdom Government is concerned that "lending at soft rates might have repercussions on the terms of treasury lending to domestic borrowers, such as the nationalized industries." Several governments feel that they cannot afford subsidies from budgetary funds required by soft terms of lending: "The budgetary and financial position of their countries limits their ability to increase the proportion of loans at lenient terms." Italy and Japan also feel that for balance-of-payments reasons they cannot exceed relatively short repayment periods. We have this same reason for exerting greater caution in lending on soft terms; the burden falls not only on the taxpayer but also on the balance of payments.

The special Committee to Strengthen the Security of the Free World, of which General Lucius D. Clay is chairman, recommended last March that Europe and Japan soften the terms of their lending to less-developed nations. At the same time, it recommended that U.S. loan terms be determined "on a more flexible basis" after a country-by-country analysis of debt-servicing capacities. "Loans to countries with adequate debt-servicing capacity in the foreseeable future should be made on harder terms." Last April, the OECD Development Assistance Committee, which includes Japan, reportedly reached an agreement to secure more uniform lending terms, with the stricter lenders softening theirs.

On broad economic principles, projects that can pay their way out, in terms of principal and interest, should have precedence over projects that cannot. In other words, subsidized lending becomes political lending.

The danger in soft lending is that bad loans may drive out the good, invite improvidence and penalize good fiscal management. Americans object on principle to taxation of their private enterprise to subsidize foreign public enterprise. In the final analysis, soft lending can drive private enterprise right out of business. If capital is sorely needed, borrowers should be able to pay what savers can command from other borrowers.

Respect for the dollar—and the resolution of our unsolved balance-of-payments problem—depends in no small way on discretion in government spending, with special accent on overseas spending. And unsound spending-lending on our part can induce unsound spending-investing on the part of recipient nations. As the German Government observed in the OECD document quoted above:

> ... loans at soft terms may impair the role of private capital, distort competitive positions and weaken the function of interest rates in allocating scarce capital among competing uses. Care must be taken . . . to ensure that the granting of loans at soft terms does not constitute a substitute for monetary and financial discipline on the part of the recipient countries.

Capacity to repay loans depends vitally on the policies a country pursues. If loans are really development loans, and are used efficiently, they should help expand output and strengthen balances of payments more than enough to cover the debt service at market rates of interest and over periods shorter than the life of the investment. Capital has scarcity value. It needs to be used where it can return the most. That, at least, is the rule provident people live by. And without provident people there can be no generation of capital for national and international economic development.

## Depreciation of Money

In the accompanying table, we again present our annual round-the-world survey of the shrinkage in the value of money. As in the past, we measure this shrinkage by the decline in the domestic purchasing power of the various national currencies, as calculated from official cost-of-living or consumer price indexes compiled in 43 countries.

In 1962, and for the 1952-62 decade as a whole, the performance of the U.S. dollar held close to the top of the list. Yet even our ten-year average rate of shrinkage, 1.3 per cent per annum, if projected over the life of the latest long-term U.S. Treasury bond issue, will reduce by one third the real value of the bonds by final maturity in 1994. People take this into account in wanting interest rates around 4 per cent on U.S. bonds and over 5 per cent on real estate mortgages. But the fact that vast amounts of long-term borrowing and lending are being carried out in the interest rate range of 4 to 6 per cent represents an expression of confidence that the dollar will fare no worse in the future than it has in the past. The situation is different in many other countries where indulgence of inflation has weakened or even destroyed faith in long-term promises to pay.

While a number of important countries, including the United States, have moved closer to overall price stability, wage-price spiraling has broken loose in a number of industrialized countries, including Western Europe rather generally. Among South American countries whose currencies have suffered the most serious losses in purchasing power, the performance of Chile has been significantly improved while deterioration has accelerated in Brazil and Argentina. This is apparent from a comparison of the annual rates of depreciation for 1961-62 with those for the 1952-62 decade.

The Working Party on Economic Development and Planning, an arm of the United Nations' Economic Commission for Asia and the Far East (ECAFE), recently added its voice to those of responsible officials who have been stressing the need for development of financial institutions and markets as means to faster economic progress. In Far Eastern countries, as elsewhere, family households do most of the national saving. Out of long experience with price inflation, the tendency is to put savings into tangible assets—gold, silver, real estate and works of art. But a greater proportion of household income is saved and made available for economic growth in those places, notably Japan, where people feel secure enough in their currency to entrust their savings to financial institutions that in turn can channel the money into major productive projects. Where such intermediaries do not play a prominent role, sizable investment projects remain limited to those that can be financed by plowing back profits, by foreign money, by taxes—or by shortsighted and self-defeating recourse to the printing press.

| | Indexes of Value of Money | | | Annual Depreciation | |
| | 1952 | 1961 | 1962 | '52-'62* | '61-'62 |
|---|---|---|---|---|---|
| Ceylon | 100 | 95 | 94 | 0.6% | 1.0% |
| Venezuela | 100 | 93 | 93 | 0.7 | —1.0 |
| Guatemala | 100 | 94 | 92 | 0.8 | 2.0 |
| El Salvador | 100 | 91 | 91 | 1.0 | .. |
| Canada | 100 | 91 | 90 | 1.1 | 1.0 |
| Philippines | 100 | 94 | 89 | 1.1 | 5.4 |
| Belgium | 100 | 90 | 89 | 1.2 | 1.0 |
| Ecuador | 100 | 92 | 89 | 1.2 | 2.8 |
| Switzerland | 100 | 92 | 88 | 1.2 | 3.7 |
| United States | 100 | 89 | 88 | 1.3 | 1.0 |
| Lebanon | 100 | 89 | 87 | 1.4 | 1.9 |
| Portugal | 100 | 92 | 87 | 1.4 | 4.6 |
| Germany | 100 | 89 | 86 | 1.5 | 3.7 |
| Italy | 100 | 84 | 80 | 2.2 | 4.6 |
| South Africa | 100 | 81 | 80 | 2.2 | 1.0 |
| Austria | 100 | 84 | 79 | 2.3 | 5.4 |
| India | 100 | 82 | 79 | 2.3 | 3.6 |
| Australia | 100 | 79 | 79 | 2.4 | .. |
| Netherlands | 100 | 81 | 78 | 2.4 | 3.7 |
| Pakistan | 100 | 78 | 78 | 2.5 | .. |
| Denmark | 100 | 81 | 76 | 2.8 | 7.0 |
| Ireland | 100 | 79 | 75 | 2.8 | 4.6 |
| Norway | 100 | 79 | 75 | 2.9 | 5.4 |
| United Kingdom | 100 | 78 | 75 | 2.9 | 3.7 |
| Sweden | 100 | 77 | 74 | 3.0 | 4.5 |
| New Zealand | 100 | 76 | 73 | 3.1 | 3.6 |
| Japan | 100 | 77 | 72 | 3.2 | 5.9 |
| France | 100 | 73 | 70 | 3.5 | 4.2 |
| Finland | 100 | 72 | 69 | 3.6 | 3.6 |
| Greece | 100 | 66 | 66 | 4.0 | .. |
| Mexico | 100 | 62 | 62 | 4.7 | 0.9 |
| Spain | 100 | 63 | 60 | 5.0 | 5.1 |
| Iran | 100 | 54 | 54 | 6.0 | 0.8 |
| Peru | 100 | 53 | 50 | 6.7 | 5.9 |
| Colombia | 100 | 51 | 50 | 6.8 | 2.4 |
| Israel | 100 | 51 | 46 | 7.5 | 9.0 |
| China (Taiwan) | 100 | 45 | 44 | 7.9 | 2.1 |
| Turkey | 100 | 41 | 39 | 8.9 | 4.2 |
| Uruguay | 100 | 23 | 21 | 14.6 | 9.2 |
| Argentina | 100 | 14 | 11 | 19.7 | 21.8 |
| Brazil | 100 | 13 | 9 | 21.5 | 33.8 |
| Chile | 100 | 6 | 6 | 25.0 | 12.1 |
| Bolivia | 100 | 1 | 1 | 35.2 | 5.3 |

* Compounded annually.
Note: Depreciation computed from unrounded data. Value of money is measured by reciprocals of official cost-of-living or consumer price indexes.

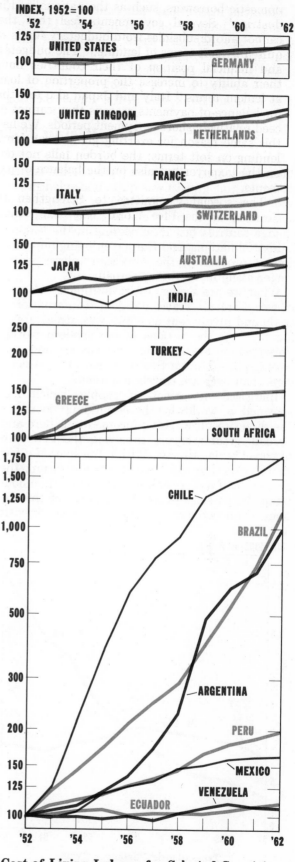

Cost-of-Living Indexes for Selected Countries, 1952-62

Financial institutions that can mobilize small savings are unlikely to flourish, as the U.N. experts recognized, when there is unchecked inflation. In too many places, as our table shows, this lesson has not been applied.

As Reinhard Kamitz, president of the Austrian National Bank, said at the annual meeting of the National Industrial Conference Board, May 17: "The rates of monetary depreciation in the free world, which prevailed during the last 10 years, must be considerably reduced, if we really want the best possible results of modern economic policy and the highest possible standards of living."

## The Rising Tide of World Travel

Tourism today is not only big business; it is one of the most vigorous of growth industries. Although this growth was quite one-sided in the first decade following World War II, it is now blossoming on a truly global scale. With exchange controls fast disappearing in the leading industrial nations, and Europe enjoying unprecedented prosperity, the American tourist is no longer alone in venturing abroad.

What we are seeing is a revolutionary change in world travel. Travel has joined international trade and investment as a two-way street drawing together the nations of our modern world. Foreigners in ever-growing numbers are now discovering the United States, while more Americans than ever are traveling abroad.

Increased movement of people—which has spawned a worldwide hotel-building boom—is the direct result of rising income levels here and abroad, greater leisure time and the new ease of travel by jet aircraft. Within the span of a few short years, the jets have effectively shrunk the globe to half its former size, while more than doubling the passenger-carrying capacity of the airlines. On a two-week vacation a person can visit a half dozen countries, as distant as his budget will allow. There is scarcely a major city left that is now more than a day's journey by plane. Thus, businessmen, diplomats, holiday seekers and students are all moving about the world as never before.

### Another Record-Breaking Year

As the summer vacation season gets into full swing, all signs point to another record-breaking year for American travel abroad. U.S. passport applications are running 14 per cent ahead of last year, when 1.8 million citizens went overseas for sightseeing, business or study, compared with only 800,000 a decade ago. Americans numbering 6.6 million took overland vacations or business trips (of more than two days' duration) into neighboring Canada or Mexico last year. Total U.S. spending on foreign travel—$2.9 billion in 1962 (including $430 million paid to U.S. carriers)—has more than doubled in the past eight years and is growing nearly twice as fast as disposable personal income.

The United States, in turn, was host to more than 700,000 visitors from overseas in 1962, plus nearly 5.5 million tourists from Canada and Mexico. This influx has doubled in the past decade, with U.S. earnings from this source totaling more than $1 billion in 1962.

Through the United States Travel Service, established just two years ago, this country is now actively supplementing the long-time efforts of major U.S. carriers to attract more foreign visitors here. There is evidence that the expanded effort is meeting with success. During 1962, the total number of overseas visitors to this country rose by more than 14 per cent, and so far this year a further gain of 22 per cent has been reported. During the past three years, partly in anticipation of the 1964-65 World's Fair, the transient hotel capacity of New York's Manhattan Island has been enlarged by 8,700 rooms, a 10 per cent increase involving 13 new hotels.

### Dynamic Growth Industry

The magnitude of the postwar travel boom is seen in the roughly $7 billion global total of foreign tourist spending last year, estimated on the basis of balance-of-payments data submitted to

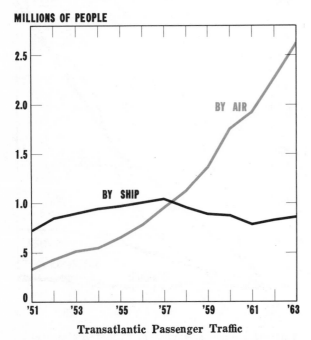

**MILLIONS OF PEOPLE**

BY AIR

BY SHIP

**Transatlantic Passenger Traffic**

Source: International Air Transport Association and Trans-Atlantic Passenger Steamship Conference. Figures for 1963 estimated.

the International Monetary Fund. For Western Europe as a whole, total tourist earnings were placed at $3.7 billion in 1961, with one sixth of this spent by Americans.

Nearly a million Americans are expected in Europe this year, compared with 900,000 in 1962. Although Britain, France and Italy are still the top attractions for U.S. travelers, out-of-the-way spots are gaining favor, for example the Greek Islands and Yugoslavia's Dalmatian Coast. The tripling of American tourist traffic to Europe over the past decade has been handled largely by the airlines. Although more than 75 per cent of all U.S. transatlantic travelers now fly, compared with less than 40 per cent ten years ago, ship traffic has held up well.

The prosperous Germans have supplanted Americans as the largest travel spenders in Europe. More than eight million go abroad each year. They spent the equivalent of over $1 billion in 1962, with neighboring Austria the major beneficiary of this resurgent German wanderlust. The rapid rise of automobile ownership in Europe has increased family travel, especially southward toward the Mediterranean. Nowhere is this more evident than in Italy and Spain, which have experienced close to a tenfold growth of tourism over the past decade.

In the Pacific area, the new frontier of tourism, the visitor total has virtually tripled since 1956. Americans make up a third of all travelers to this area, and as much as one half to Japan and the Philippines. Nearly 200,000 Americans are expected in the Pacific region during 1963, a sizable gain over last year's 160,000 who spent an estimated $115 million. Probably another 240,000 U.S. Mainlanders will be welcomed this year in Hawaii, our Pacific island state where tourism has become the leading industry.

Travel to the sunny Caribbean (excluding Cuba of course) has shown spectacular growth over the past decade. These nearby islands, which first gained popularity as winter-vacation resorts for North Americans, are now actively fostering off-season traffic. *Turismo* has become the most dynamic sector of the Puerto Rican economy, and the same can be said for a dozen other tropical islands.

South America's share of U.S. travel spending, in contrast, has actually declined. The entire continent earned only $55 million from this source last year—less than .2 per cent of what we spent journeying abroad. A larger potential obviously exists, but it is equally clear that it will not be achieved without more vigorous promotion, coupled with political stability. These South American republics have managed to reduce the red tape formalities of getting into and out of a country, which can take much of the pleasure out of travel.

Closer to home the tourist volume goes up sharply. Tourism is Mexico's largest dollar earner, and it has long offset the country's sizable trade deficit. Canada, because of its proximity to major U.S. cities, is the No. 1 foreign destination for Americans. But Canadians too are avid travelers, so that Canada, like most other prosperous nations, consistently spends more abroad than other peoples spend in Canada.

### Learning from Success

The travel industry looks to the decade ahead with great expectations. Predictions abound for a further doubling or tripling of global tourism, boosted by rising incomes, more leisure time and the steady upgrading of worldwide travel facilities. And looming somewhere in the future is the advent of the supersonic passenger plane that will shrink distances even more.

Already a matter of record, however, is the invaluable contribution of tourism to the economic well-being of many nations, some highly developed and others more recently on the road to self-advancement. In Austria, Italy and Spain, catering to foreign visitors earns more than any single export. In many countries, tourist earnings make up the difference between surplus or deficit in international payments. And in the Caribbean, there are numerous examples of islands that have achieved rising income and employment through intelligent promotion of tourism and relatively small public investment.

This success can serve as an example to the many newly-independent nations now striving to develop their economies. For most, promoting tourism will yield far greater return than a costly prestige airline or a state-owned steel mill. In fact, tourism is usually an ideal industry for a developing country. It focuses on the use of domestic resources, no matter what they may be. The end-product has the low import content and high ratio of employment to investment characteristic of a service industry. Needed skills are easily acquired. Furthermore, tourism gets people acquainted, often with spectacular results. Puerto Rico's experience has shown that today's vacationing businessmen may be active investors in tomorrow's economy.

## FIRST NATIONAL CITY BANK

# If you have trouble scoring with your investments, stop in and see the pros at First National City!

**OUT OF THE ROUGH**

Do-it-yourself investing can be painful—particularly where important sums are involved. The stock market is no place for guessing games! Selecting securities today is a full-time job. △ Serious investors look to an organization like ours for continuing investment management. We're not infallible, but we give it our very best. Our staff, resources, research, and experience are all extensive. In a major sense, investing is our business. △ We tailor investment programs to your wants and needs. We are able to practice <u>flexibility</u> in investing. Our Investment Advisory Service includes full custodianship, and its modest cost is usually tax deductible. "Successful Investing in the 1960's & 70's" tells more about it. Write for a copy today. **FIRST NATIONAL CITY BANK**

TRUST DIVISION, DEPARTMENT F, 399 PARK AVENUE, NEW YORK 22, NEW YORK • MEMBER FEDERAL DEPOSIT INSURANCE CORPORATION

PRINTED IN U.S.A.

# Monthly Economic Letter

## General Business Conditions

The strong and steady course of business activity was overshadowed during July by action on the balance-of-payments front, the nagging possibility of a railroad strike and concern over growing civil rights disputes. Another major event was the agreement late last month on a treaty between Russia, Britain and the United States providing a partial nuclear test ban. It could be a first step toward moderation of long-standing East-West tensions which cost all three countries vast efforts that could be expended to better advantage.

The major development eclipsing business news in July was the announcement from Washington of a program to deal more vigorously with the stubborn balance-of-payments deficit. The most surprising proposal, aimed at diminishing the outflow of long-term capital, was for a graduated tax on purchases of foreign securities by Americans and by foreigners residing in the United States.

To stem the outflow of short-term capital, the Federal Reserve reinforced an eight-week upward trend in Treasury bill rates with an increase in the discount rate from 3 to 3½ per cent. The monetary authorities made it clear that this action was designed "to aid in the United States' efforts to combat its international balance-of-payments problem." It marked the first time in more than 30 years that a discount rate increase has been employed solely to deal with an international situation. Usually the discount rate has been raised for domestic reasons to resist inflationary pressures accompanying economic expansion.

The Federal Reserve explained that "these actions . . . do not constitute a change in the System's policy of maintaining monetary conditions conducive to fuller utilization of manpower and other resources in this country." It is the sustainability of the current growth rate and strength of the domestic business picture that enable monetary authorities to tighten up a bit without an adverse effect on the economy.

### Strength in the Economy at Midyear

Industrial activity in June continued to forge ahead. A 5 per cent decline in steel ingot production was more than offset by a broad advance in other lines, particularly automobiles and business equipment. The Federal Reserve production index (seasonally adjusted, 1957-59 = 100) advanced to a new high of 125 in June, up 1 per cent from May and a gain of 5 per cent since the start of the year. During July, however, production figures for certain major industries suggested a leveling off in the index.

General economic activity, as measured by the gross national product, also reached a new record during the second quarter. Preliminary estimates of GNP indicate a gain of $7.2 billion to a seasonally adjusted annual rate of $579 billion; the increase slightly exceeded the first quarter rise of $6.6 billion. The general consensus is that GNP for the full year will be in the neighborhood of $580 billion, which implies a somewhat slower rate of growth during the second half.

The increased pace of expenditures for producers' durable equipment, residential construction and consumer services accounted for the bulk of the second quarter rise. One favorable aspect is that inventories, generally speaking, are still low relative to sales. The annual rate of accumulation declined from $5.1 billion in the first quarter to $3.5 billion in the second. On the other hand, the inflow of manufacturers' new orders has weakened perceptibly in some lines and, of course, quite abruptly in the special case of steel. However, order backlogs outside the steel industry are still relatively high.

### $100 a Week

Reflecting continued high business activity, corporate profits pushed ahead in the second quarter, as described in a later article. Most other recent economic reports were also favorable, including employment data. Teenagers in the labor force increased 2 million in June, and about two thirds of that number were apparently successful in finding jobs, raising total employment (including the armed forces) to a record of 73 million. Unemployment rose less than seasonally, as evidenced by the fact that the seasonally adjusted unemployment rate dipped to 5.7 per cent of the civilian labor force from 5.9 per cent in May. Employment, hours and wage rates in manufacturing all rose in June, boosting average weekly earnings of production workers past the $100 mark for the first time.

Supported by increased employment at rising wages, total personal income reached a record seasonally adjusted annual rate of $462 billion in June. Consumers have been spending freely from these increased earnings, and have also been using them as a basis for buying on the instalment plan. During the twelve months ended May 31, instalment debt outstanding rose $5 billion—close to the record pace of the years 1955 and 1959.

During the first half of 1963, retail sales ran 5 per cent higher than in the corresponding period of 1962; most retailers look for this year-to-year margin of improvement to continue during the second half, according to a recent survey by the National Retail Merchants Association. *Ward's Automotive Reports* notes that automobile dealers are looking for sales of 1.5 million new cars in the third quarter, 10 per cent more than a year earlier but 23 per cent below the unparalleled sales performance in the third quarter of 1955. A satisfactory cleanup of this year's models in dealers' hands is indicated, preparing the way for introduction of '64 models during the fourth quarter.

Appliance and furniture stores have also been reporting better-than-average sales gains, and as a result factory sales of television sets, refrigerators, air conditioners and dishwashers so far this year have increased substantially over a year earlier. In part, this heavy demand reflects the high rate of new home construction. Residential building permits issued, contracts written and dwellings started during the spring indicate continued high homebuilding activity during the rest of the summer as projects are carried to completion.

## New Balance-of-Payments Moves

The U.S. balance-of-payments deficit remains uncomfortably large. Hopes for decisive improvement have been disappointed. Special government transactions overseas are holding down the deficit without, however, cutting into its hard core. Even with this help we find that the payments gap remains at an annual rate beyond $3 billion. Less gold is going out but short-term indebtedness keeps accumulating.

Our export trade surplus continues to be the mainstay of our international payments. The commercial surplus on goods and services account strictly defined—i.e., excluding exports financed by U.S. Government aid but including earnings on our $60 billion of overseas investments—was running at a $4-billion annual rate earlier this year. This is in line with the 1962 performance if allowance is made for the impact of the dock strike early this year. It is not, however, proving easy to enlarge the surplus. While exports are growing, so are imports.

The immediate trouble spot lies in the capital account. During the first half of this year, short-term outflows were much less than two or three years ago, partly in response to higher money rates here. Nevertheless they continued on a substantial scale. Direct investments in productive plants abroad were holding at a rate of $2 billion a year. On the other hand, investments in foreign bonds were exceptionally large, swollen by particularly heavy placements in the New York market by Canadian governmental units.

The more fundamental difficulty is the load of defense and foreign aid expenditures which the U.S. Government has assumed throughout the world. The direct foreign exchange costs of U.S. Government expenditures abroad were running earlier this year at an annual rate of $2 billion for net military outlays and $1 billion for untied aid. These figures are conservative because they assume that none of the exports financed by U.S. aid would have been sold in the absence of that aid. In a recent speech, Allan Sproul, former President of the Federal Reserve Bank of New York, described foreign aid as "a special kind of export of capital." Endorsing in general the recommendations of the Clay Committee, he expressed the opinion that it is past time for "a severe tightening up in our foreign military and economic aid."

### The President's Message

It was against this background that the President, on July 18, sent to Congress a special message on the balance of payments. Noting that long-range forces are working in our favor, he listed a "series of more immediate and specialized efforts":

· export expansion;
· encouragement of domestic tourism;
· restraint on federal military and economic aid expenditures abroad to bring them, by 1965, to a level $1 billion below those for 1962;
· Treasury-Federal Reserve actions to raise short-term interest rates, while maintaining ample credit availability, to make short-term dollar investments more attractive;
· proposal for a special excise tax on purchases of foreign securities by Americans everywhere and foreign residents of the United States;
· arrangement of a stand-by credit from the International Monetary Fund in the amount of $500 million, something less than half the gold the U.S. has contributed to the Fund.

The President's message came two days after most Federal Reserve Banks raised their discount rates from 3 to 3½ per cent, a move which had been foreshadowed by an officially encouraged rise in 91-day Treasury bill yields from about 2.90 per cent toward 3.25 per cent over the preceding eight weeks. At the same time, the Federal Reserve Board raised the ceilings on rates of interest banks may pay on time deposits. The helpful impact of the discount rate action on respect for the dollar was somewhat blunted by a statement that the President had been assured by Treasury and Federal Reserve officials that they intended "to do everything possible through debt-management policy and open-market operations to avoid any reduction in domestic credit availability and any upward pressure on long-term interest rates while the economy operates below capacity without inflation."

While preserving a free and open capital market, and acting as banker to the world, the United States cannot insulate any of its interest rates from degrees of foreign influence. The world has simply gotten too small.

### Interest Equalization

The excise tax on American purchases of foreign securities is officially described as a special and temporary levy, designed to be effective from July 19, 1963 down through the end of 1965. As originally proposed, it represented an intellectual effort at interest equalization, as between the capital markets of the United States and other developed countries, consistent with the essential freedom of our trading and financial markets and fulfilling what the President called "our special responsibilities at the center of the financial system of the Free World." The proposal recognizes the importance of credit for financing exports by exempting securities or loans that mature in less than three years. It also recognizes the foreign exchange earning power of overseas investments of American corporations by exempting direct investments.

The proposal demoralized stock exchanges in Canada and Japan and brought international trading in stocks and bonds temporarily to a halt. In light of these impacts, and representations by foreign countries most vitally affected, the plan has been modified. Normal business cannot be resumed until investors regain positive assurance that specific transactions will not be subject to the special tax. Canadian officials asked for a general exemption based on the special economic relationships between our two countries. They, and the Japanese as well, pointed to the importance to them of selling bonds here to finance their normal trade deficits with the United States. Indeed, the countries affected might face the necessity to retaliate by restrictions upon their imports.

The Administration, in the circumstances,

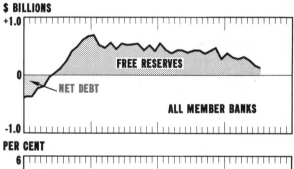

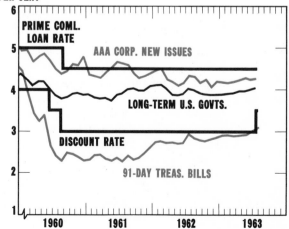

**Member Bank Reserves, Bond Yields and Money Rates**

Monthly averages except prime rate and discount rate; July figures preliminary.

found itself impelled to make adjustments in the proposal to practical realities. At this writing, the legislation has not been formally drafted but an understanding has been reached that new issues of Canadian securities, at least, will be exempted. Since Canada is by far the biggest borrower at long term in the U.S. market, the whole scheme loses most of its potential usefulness as a means of significantly reducing our balance-of-payments deficit.

The tax as proposed would apply simply to a specified list of 22 foreign countries, classified as developed. This selection, subject to change by Executive Order, involves some difficulties of drawing the line. For example, Portugal would be exempt but not Spain, the Philippines but not Hong Kong, Finland but not Norway. One observer has characterized the tax proposal as a discriminatory tariff imposed upon imports of stocks and bonds.

In this whole context it needs to be understood that developed countries, including the United States, are nevertheless still developing and in need of the broadest possible distribution of their securities. Developed countries have needs for continuing imports of capital to finance imports of machinery and equipment or to overcome temporary balance-of-payments pressures. Indeed, we ourselves have to rely on foreign buying interest in our securities to keep our international accounts in order. The President, in his message, expressed the hope that a better climate for investment here, created by the proposed income tax rate reductions, will promote exports of securities of U.S. companies. The free world has everything to lose by a policy of narrow nationalism that would cut pipelines of international investment.

The reaction to the proposal has served the constructive purpose of bringing to public attention the importance of private capital flows among the so-called more developed countries.

We should not get diverted by devices which are offensive to what the President calls "our basic precept of free markets" and which, while gaining some time, do so by checking the growth of our foreign assets and hastening the buildup of our foreign liabilities. We must keep our eyes fastened on the fundamentals of fiscal, monetary and wage policies. These form the three-legged milk stool upon which economic growth without inflation depends.

## First Half Corporate Earnings

The continuing business upswing, together with an unusual concurrence of temporary developments in several industries, brought a decided improvement in profits in the April-June period. This bank's tabulation for 952 nonfinancial corporations reporting to date shows aggregate after-tax earnings of $4.1 billion in the second quarter, up 12 per cent from the preceding quarter and 16 per cent from the like period a year earlier. This raised earnings in the first half to a level 10 per cent above the first half of 1962.

Among manufacturing companies alone, 713 firms reported profits of $3.2 billion, representing an increase of 17 per cent from the March quarter and a gain of 16 per cent from second quarter 1962. For the first half, earnings were 11 per cent above a year earlier.

For manufacturing firms reporting sales figures, the average profit margin in the second quarter rose to 6.6 cents per sales dollar, compared with 6.1 cents in the March quarter and 6.1 cents a year earlier. Another key indicator of the business trend is the seasonally adjusted percentage of manufacturing companies showing increased earnings from the preceding quarter. In the June quarter, 74 per cent reported higher profits. After seasonal adjustment, the figure comes to 59 per cent. This compares with 50 per cent in the March quarter and 56 per cent in last year's fourth quarter.

Outside of manufacturing, the most notable year-to-year gains were scored in the long-de-pressed railroad and mining industries. Substantial gains were also recorded in the trade, trucking and utilities fields, while in the service group, which was pulled down by the deficit of a single company, most firms actually had higher earnings.

In evaluating the over-all results, however, allowance must be made for special factors that gave an extra lift to second quarter results. Most widely publicized of these temporary boosters was the strike-hedge inventory buying by steel users, which not only brought added sales to the mills but generated more business for the railroads, coal mining and other supporting industries. Extra shipments to make up for billings lost during the East Coast dock strike or held up by the unusually severe winter added to second quarter volume in many lines. The run-up of sugar prices to near-record levels in May brought non-recurring inventory profits to refiners. Diminished price-cutting on gasoline, raising oil company earnings, may also be regarded as somewhat adventitious.

Nevertheless, the basic reason for the over-all improvement was the generally favorable trend in the fundamental factors of demand, costs and prices. On the demand side, the moderate upswing in capital goods programs, and high consumer spending for big-ticket items—autos, appliances, television sets and home improvements—has tended to spread improved sales volumes throughout industry. Production costs, meanwhile, have responded to management efforts to control expenses and gain improvements in productivity. There has been some firming of prices realized in recent months, though the situation has shown little or no improvement in such industries as chemicals, plastics, paper and aluminum, where intense competition among both domestic and foreign producers has kept prices weak.

### Industry Trends

Following its usual feast-or-famine pattern of recent quarters, the steel industry led the way in year-to-year gains for the various industry groups. As a result of the peaking of shipments in the second quarter and the modest price increase in flat-rolled products, a number of producers were able to report their best quarterly earnings since second quarter 1959.

Detroit, which is not taking a back seat to anyone this year, continued its profitable ways in the second quarter as auto assembly lines rolled at near-record rates and truck production continued to climb. Earnings, as a result, topped any previous quarter. With tire prices beginning to firm at last, the rubber industry has begun to share somewhat belatedly in the auto industry's prosperity.

The revival of capital goods spending at a time when demand for consumer hard goods is also strong is reflected in the general improvement of the heavy engineering groups—machinery, electrical equipment and fabricated metals. While such lines as construction machinery and office equipment have been doing well for some time, the pickup in appliances and industrial machinery has bolstered earnings in the machinery group. Similarly, the electrical equipment and electronics industries have benefited from both an expansion of capital spending by public utilities and brisk sales of electrical appliances and television sets.

Though the oil industry has been steadily improving its earnings performance since its depression year, 1958, the second quarter turned out to be especially good for both domestic and international companies. Continued gains in production and sales abroad bolstered earnings of international companies.

The chemical companies as a group managed to chalk up a moderate year-to-year gain in the second quarter despite price weaknesses in many lines as rising industrial activity stimulated increased demand. Earnings in aluminum, reflecting the impact of low ingot prices, dropped from a year earlier even though metal shipments reached a new high. Profits in paper also declined and the reason again was depressed prices.

In the consumer soft goods area, profits generally rebounded from lackluster first-quarter performances. The beverage and tobacco groups, which had shown year-to-year declines in the initial quarter, registered substantial increases in the latest period, while the food and the drugs-soap-cosmetics groups also attained better than seasonal improvement over the March quarter.

## Net Income of Leading Corporations for the Second Quarter and First Half Year
### (In Millions of Dollars)

| No. of Cos. | Industry Groups | Reported Net Income Second Qr. 1962 | Reported Net Income First Qr. 1963 | Reported Net Income Second Qr. 1963 | % Change from Second Qr. 1962 | % Change from First Qr. 1963 | Reported Net Income First Half Year 1962 | Reported Net Income First Half Year 1963 | Per Cent Change |
|---|---|---|---|---|---|---|---|---|---|
| 34 | Food products ...............$ | 65.1 | $ 74.5 | $ 69.1 | + 6 | — 7 | $ 134.0 | $ 143.6 | + 7 |
| 11 | Beverages ................... | 20.0 | 15.9 | 23.0 | +15 | + 44 | 37.5 | 39.0 | + 4 |
| 8 | Tobacco products ............. | 66.6 | 58.7 | 71.6 | + 7 | + 22 | 127.3 | 130.3 | + 2 |
| 31 | Textiles & apparel ........... | 21.9 | 24.0 | 24.1 | +10 | + 1 | 44.6 | 48.1 | + 8 |
| 16 | Rubber & allied products .... | 36.7 | 30.6 | 43.7 | +19 | + 43 | 66.6 | 74.3 | +11 |
| 31 | Paper & allied products ...... | 60.1 | 49.8 | 58.5 | — 3 | + 18 | 109.7 | 108.4 | — 1 |
| 21 | Printing & publishing ........ | 14.9 | 7.1 | 16.4 | +11 | +132 | 26.9 | 23.6 | —12 |
| 52 | Chemicals, paint, etc. ........ | 297.2 | 253.9 | 317.3 | + 7 | + 25 | 547.0 | 571.2 | + 4 |
| 35 | Drugs, soap, cosmetics ........ | 95.1 | 115.1 | 107.2 | +13 | — 7 | 203.0 | 222.4 | +10 |
| 35 | Petroleum prod. & refining .. | 629.1 | 842.4 | 769.7 | +22 | + 9 | 1,354.7 | 1,612.1 | +19 |
| 38 | Cement, glass, & stone ...... | 89.7 | 39.5 | 92.1 | + 3 | +133 | 136.4 | 131.6 | — 3 |
| 42 | Iron & steel ................. | 137.9 | 134.8 | 267.9 | +94 | + 99 | 345.7 | 402.7 | +16 |
| 26 | Nonferrous metals ........... | 88.1 | 62.0 | 75.7 | —14 | + 22 | 168.0 | 137.6 | —18 |
| 53 | Fabricated metal products .... | 73.3 | 58.6 | 78.9 | + 8 | + 35 | 129.9 | 137.5 | + 6 |
| 91 | Machinery ................... | 162.0 | 137.7 | 176.7 | + 9 | + 28 | 293.0 | 314.4 | + 7 |
| 73 | Electrical equip. & electronics | 124.3 | 117.5 | 127.2 | + 2 | + 8 | 241.0 | 244.7 | + 2 |
| 27 | Automobiles & parts ........ | 583.0 | 595.8 | 693.4 | +19 | + 16 | 1,108.5 | 1,289.2 | +16 |
| 24 | Aerospace & railway equip. .. | 61.7 | 61.8 | 75.4 | +22 | + 22 | 119.1 | 137.2 | +15 |
| 65 | Other manufacturing ........ | 116.0 | 93.4 | 119.2 | + 3 | + 28 | 211.8 | 212.6 | +..* |
| 713 | Total manufacturing ....... | $2,742.7 | $2,773.1 | $3,207.2 | +17 | + 16 | $5,404.6 | $5,980.3 | +11 |
| 16 | Mining & quarrying .......... | 25.1 | 27.7 | 27.5 | +10 | — 1 | 54.9 | 55.2 | + 1 |
| 55 | Trade (retail & wholesale) .... | 53.9 | 54.9 | 58.8 | + 9 | + 7 | 104.8 | 113.8 | + 9 |
| 38 | Service & amusement ......... | 19.1 | 11.5 | 16.4 | —14 | + 43 | 32.5 | 27.9 | —14 |
| 38 | Railroads ................... | 78.5 | 59.0 | 130.1 | +66 | +121 | 138.1 | 189.0 | +37 |
| 18 | Common carrier trucking .... | 8.3 | 3.9 | 9.0 | + 9 | +128 | 12.4 | 13.0 | + 5 |
| 67 | Electric power, gas, etc. ...... | 222.0 | 325.5 | 232.5 | + 5 | — 29 | 525.9 | 558.0 | + 6 |
| 7 | Telephone & telegraph ........ | 375.4 | 378.1 | 394.4 | + 5 | + 4 | 736.0 | 772.5 | + 5 |
| 952 | Grand Total ................. | $3,524.9 | $3,633.7 | $4,076.0 | +16 | + 12 | $7,009.1 | $7,709.7 | +10 |

* Increase of under 0.5%.

# The Case for a Tax Cut — Now

The moves in Washington last month to deal with the balance-of-payments problem serve as a reminder of the pressing need to get on with the job of cutting federal income taxes. At his press conference on July 17, President Kennedy reminded Americans that "the most urgent economic business before the nation is a prompt and substantial reduction and revision of federal income taxes." In his balance-of-payments message the next day, he termed early passage of his tax program "the single most important step that can be taken to achieve balance abroad as well as growth here at home." Positive measures to improve the climate for enterprise in the United States are both more appropriate and potentially more effective than negative measures to obstruct American investments selectively within the Free World.

The House Ways and Means Committee has been hard at work on a tax bill during the six months that have elapsed since the President's message on taxes in January, and has reportedly reached a number of tentative decisions. Yet, a combination of circumstances—including a three-week recess in Committee deliberations and Congressional preoccupation with civil rights legislation and the rail dispute—has slowed progress toward final enactment.

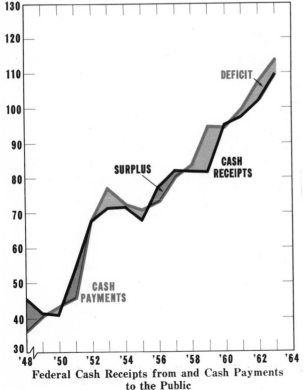

**$ BILLIONS**

CASH PAYMENTS

SURPLUS

DEFICIT

CASH RECEIPTS

**Federal Cash Receipts from and Cash Payments
to the Public**

Fiscal Years 1948-63

It will be recalled that the President proposed cutting individual income tax rates to a range of 14 to 65 per cent, from the present 20 to 91 per cent, while the corporate rate would be reduced from 52 to 47 per cent. The cuts were to be made over a three-year period, ultimately adding up to $13.6 billion a year. However, the President coupled these proposed rate cuts with a large number of revenue-producing "reforms," so that the net reduction in tax payments was estimated at $10.3 billion a year.

What the Ways and Means Committee has done is to take up the various "reform" proposals, many of them controversial, before tackling the vital question of rates. Some of the President's proposals have been rejected; most others have been substantially modified. The major reforms reportedly adopted by the Committee by late July are summarized in the accompanying box. These decisions are informal and tentative and could be reversed when the Committee gets down to formal voting.

Perhaps the most important change relates to capital gains, taxes on which would be reduced to a maximum rate of 19.5 per cent where an individual has held certain "true" capital assets at least three years. The present 25 per cent maximum rate would continue to hold for other types of capital gains. Significant changes have also been tentatively approved in the rules governing personal deductions—most notably the removal of deductibility of state and local excise taxes on gasoline, cigarettes and many other items.

While some of the Committee's decisions would cut rather than gain revenue, on balance they are expected to add about $600 million to federal tax receipts—far less than the $3.3 billion President Kennedy had anticipated raising through such revisions. It seems likely, therefore, that the Committee will adopt rate cuts shallower than those the President requested.

## Taxes and the Budget

The size and nature of any tax cuts ultimately voted will be influenced strongly by the budgetary outlook and our balance-of-payments position, as well as by the economy's longer-term needs. In addition, tax policy must be coordinated effectively with the government's spending, debt-management and monetary policies.

From a purely domestic point of view, the performance of the economy in the first half of 1963 exceeded nearly everyone's expectations, and economists generally foresee some further expansion in the remainder of the year. One benefit of the advance has been a sharp improvement in federal budgetary accounts.

When the President proposed his tax cut last January, his budget message called for record expenditures of $98.8 billion and a whopping deficit of $11.9 billion in the administrative budget for the fiscal year ending June 30, 1964, on top of an estimated deficit of $8.8 billion for fiscal '63. The anticipated deficit in the cash budget for fiscal '64 was almost as large, $10.3 billion; but only $2.7 billion of this was expected to result from the tax cut. Understandably, many people have been reluctant to support major tax reductions until expenditures are brought under better restraint, and this is one reason why action on the tax front has been held back.

Now, however, comes the heartening news that the cash deficit for fiscal '63 turned out to be $4.1 billion, only half that expected in January. The administrative budget also showed improvement —the actual deficit was $6.2 billion, compared with the official forecast of $8.8 billion. As yet, revised estimates for fiscal '64 have not been published. But if the Congress and the Administration show vigilance in keeping the lid on government spending, rising tax yields should shrink the budget deficit projected for the fiscal year ending next June 30.

All this lends support to the view that a tax cut oriented toward accelerating our growth rate—one that is aimed mainly at fostering investment, enterprise and increased effort—would be fully consistent with widespread aspirations for a balanced budget if coupled with effective control of expenditures.

### Taxes and the Balance of Payments

The relevance of our tax system to the balance-of-payments problem does not always receive proper recognition. Taxes, along with wages, are costs of doing business. Easier taxes and greater discrimination in programing government expenditures can help American industry maintain price-level stability and compete more effectively for overseas business.

The recent moderate shift in monetary policy adds a new dimension to the discussion. The increases in Federal Reserve discount rates to 3½ per cent in July, and the associated rise in short-term money rates in recent weeks, were undertaken for balance-of-payments reasons. These increases are not likely to have an adverse effect on the economy. Nevertheless, it becomes increasingly important that reliefs be undertaken so that our business activity can be sustained without the crutch of artificially cheap money which tends to create distrust of the dollar and invites excessive foreign demands upon our money and capital markets.

Moreover, as President Kennedy stressed in his balance-of-payments message, a tax cut could con-tribute to the solution of our payments difficulties by providing a better climate for investment in the United States, for Americans and foreigners alike. The President pointed out that foreign purchases of U.S. corporate securities in 1962 amounted to less than $150 million. Securities of U.S. corporations, he said, "could be and should

---

**Major Tax Changes Reported as <u>Tentatively</u> Approved by the Ways and Means Committee**

*Personal deductions*

- limit deductibility of state and local taxes to property, income and general sales and use taxes.
- raise ceiling on deductions for contributions to publicly supported and controlled organizations from 20 per cent to 30 per cent.
- raise child care deductions to $900 for widows or widowers with two or more children.
- allow casualty deductions only for losses over $100.
- liberalize treatment of moving expenses to new jobs.
- exclude sick pay only after 30 days of illness.

*Income averaging*

- allow taxpayers whose income fluctuates markedly to spread income over five-year periods.

*Capital gains*

- reduce the taxable part of gains on certain "true" capital assets held three years to 30 per cent, as against 50 per cent currently; maximum tax on such gains lowered from 25 per cent to 19.5 per cent.
- allow net capital losses to be carried forward indefinitely.
- compute gain from sale of inherited property on cost basis of decedent (or market value at death, if lower), plus allocable portion of estate tax.
- exempt gain attributable to first $20,000 of sale price of a home owned five or more years by a person aged 65 or over.
- tighten stock option rules; three-year holding period required for option stock to qualify for full tax benefits.

*Mineral properties*

- restrict lumping of high-allowance and low-allowance properties in figuring depletion allowances.
- eliminate capital gains treatment of profit on sale of such properties to the extent of development costs taken as business deduction after Jan. 1, 1964.

*Consolidated corporate returns*

- lift the 2 per cent penalty on companies that file consolidated returns; apply a 3 per cent penalty to affiliated companies unless they file a consolidated return or forego multiple surtax exemptions.

be one of our best selling exports."

Even more important, American businesses would tend to invest more in this country, creating more jobs, boosting productivity and improving the competitive power of our products in world markets.

### What Kind of Tax Cut?

The case for tax revision rests fundamentally on the urgent need to strengthen the incentives to business enterprise that build our economic muscle. Lower taxes and structural revisions would provide the foundation for solid long-term economic expansion and create the jobs our growing population must have.

Unemployment is still too high, despite the current business expansion. Furthermore, the labor market is starting to feel the pressure of the large number of "war babies" growing up into adults looking for work. Job insecurity is an important underlying factor in the disputes over civil rights, automation and featherbedding that have been dominating the headlines. A tax cut would go far toward creating an economic atmosphere in which these conflicts could be more smoothly resolved.

From every point of view the case for an immediate tax cut is strong. It could help put an end to the troublesome deficits plaguing us—the deficit in the federal government's budget, the deficit in our balance of international payments and the deficit in jobs. Moreover, the existence of unused resources and the recent steps toward less monetary ease imply that taxes can be cut with safety.

The remaining questions are how large a cut should be made and what kind of a cut it should be. Any old kind of tax cut will not do. And least of all a big expensive cut that will lack power to stimulate investment and enterprise. On the other hand, a significant reduction of corporate income tax rates would:

- provide additional capital needed for faster growth;
- encourage the cost-reducing modernization of our plant and equipment needed to make American exports more competitive with the rest of the world;
- help restore full employment by stimulating private demand for goods and services;
- permit lower product prices in many industries where present corporate taxes are, at least in part, passed on to consumers;
- help reverse the present large net outflow of long-term investment from the United States by improving investment yields in this country.

These same objectives would also be advanced by a different kind of tax cut—one that is dedicated, at long last, to moderating the severely progressive rate structure of our present individual income tax. We need to cut the Gordian knot that shackles the power of personal effort and enterprise.

## The Invisible Costs of Government

As everybody knows, government costs a lot of money. Revenues of all our governments—federal, state and local—are running up past $150 billion a year, equivalent to $1,400 for every adult in the United States. While devoting tens of billions to putting a man on the moon—described by former President Eisenhower as "a mad effort to win a stunt race"—government has taken on dependents all over this earth. Checks go out to more than 40 million persons at home: 12 million to employes and the others to welfare beneficiaries. Abroad, no less than 95 countries and territories are receiving U.S. aid.

The true cost of government runs far beyond $150 billion a year. Many people, after gathering figures and receipts all year long, worked on into the night last Easter on governmentally prescribed arithmetical exercises, filling the forms for federal (and perhaps also state) income tax returns due the next day, April 15. No one has tried to calculate the manhours of dismal drudgery going into the preparation of tax returns. The rates of tax rise progressively. And so does the effort demanded. The more a man earns—and the more his time is worth—the greater the obligation imposed to amass detailed records and comprehend the complications of the law.

Form 1040, which 35 million persons find it necessary to use, can require upwards of 500 entries (including supplemental schedules) and as many as 200 additions, subtractions, multiplications and divisions. The Superintendent of Documents in Washington has on sale a 144-page volume which elucidates some of the major technicalities. Yet no one can settle back and say he understands the whole of the law. Not only is the law itself in process of repeated change, but the regulations are changed and court decisions alter the interpretation of law and regulations. The Internal Revenue Service itself has a major problem of training qualified agents, numbering some 30,000. Publishing technical books on taxes, and advising people on taxes, have become big business. The core of tax experts outside government is represented in the 71,000 "enrolled practitioners" recognized by the IRS.

The work imposed on individuals is nothing compared to that imposed on employers. Not only are there many more forms but employers must serve as uncompensated tax collectors, taking money out of the pay envelopes of workers according to formula and, often, adding a tax bite assessed on customers. The IRS has a total staff of 64,000 and a budget of $674 million. These are big figures. But there is little doubt that business firms collectively employ even more people and spend even more money gathering in tens of billions of revenues.

And burdens of calculating and assessing taxes are just part of the story. Besides the IRS and state and local tax authorities, there are thousands of government offices and agencies with overlapping jurisdictions over business. Thus, lying beneath the visible costs—set out in the budgets prepared at various levels of government—is an iceberg of invisible costs.

### Size of the Problem

Such costs take an infinite variety of forms, ranging from a simple postcard report for an official agency to interminable procedures required by regulatory authorities and tedious investigations launched by Congressional committees or Executive departments—all too often simply uncovering facts already known to anyone who has taken the trouble to find them. A major company may be called upon to supply hundreds of thousands of figures in a year's time. Many valuable statistics emerge from official compilations but the truth is that the quantity of data overwhelms the capacity of statisticians to digest them. Some required forms have no more important use than getting bundled up for sale as waste paper.

The second Hoover Commission gave some idea of the dimensions of the problem at the federal level. As of 1955 it was estimated that paperwork within the Federal Government cost $4 billion a year, consumed 25 billion sheets of paper, required office space equal to 36 Empire State Buildings and storage space equal to 7 Pentagons. Paper handling is a more popular exercise than 50-mile hikes. It fans out across the country.

Forms go out to business firms and individuals to be completed and returned for regulatory, statistical or tax purposes. Though the Hoover Commission made no over-all estimate of the total costs involved, it pointed out that the private cost "is far greater than the government's cost of totting up the figures."

Since 1955, both costs have grown. By latest count, the Federal Government has some 5,300 forms in use for regular reporting. And this does not include reports to the IRS, certain other agencies of the Treasury Department, and the several layers of banking authorities, which are exempted from the Federal Reports Act.

There are, besides, reports for state and local government units. The Hoover Commission found that state and city governments impose "more than 50 per cent of the nation's burden of paperwork."

As John E. Swearingen, president of the Standard Oil Company of Indiana, describes the situation:

> We have arrived at the unhappy point at which the Cyclopean eye of some almighty regulatory agency is upon us when we buy or sell, ship or receive, hire or fire, grow or manufacture, save or spend, drink or diet, profit or lose, talk or listen.

Amid all the hue and cry about accelerating economic growth—which means cutting out useless effort and getting more production per manhour—we tend to ignore the multiplication of burdens placed upon people to comply with laws. And while we lament the shortage of employment opportunities, we overlook the endless rules and regulations that discourage people from going into business or invite them to get out.

### Costs of Tax Reporting

The most familiar kind of invisible cost to the average American is the paperwork involved in his income tax return. Partly because the tax rates are so high, the government takes a proprietary interest in the money a man earns. And all the time people are being put to more and more trouble to defend their take-home pay. Even so, there was considerable public support for changes in expense account rules—including the requirement for the keeping of a day-to-day diary—put into the Revenue Act of 1962 as a means of checking abuses. This makes bookkeeping a large part of the job of everyone who has responsibilities to pay out money in connection with business travel.

In response to businessmen's advice, the IRS later loosened up a bit on the rules. But all this paperwork becomes a burden to the employer's tax department. One corporate executive, quoted by *Business Week*, predicted that "we'll have to rent a separate warehouse for the literally millions of pieces of paper we'd have to keep." No one will ever have a chance to go through them all. Nevertheless the law requires that they be there for years until the related tax returns are audited and approved or the statute of limitations mercifully permits disposal of the waste.

The scope for additional layers of state and local government taxation has been broadened by Supreme Court decisions giving them greater leeway for taxing out-of-state corporations. What this has meant in terms of paperwork burdens was effectively presented before the Special House Subcommittee on State Taxation of Interstate Commerce in June, 1962 by Werner N.

Davidson, secretary-treasurer of the Caloric Corporation:

> The cost of additional help to file only for state tax purposes, the space required for the storage of such otherwise useless records, the cost of one additional invoice copy for each charge to our customer, will add at least $20,000 annually to our cost of doing business. . . .
>
> By taking into account machine time, salaries paid to our people who perform the tax reporting function, subscriptions for tax services, endless correspondence with taxing authorities to support our returns, payment of travel and per diem allowances to tax auditors of foreign states, we spend an additional $50,000 per year.
>
> Our corporation and its subsidiaries file a total of 999 tax returns of all kinds per year and the cost of each tax return amounts to $70.

Just in the year since his testimony, Mr. Davidson reports that the number of tax returns has risen further to 1,140. Larger companies have even more. In 1959, the Union Carbide Corporation was filing 3,600 tax forms a year.

### Case Studies from Business Experience

Some other cases were presented in a 1959 report of the House Subcommittee on Census and Government Statistics. One of the most striking was that of a large midwestern manufacturer, which kept a detailed record for one year:

> In the year, the company handled 173 different federal forms ranging in frequency of filing from daily to annual, and involving the filing of 37,683 reports. The workload amounted to 48,285 hours. In addition, the company received a number of other federal forms, presumably voluntary, which it did not respond to because it objected to the apparent duplication, felt that the data requested were confidential, or for other reasons. . . . Requests from state agencies which were complied with included 63 different forms, involving the filing of 1,145 reports at a cost of 3,266 hours.

While it is difficult to generalize, reporting requirements arise at the birth of a fledgling enterprise and ever after distract from the work of keeping alive. The requirements tend to be heaviest for the biggest companies, for firms in regulated industries, for corporations holding government contracts and for firms dealing in agricultural products.

Regulated industries typically have much more government-imposed reporting and record-keeping expense than business generally. After the **Hoover Commission** study in 1955, some progress was made toward simplifying and thinning out reporting workloads in certain industries. The contrary drift is exemplified in the field of banking where financial institutions this year are being required to file information returns on each account with interest payments of $10 or more. Also, along with other payers of interest or dividends, banks are devoting a good deal of time and money to obtain social security numbers from customers to be put on reports to the IRS.

The classic case, of course, is that of the railroad business, put under the Interstate Commerce Commission in 1887. Over the decades, reports required to meet the needs of the day were enlarged until the industry found itself preoccupied with paperwork. The last time the Association of American Railroads made a listing of the reports required by federal agencies—in 1954—it took 10 pages to give the titles of 164 separate reports. This list did not include reports connected with the handling of mail.

Some reports are required annually, others semi-annually, quarterly, monthly, weekly, daily or as certain events occur. The longest annual report, "Form A" of the ICC, runs to 117 pages of detailed schedules.

One monthly report for the Department of Agriculture is labeled:

> Report to USDA, San Francisco, of number of carloads of corn westbound passing Needles, California.

Such detailed reports are only one aspect of a general problem of overregulation of the railroads; reporting to the ICC alone is figured as costing more than $5 million a year.

Similar problems are found in other public utility fields. The Hoover Commission reported in 1955 that it cost gas and electric companies more than $14 million a year to prepare requests for rate changes. It cited one example of how expensive rate proceedings can be:

> One company fills its plane with several tons of documents and exhibits for such a case. Company executives are forced to fly to Washington separately in commercial airlines. Normally one or more Federal Power Commission representatives then visit the utility.
>
> Some measure of how lengthy a process this is, is the fact that the government man commonly buys or rents a house in the locality, checks on schools for his children, etc. There he audits the company's books to see if they support the facts in the reports. In practice he seldom agrees with costs claimed by the company. His suggestions, therefore, cause the company to revise the voluminous data originally compiled.

Industry sources say $14 million is still a conservative estimate of rate proceeding costs, and that instances like the case cited above are not unusual.

### "Nightmares at High Noon"

Even if a manufacturer or distributor is not in a regulated industry, it may still find itself immersed in a similarly expensive procedure. An everpresent danger is the possibility of running afoul of the vague but potent antitrust laws.

In 1959, for example, three salt companies— Morton, International and Diamond Crystal—

were charged with fixing prices of rock salt. Two and a half years later, a federal jury found them not guilty. In the interim, the work of assembling data and materials to defend themselves—plus lawyers' fees — had cost the three firms $775,000, a sum far greater than the $150,000 maximum in fines they might have been liable to pay if found guilty. But the invisible costs go beyond these figures. As reported by the *Wall Street Journal*, Morton Salt Company president Daniel Peterkin described the lingering effects:

> We've been in business more than 100 years and we think we have a fine reputation. Anytime you're accused of violating the law, particularly the anti-trust laws, it's extremely damaging to you. After acquittal, the damage still exists. The mere fact that you're accused is enough to hurt you in many people's minds.

A similar, but much lengthier, case involved Standard Oil of Indiana, which was cited for alleged price discrimination by the Federal Trade Commission in 1940. After extensive litigation involving two trips to the Supreme Court, the company finally won its case in 1958.

President Swearingen, however, found the victory worth the cost:

> In our judgment, the net effect was to preserve a competitive system for American business, but it took 17 costly and trying years of litigation to do it. And, to preserve our right to compete, we had to fight off a federal agency originally established to insure the continuance of effective competition. . . .
>
> I submit that this is the kind of thing that can give any responsible businessman nightmares at high noon. In our instance, the continuing threat to our ability to compete also threatened the interests of our thousands of stockholders and employes.

### Attempts to Stem the Tide

While the growing burden of paperwork and other expenses imposed by government has naturally evoked recurrent protests, attempts to stem the tide have met with only limited success.

In 1942, when World War II had stimulated a vast outpouring of government regulations and requests for information, Congress passed the Federal Reports Act, authorizing the Bureau of the Budget to coordinate federal reporting with a view toward eliminating duplications and minimizing burdens. In 1951, during the Korean conflict, this authorization was supplemented by an Executive Order.

The Budget Bureau's Office of Statistical Standards, charged with carrying out this function, has been largely responsible for making the federal statistical system more orderly and appreciative of the needs of the public and of the problems of respondents. Helping to accomplish this has been an Advisory Council on Federal Reports, sponsored by five national business groups.

The work of these groups was given impetus by the Hoover Commission. But, as the Office of Statistical Standards has pointed out, progress is slow and requires continuing, persistent efforts because changes in administrative reports "involve legal or policy problems."

### The Nub of the Problem

Therein lies the nub of the problem. The growth of "invisible costs" has accompanied the expansion of government activities—through the Great Depression, two major wars and the post-war burgeoning of the welfare state.

As more and more money is disbursed by public agencies and as more private activities are regulated by government, public officials want at hand more minute information about what's going on. Hence, more paperwork.

It is perhaps no accident that the agency with the largest number of regularly required reports—the Agriculture Department—is the one that encountered outright rebellion last May when wheat growers, in a national referendum, rejected high price supports and tighter controls. There comes a time when self-respecting individuals resist encroachments upon their privacies and freedoms.

About the worst thing that can happen to a people is to become servants of the state. It is well to recall the warnings of Alexis de Tocqueville, more than a century ago, describing how despotism might conquer a democratic society:

> Above this race of men stands an immense and tutelary power, which takes upon itself alone to secure their gratifications and to watch over their fate. That power is absolute, minute, regular, provident, and mild. . . .
>
> After having thus successfully taken each member of the community in its powerful grasp and fashioned him at will, the supreme power then extends its arm over the whole community. It covers the surface of society with a network of small complicated rules, minute and uniform, through which the most original minds and the most energetic characters cannot penetrate, to rise above the crowd. The will of man is not shattered, but softened, bent, and guided; men are seldom forced by it to act, but they are constantly restrained from acting.
>
> Such a power does not destroy, but it prevents existence; it does not tyrannize, but it compresses, enervates, extinguishes, and stupefies a people, till each nation is reduced to nothing better than a flock of timid and industrious animals, of which the government is the shepherd.

**FIRST NATIONAL CITY BANK**

*"They only dive for First National City Travelers Checks*
*—they're better than money."*

Why should the divers—or you—settle for less than FNCB Travelers Checks? They're better than money because you can get an on-the-spot refund if they're lost or stolen. You'll get a prompt refund through any of FNCB's global network of thousands of refund agents. They are spendable anywhere—here and abroad—but only by you. And they are backed by First National City, best-known name in world-wide banking. Ask for them by name at your bank.

**Fastest refund in case of loss or theft**—
Checks missing? Anywhere in the U.S. except Alaska and Hawaii, simply phone WESTERN UNION OPERATOR 25 for nearest refund location. For information concerning refund points in other countries, Alaska and Hawaii, ask at principal hotels.

# FIRST NATIONAL CITY BANK
# TRAVELERS CHECKS

Member Federal Deposit Insurance Corporation

PRINTED IN U.S.A.

September 1963

# Monthly Economic Letter

FIRST NATIONAL CITY BANK
1812 · 1963
NEW YORK

## General Business Conditions

As the economy moves into the fall season, business sentiment is generally good, reflecting better-than-expected sales and profits so far this year, renewed buoyancy in the stock market and some tangible progress on the tax bill.

There has been no summer holiday for the nation's pressing policy problems. This is evidenced in the length of the Congressional session which usually ends up in the heat of the summer but now seems likely to go on right through the fall. It is only now in September that the big tax bill will reach the House floor for debate. Meanwhile, emergency actions to deal with the balance of payments, and the threat of a railway strike, were added to the Congressional agenda. Decisions on these issues will affect not only the current course of business, but more importantly, the long-term pattern of our national development. However, overhanging problems of national policy have not dimmed businessmen's expectations for sustained good business in the remaining months of 1963.

Recent business reports betray no faltering of the pace of activity. In July, the industrial production index picked up another point, to 126.5, on top of the six-point gain in the first half. While unemployment, at 5.6 per cent of the civilian labor force, was equal to last year's average, total employment (including the armed forces) reached a seasonal peak of 73.6 million persons, up 1.2 million from July 1962. The May-to-July increase in teenage employment (14-19 years) was about on a par with the 2 million increases for similar periods of the last three years. The summer crop of young people looking for jobs was larger this year, so that unemployment in this group was greater than the year before.

The decline in steel bookings leveled off in July and total new orders received by manufacturers rose a bit. In late August, reports of improved ordering of steel for fall delivery were accompanied by a bottoming out of production. The industry remains confident that fall business will bring the year's output above 100 million tons for the first time since 1957. Retail sales in July and August maintained their margin of about 5 per cent gain over a year earlier. A further sign of good business was a stiffening in price quotations for a number of nonferrous metals and some finished products, suggesting that production was moving closer to capacity and pointing toward sustained or even improved profit margins if the recent stability of costs can be preserved.

### A Record Model Year

During the '63 model year, a record-setting 7,340,000 passenger cars were assembled, a 16 per cent gain over the '62s. Yet, in August, the relatively low stocks left in dealers' hands were already limiting sales of some makes. The outstanding sales performance of the '63 models has been the most dramatic element in the renewed vigor of the business upswing this year. Auto industry spokesmen, understandably cautious when they remember the letdown after the last record year, in 1955, are talking of 7,000,000 as a reasonable expectation for 1964. It is a nice round figure. The public will decide what is right after reconciling the appeal of the new models against practical considerations of what they can afford and competing needs and enjoyments.

Observers are looking to growth in plant and equipment expenditures by business to step into the breach as other expansionary factors diminish. This is what happened in 1956-57, under the spur of tax reduction. Currently, the output and orders picture in the capital goods area is improved but not strong. Reflecting improved cash flow from profits and depreciation, corporate borrowing in the bond market and from banks has been moderate.

### Progress on Tax Reductions

Tax reduction remains the principal hope for encouraging more investment. The Ways and Means Committee has finished work, except for final drafting, on a tax-cut bill expected to reach the House floor in mid-September. This package calls for cuts amounting to $11.7 billion and revenue-raising reforms of $565 million. The net tax reduction of $11.1 billion would be spaced over two years with roughly two thirds coming on January 1, 1964, and the rest a year later.

This is a big tax bill. Its enactment would represent a bold—and doubtless successful—effort to show what easier taxes can do to stimulate the economy. It will be safe to proceed with cuts approaching such dimensions only if we are prepared to pay interest rates required to finance deficits in a noninflationary manner and to tailor government expenditures in light of prospective revenues. President Kennedy gave some reassurance on this latter point in a letter to Ways and Means Committee Chairman Wilbur D. Mills on August 21, when he promised that the deficit he would propose in the fiscal '65 budget would be smaller than the $9.2 billion presently foreseen for fiscal '64.

### Featherbedding—A Challenge to Progress

After more than four years of tortuous negotiation, fact-finding studies, mediation efforts and court decisions, the "featherbedding" dispute on the nation's railroads was put on the track to compulsory arbitration at the eleventh hour.

As in the old-time movie serials of the "Perils of Pauline," which often left the heroine tied to the tracks in the path of an onrushing steam locomotive, the public from week to week has found itself threatened with an intolerable, paralyzing rail strike.

We do not have steam locomotives any more and it is the obsolescence of the occupation of railroad firemen that crystallizes the dispute. Hence we have the paradox that men want to keep jobs that do not exist. Two Presidential panels have upheld the railroads' contention that unneeded jobs be gradually eliminated. Congress, however, had been loath to enforce arbitration of the dispute because this might set a precedent that would undermine collective bargaining and force Congressional action or other government intervention in more and more labor disputes.

It is easy to understand the resistance of men faced with a need to look elsewhere for work. These things happen every day. And many men are helped by shaking loose from old moorings. They find satisfaction in productive achievement, doing work that is wanted and needed. Union power is great. But it should be applied neither to threaten the economy with strangulation nor to challenge the ultimately irresistible power of progress.

## Brookings Report on the Balance of Payments

The deficit of the United States in its balance of payments with the rest of the world has returned to the forefront of public discussion. Hopes that the deficit could be wiped out by the end of 1963 have been disappointed. It seems now that this year's deficit will range somewhere between $2 and 4 billion for the sixth consecutive year. While the gold loss is less than in 1962, the rate of accumulation of U.S. short-term indebtedness overseas is somewhat greater.

The obstinacy of the problem has led to new measures and fresh reappraisals. During July, in quick succession, the Board of Governors of the Federal Reserve System approved increases from 3 to 3½ per cent in Federal Reserve Bank discount rates; President Kennedy followed up with a Special Message on the Balance of Payments; the Congressional Joint Economic Committee released the provocative Brookings Institution report on *The United States Balance of Payments in 1968.*

The Brookings report was initiated in the spring of 1962 when President Kennedy asked his Council of Economic Advisers to consider the outlook for the balance of payments over the next several years. The Council commissioned the Brookings Institution to make a comprehensive and independent study and this was undertaken by six economists under the direction of Walter S. Salant of the Brookings staff. The report was transmitted to the Council in January and is being published with some revisions and the addition of a chapter on policy recommendations.

### The Balance of Payments in 1968

The Brookings group tried to figure out what the U.S. balance of payments may look like five years hence, in 1968, on the basis of "initial assumptions" provided in part by the President's Council, and with help of statistical and theoretical studies prepared by scholars in the universities, government departments and the International Monetary Fund. The authors hold no brief for the exactitude of the numerical projections; they are "highly speculative" guesses which emerge out of the assumptions and techniques used.

The report has attracted widespread interest for its findings, for the assumptions chosen, for its description of the dollar as "a weak currency," and for the dark implication that even elimination of the deficit "may not suffice to restore the dollar's strength because that alone might not increase the attractiveness of the dollar for foreign and domestic holders."

### The Assumptions

While deprecating the importance of the U.S. balance-of-payments position, the Brookings group calculates that—under its "initial assumptions"—our basic balance of payments in the year 1968 will have moved into a surplus position of $1.9 billion. Figures are also given under an alternate, less optimistic set of assumptions which would leave a modest deficit of $0.6 billion in 1968. But the authors offer as their "best guess" that the basic deficit will be eliminated.

The *basic* deficit is one which leaves certain items out of account, principally changes in private short-term investments abroad and "net errors and omissions" believed to represent largely unrecorded flows of such funds. The "nonbasic" transactions have added an average of $1.2 billion to the annual deficits in the last three years.

The charts published in this issue are mainly drawn from the Brookings report and reflect the judgments of its authors on questions of classification. There are many differences of opinion as to how balance-of-payments data should be presented and a special expert group has been appointed to study the matter. A number of students, while agreeing to the seriousness of the problem, believe our official figures overstate the deficit.

The assumptions used by the authors are of interest for the implied forecasts of the shape of U.S. financial policy and world economic developments. The following are among those of critical importance:

1. The United States will improve its performance relative to that of Continental Western Europe in gross national product, output per manhour and utilization of productive resources. Specifically, it is assumed that unemployment in the United States will be "rapidly" reduced to 4 per cent of the labor force. Europe, it is assumed, will remain fully employed.

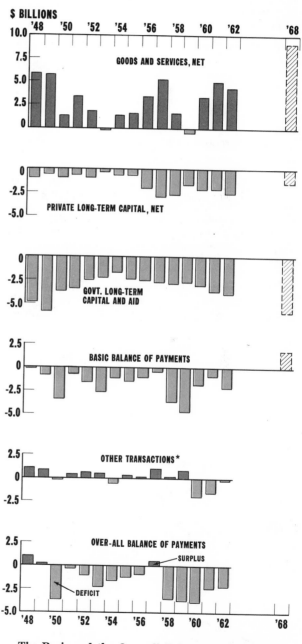

The Basic and the Over-all Balance of Payments

\* Short-term capital flows, prepayments by foreigners of U.S. Government loans and other special transactions, and "errors and omissions." Source: The Brookings report. In all charts, projections for 1968 are those based on "initial" (more optimistic) assumptions.

2. The rise in average hourly earnings in the United States will run at a rate of 4.4 per cent a year, which is described as "in line with experience in recent years." Exceeding a projected 2.9 per cent a year rate of productivity increase, this will raise prices here an average of 1.5 per cent a year. This figure refers to a price index for everything going into the gross national product; its rise over the past 10 years has been 1.8 per cent per annum. (The annual average rise in the cost-of-living index has been 1.3 per cent.)

3. The rise in hourly earnings in France, Italy and Germany will average 8.7 per cent a year, exceeding a 4.9 per cent a year productivity increase. This will not only squeeze down profits in Western Europe but also force prices up to the tune of 3 per cent a year. (Figures for the United Kingdom would fall between those of the United States and the Continent.)

4. The presumed improvement in our international competitive position would help lift U.S. exports from $20.5 billion in 1962 to $31.4 billion in 1968. With imports rising from $16.1 billion to $23.3 billion, the favorable balance on merchandise trade would move up from $4.4 billion to $8.1 billion.

5. Government long-term capital and aid extended abroad will rise from $3.9 billion in 1962 to $5.8 billion in 1968.

6. Direct investment by American business overseas will shrink from $1.6 billion in 1962 to $0.9 billion in 1968, while foreign investments in the United States (direct and portfolio) will increase from $0.3 billion to $0.6 billion. Nevertheless, net dividend and interest earnings on private account are figured to rise from $3.2 billion to $4.3 billion.

The assumption numbered 1 hopefully can prove correct. It is nothing to take for granted. To improve our performance will take real effort.

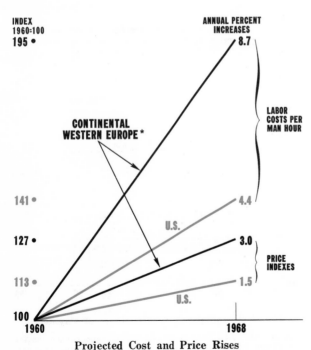

INDEX 1960=100

ANNUAL PERCENT INCREASES

CONTINENTAL WESTERN EUROPE *

LABOR COSTS PER MAN HOUR

PRICE INDEXES

Projected Cost and Price Rises

* France, West Germany and Italy.
Source: The Brookings report.

The spirit of enterprise will have to be encouraged by income tax rate reforms and better understanding of the key role of profits among political, intellectual and labor leaders.

Assumption 2 represents a projection of past experience in the United States: that the Council of Economic Advisers' guideposts to noninflationary wage settlements will be exceeded sufficiently to create a continuing upward creep in prices. The late Per Jacobsson offered the wise counsel that we could more quickly improve our balance-of-payments position, and reduce our unemployment, if we maintained stable wages or had wage increases less than the increase in productivity. Then the benefits of progress would assert themselves in lower prices for the benefit of everyone.

### European Wage Inflation

The third assumption is dubious. We reported in these pages last May on European wage-price inflation since 1959. The Brookings report projects these trends five years on into the future with the implication that, from 1962 to 1968, the currencies of France, Italy and Germany would lose one fifth of their buying power. Assuredly, this would help U.S. competitive power in world markets—if we meanwhile resist the same disease. But continuous wage-price spiraling is neither politically nor economically acceptable to Western Europe.

As a matter of fact, one of the smaller nations, Denmark, let wage-price inflation get out of hand, and was led last March to prohibit strikes and establish strict regulatory controls over wages, prices, gross profits and dividends. In Germany, at the expense of a temporary shutdown in its metal-working industries, the pace of wage inflation has been measurably slowed. The Organization for Economic Cooperation and Development, with advisory help from business and labor groups, has been giving earnest attention to the problem of bringing a halt to the rise in costs and prices in Europe. We cannot expect, and should not want, Western Europe to imperil its own progress, prosperity and stability in order to bail us out of our difficulties.

International payment imbalances should be redressed by means consistent with internal price stability and liberal trading policies. In 1961 Germany and the Netherlands upvalued their currencies by 5 per cent, thus correcting excessive devaluations undertaken in 1949. Many students diagnose the improvement in French reserves as evidence that the last devaluation of the franc, in 1958, was excessive to the needs. For political reasons countries tend to put off needed devaluations too long; then, for economic reasons, they devalue too much.

The Brookings report recognizes the virtues of fixed exchange rates:

> . . . Fixed rates remove much of the uncertainty which would otherwise be inherent in international movements of goods, services and capital. They tend to increase the volume of trade and productive international investment, thus contributing to efficient use of world resources and to economic welfare. . . .

> If confidence in the maintenance of exchange rates becomes firmly established, it is likely that the process of adjusting balances between countries will begin to resemble more closely adjustment among different regions of a single country, in which equilibrating movements of capital induced by small differences in interest rates play a major role. . . .

> In addition, by increasing the economic interdependence of the Free World countries, it may tend to increase their political cohesion.

The report rejects the idea of dollar devaluation. As a matter of fact, the United States lacks effective power to devalue its currency; the dollar is the common benchmark against which the values of other currencies are stated. The United States can hardly have a "floating dollar" when the dollar is the sea on which other currencies float. In this situation, we stand at the mercy of other countries, excessively devaluing their currencies to the disadvantage of our balance of payments.

Countries convinced that the dollar is overvalued in terms of their own currencies should upvalue, though not before testing them out against the full strength of the dollar, removing import barriers and giving their citizens freedom to invest in the American market as much as they please.

### Government vs. Private Enterprise

Assumptions numbered 5 and 6, if realized, imply a reversal of basic American policy since World War II of encouraging private capital to fill the gap of financial needs overseas and replace aid programs financed by our taxpayers. The projections have the role of government growing, and that of private capital shrinking.

This drift of prospective events requires searching reappraisal. It implies constriction of opportunities for private enterprise abroad as well as at home, greater burdens for American taxpayers and more "federal funds for free" to nations abroad. We cannot let this happen if we are to re-establish self-reliance as the first principle of economic progress.

In short, the report has the wrong combination of assumptions for the elimination of the deficit. Instead of indulgence of wage-price spiraling by Europe, we must have better discipline over our own business costs and prices. Instead of assumed

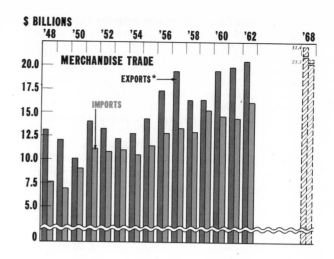

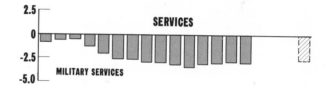

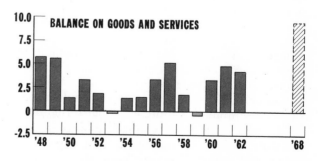

U.S. Trade in Goods and Services

\* Exclude military aid shipments but include other exports financed by foreign aid. † Include primarily travel, transport and private remittances.

Source: The Brookings report.

enlargement of the role of government, and intergovernmental grants and aids, we must release, from the constraints of excessive taxes and regulations, the full power of which a free society is capable.

### Subordination to Higher Priority Objectives?

Some of the most tantalizing language in the report is found in a section which sets out four national objectives that should have priority over balance-of-payments discipline:

> 1. Achieving domestic economic stability and sustained growth at full employment.
>
> 2. Maintaining the military strength of the Free World.
>
> 3. Promoting and supporting economic development of underdeveloped areas and avoiding injury to the continued growth of other countries.
>
> 4. Assuring the greatest possible freedom of economically productive international transactions in the Free World.

The authors say that balance-of-payments discipline "is not desirable if it requires the subordination of higher priority objectives." This sounds as though a nation, willy-nilly, can decide to have any dimension of balance-of-payments deficit it chooses. But someone has to be willing to pick up the IOUs. And this is the rub. We are badly deluded if we think that the world (i.e. Western Europe) owes us an obligation to pile up dollar holdings and make good, in the tangible terms of goods and services, on all the helps—military and economic—we want to give abroad.

Certainly the enumerated four objectives are vital goals. Yet we do not "maintain the military strength of the Free World" when we ship out dollars without a counterpart of exports but instead expect other nations to provide the goods and accept and hold the dollars. The same is true in "promoting and supporting the economic development of underdeveloped areas." Indeed, we injure the solid growth of other countries if, through balance-of-payments deficits, we export inflation. Our continuing balance-of-payments deficits do not assure "the greatest possible freedom of economically productive international transactions." They have led us to "tie" aid, at additional expense to the taxpayer, and to consider a discriminatory "interest equalization tax."

The first high priority objective—"achieving domestic economic stability and sustained growth at full employment"—is the one that has the largest appeal. No one would seriously ask that the United States accept spiraling deflation, with all the unemployment and business failures inevitably involved, as a price for cor-

recting the balance-of-payments deficit. No one is asking us—in William Jennings Bryan's words—to "crucify mankind upon a cross of gold."

The real importance of balance-of-payments discipline is that it is inducing us to take measures for our own good, protecting the buying power of the dollar—the real values in the social security check, in the workman's pay envelope, in the goods we have to sell at home and abroad.

We need to see that financial improvidence obstructs, rather than advances, real accomplishment. As Chairman William McC. Martin of the Federal Reserve Board said to the Congressional Joint Economic Committee earlier this year:

> There is no set of policies that is truly good for the domestic economy, but bad for the dollar; and there is no course of action that is really good for the dollar, as an international currency, which is not good for the American economy.

### New Monetary Machinery?

The central conclusion of the report is one quite unrelated to the projection of a basic balance by 1968:

> . . . no position of the balance of payments — whether surplus, deficit, or balance — would simultaneously free the United States from undesirable constraints and provide for needed expansion of international monetary reserves. It is clear, therefore, that the present problem is not primarily a balance-of-payments problem. More fundamentally, the problem is the basic inadequacy of the international monetary mechanism in relation to requirements of the Free World.

The balance of payments is a complicated subject. It is tempting to believe that there may be some easy escape through rebuilding the international monetary mechanism. But, before we venture afield, we should be clear in our own minds what we want to accomplish and what price we want to pay.

People have a right to know if the object is to make the inflationary bed comfortable, to get rid of the discipline of gold and to add to world money supplies so that irresistible pressures for higher wages can have effects of raising prices rather than increasing unemployment.

The report favors setting up a new super central bank, abandoning the dollar as the international standard of value, and substituting a currency unit which the bank would create and lend to various countries to give them plenty of time to finance protracted deficits in their balances of payments.

If the innovation of a new super central bank with powers of money issue were not to usher in an era of worldwide inflation, the first and most difficult task the institution would have to face would be to insist that the United States get its balance of payments in order. We should be wise enough to see this need ourselves, without prompting and without abdicating our role of international financial leadership.

People can say if they wish that the dollar is weak and unattractive. But the idea is contradicted by the fact that more private lending is done in dollars than in all the rest of the world's currencies put together. For all our problems, there is probably greater faith in the enduring value of the dollar than in any other currency.

While the dollar is good, it should be better. The attractiveness of the dollar saved can be and has been enhanced by higher interest rates. The attractiveness of the dollar earned can be enhanced by proposed easier income taxes. The attractiveness of the dollar for all purposes can be enhanced by checking the wage-price creep and the inflation of government spending. We have only to reject inflation as a way of life. The political and economic stability—the ordered progress —of the Free World demands it.

## Government Expenditures Abroad

No other nation in the world competes with us in the size of expenditures of a political or semi-political nature abroad. Bankers in Europe say we are trying to do too much. However rich a man is, however great his income, there are limits to what he can afford. We have been able to balance the federal budget in only one of the last six years. The balance of payments has been in red ink in all but one of the last 14 years.

While government expenditures abroad are most intimately related to the balance-of-payments deficit, it should be understood that the total of government spending imposes a strain on a nation's balance of payments. In fact there is no surer or more common way by which nations invite balance-of-payments crises than by financing increases in government spending by the use of money printing presses.

The technicians at the Federal Reserve and Treasury have done a skillful job of arranging credits abroad to spare our gold stock from speedier erosion. Nevertheless, as Allan Sproul, former President of the Federal Reserve Bank of New York, pointed out in a recent speech:

> . . . it is acutely in the minds of our monetary authorities, that these defenses are not impregnable and that insofar as they result in an increase in funds which we have borrowed abroad, they will have dug deeper the hole out of which we must eventually climb.

Mr. Sproul observed that it is past time "for a severe tightening up in our foreign military and economic aid." As the Brookings report arranges the figures, government long-term capital and economic aid has been rising in each of the last three years, from $2.6 billion in 1959 to $3.9 billion in 1962. This total leaves out payments on U.S. subscriptions to the International Monetary Fund, military grants, and also nearly $3 billion a year being spent for the support of our military services abroad (an item classified under "services").

The question of how much burden our overseas commitments impose on our balance of payments is a subject of active debate among economists and statisticians. By arranging the figures in various ways, they come up with all sorts of answers. A customary practice has been to exclude aids in the form of military hardware totally from the balance-of-payments data, on the theory that, while an expense to the taxpayer, they presumably would not be shipped in anything like the same amounts if foreign nations had to pay for them.

The main debate centers on the treatment of economic aid which, increasingly, is being "tied"; in other words, money provided under this heading generally is required to be spent in the United States. These programs enlarge exports but to some uncertain extent they simply pay for goods we would have sold anyway and gotten paid for.

The largest single drain probably comes from military expenditures abroad. The government has tried to persuade foreign countries to purchase military equipment here to achieve an offsetting inflow of funds. The $650 million of expenditures for American troops in Germany now appears to be fully offset by German equipment purchases. But other countries have only taken modest steps in that direction.

What can be said with certainty is that the burden on the balance of payments of government overseas expenditures in all categories runs to several billion dollars a year and is of the same order of magnitude as the total deficit.

### Cutting Back

The Administration realizes that mending the payments imbalance requires curtailment of government overseas spending. A control system—the so-called gold budget—has been set up covering all expenditures overseas by every federal agency. Our Allies have been urged to increase their own defense and aid efforts. Arrangements have been negotiated for debt prepayments, and enlarged purchases of and advance payments for military equipment manufactured here.

The President, in his message last July, committed the Administration to achieving further savings in overseas outlays: "In fact, by January 1965, these processes should result in a reduction of the rate of our federal overseas dollar expenditures by approximately $1 billion from that of 1962." If realized this could be most helpful. The present disposition of the Congress is to resist and reverse the rising trend of such expenditures as projected in the Brookings report. In the words of the Clay Committee report last spring, there is "a feeling that we are trying to do too much for too many too soon, that we are overextended in resources and undercompensated in results. . . ."

There is no denying that we live in a perilous world in which there are large tasks for the government to perform. One of the paramount tasks is to defend the dollar as a strong and reliable currency not only for ourselves but for the entire Free World. It would be self-defeating if the government, to accommodate its own spending and lending overseas, should take away freedoms of Americans to travel or invest abroad or should weaken the usefulness of the dollar as an international currency.

### Exporting Inflation

The chronic deficits in our balance of payments show that our financial generosity exceeds our economic generosity. In other words, we are not exporting equivalences of goods and services for the money we are spending and lending abroad. Thus excesses of dollars pile up among nations which are more conservative in their overseas undertakings.

As the Brookings report persuasively argues— U.S. balance-of-payments deficits tend to become the balance-of-payments surpluses of Continental Western Europe. The underdeveloped countries, as a whole, rarely can afford to build cash reserves; they are short of capital and tend to use promptly whatever extra reserves come into their possession. In the United Kingdom, Canada and Japan, reserves fluctuate up and down without trends toward continuing accumulation.

In technical terms, we have a transfer problem, reminiscent of the transfer problem that arose from German reparations payments and Allied war debts after World War I. This time the obligations are ones we have assumed. They do not arise from reparations we must pay but from helps which are voluntarily given and for that reason should be more easily controllable.

As De Nederlandsche Bank (the Netherlands' central bank) states in its 1962 annual report:

> A deficit of over $2 billion . . . is too great to be lastingly squared in the normal manner, that is to a large extent by parting with gold; it is moreover so great that it cannot fail, sooner or later, to exert an appreciable inflationary influence on the rest of the world.

### Advice from Abroad

As the Nederlandsche Bank report points out, the problem is two-sided and can be worked out by corrective actions taken on both sides of the Atlantic. That done, and with the help of the effectively functioning International Monetary Fund, talk of needs for drastic changes of the international monetary system to increase international liquidity can wither away.

Europe has as little wish to build reserves to the moon as we have to run balance-of-payments deficits until our international credit is exhausted. The authors of the Brookings report, with all their accent on needs for additional liquidity, do not propose that a new super central bank should allow us to run deficits as long as we please. They admit that "it is probably necessary that the principal financial and industrial countries consult fully and frequently and coordinate policies that have substantial effects on international payments."

If we must face this problem eventually, why not now?

We need to recognize that it is past time for a tightening up of U.S. Government commitments overseas. We can exercise our powers of persuasion to get Europe to assume a larger share of military and economic aid burdens but we should not go on spilling out excess dollars and expect Europe to take the money and put up the goods.

Meanwhile, we must stimulate our economic performance by income tax rate reductions, work to lower our production costs through increased investment, restraint on wages and elimination of "featherbedding," and avoid deliberate maintenance of low interest rates.

Europe can help by accepting larger defense and aid responsibilities, opening its markets more freely to imports and improving the organization of its capital markets to reduce what the Nederlandsche Bank calls the perverse interest differential between surplus and deficit countries.

A bilateral problem requires a bilateral solution. With a spirit of mutual understanding the problem can be resolved on principles of maximizing international intercourse to the benefit of all peoples.

# The International Role of Private Capital

As the leading capitalist country of the world, with the strongest flow of saving, the United States is quite naturally the leading exporter of capital. This is another way of saying that we are a major underpinning of economic progress overseas. Capital invested in manufacturing, transportation and communication facilities makes human labor more productive and raises living standards around the world.

Our money and capital markets are international institutions. Foreigners have $13 billion invested in stocks and bonds of U.S. corporations and $14 billion in U.S. government obligations. But great as are foreign assets in this market—and the aggregate reaches $50 billion—American investments overseas are even bigger, exceeding $80 billion. Though we have a balance-of-payments problem, evidenced in a declining gold stock and in dollar accumulations overseas, the total of our foreign assets continues to grow faster than our liabilities.

It is penny-wise and pound-foolish to blame the balance-of-payments deficit on private investments overseas. Unlike soft loans and grants under government programs, private investments support the balance of payments for years into the future. Prudently made, we get our money back with interest.

Overseas investment is our natural, national destiny. Suppression of private investment is suppression of private enterprise. The ideological war can be won only by encouragements to private enterprise everywhere so that the full strength of free institutions can be mustered and unequivocally demonstrated.

### Direct Investments

The greatest part of U.S. private funds being placed at long term abroad is for direct investment. Going on in the world is a process of internationalization of business, whereby both the ownership and operations of major corporations are becoming international. A company headquartered here, and setting up branches or subsidiaries abroad, is itself likely to have many foreign shareholders. American-based companies play a leading role in bringing the benefits of our know-how to other countries as well as improving foreign markets for American machinery and components.

Income from overseas direct investments* provides a sturdy support to the U.S. balance of payments. By 1962 it had grown beyond $3 billion, nearly double the $1.6 billion of new direct investments made in that year. The Brookings report offers a calculation that a direct investment in manufacturing facilities in Europe is likely to pay back the cost imposed on the balance of payments within six years. Any funds

* Counted as service receipts in the statistics.

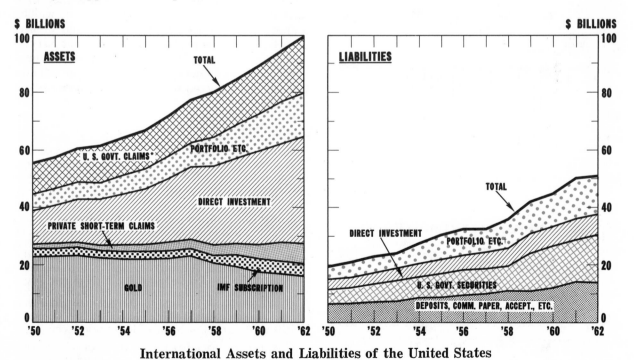

**International Assets and Liabilities of the United States**

(End of Year)

* Excluding World War I loans. † Other than U.S. Government bond and note holdings.
Source: U.S. Department of Commerce.

brought home after that represent a gain to the balance of payments, free and clear.

The outflows of new funds, as recorded in balance-of-payments statistics, are not a full measure of the contribution made by American business to capital formation in host countries. In addition to new funds sent abroad, American business year after year plows back more than $1 billion of foreign earnings. When capital flows are combined with undistributed profits, it follows that in recent years about $2.5 billion has been added annually to our equity abroad. If depreciation and depletion funds are added to this estimate of fresh capital outflows and re-invested earnings, a figure of close to $5 billion a year is obtained as a measure of American gross investment abroad.

### Portfolio Investments

Like direct investments abroad by U.S. companies, American purchases of foreign stocks and bonds increase the deficit momentarily but help the balance of payments thereafter as dividends and interest are received. A bulge in offerings of foreign government bonds was a sizable item in the deterioration in our balance of payments in the first half of this year. This led the President to propose a temporary "interest equalization tax," intended to check portfolio investments by several hundred million dollars a year.

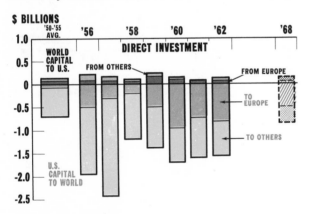

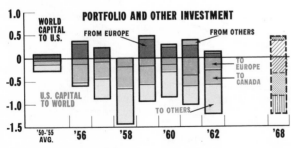

**Long-Term Private Capital Flows of the United States**

Source: The Brookings report.

Since the tax, if enacted, would apply retro-actively, the mere proposal has practically brought to a halt trading in foreign stocks and bonds between foreigners and Americans, has disrupted the international capital market of which New York is the main center and is deflecting foreign buying interest in securities to other markets. Arousing fears that it is merely the prelude to further restrictions on capital movements, the proposal is leading some money to run abroad and thus, unfortunately, may be worsening the deficit. Private capital does not like to be fenced in. We can serve our role as banker to the world, and gain deposits, only by maintaining free rights of withdrawal.

Purchases of foreign *stocks* have never been a serious factor in our balance of payments. As the Brookings report brings out, foreign holdings of American stocks are greater than American holdings of foreign stocks.

Although the fact is not well understood, the outflow of U.S. funds under the heading of portfolio investments is accounted for by *bond* issues, mostly by foreign governments. From 1946 to 1956 there were few flotations of publicly offered foreign bonds, apart from Canadian and World Bank issues. From 1957 on, however, such issues have gradually increased. Including direct placements, which account for as much as one half of the total, they reached $1 billion in the first half of this year.

The interest equalization tax proposal led to a torrent of demands for special exemptions which, if granted, would have left more holes than cheese as well as perhaps broadened the areas of Executive discretion. The New York Chamber of Commerce, in a statement for the Ways and Means Committee, objected to the whole of the proposal on principle:

It should be clearly understood that the proposed interest equalization tax is an exchange control of limited applicability. It is not a tax for revenue. It is a tax to control and restrict. It is discriminatory, and delegates to the President and to the Internal Revenue Service discretionary powers of application and exemption. . . .

We know from our own experience and that of other countries that exchange controls drive business out of the channels of legitimacy, and underground. The enforcement problems involved in administering the taxes proposed in H.R. 8000 are matters to be reckoned with. Fully effective enforcement, for example, could require censorship of international mail and telephone calls, and searching the linings of international travelers' baggage. We do not believe that this would be tolerated by the Congress, or the American people.

A tax on the purchase by Americans of foreign securities would penalize Americans and the participation of American financial institutions in international finance. It would tend to divert business to foreign financial centers where, ironically enough, transactions might still be undertaken in dollars beyond the jurisdiction of U.S. markets. In fact such diversion has already taken place as a result of the submission of the proposal. It must be underscored that the dollar is not alone our national currency. It is the World's international currency. There exists no effective substitute for it.

Rejection of the proposal by the Congress would relieve the harm done and unequivocally restate what the President has called our "historic advocacy of freer trade and capital movements."

### Borrowings in Dollars

Foreign bond issues floated here are by no means all sold to Americans. Such bonds are especially attractive to foreign buyers because they know the credits and can get higher returns than on U.S. obligations. Secretary Dillon has stated that foreigners last year bought over one third of the foreign issues publicly offered here.

One main reason foreigners come to this market to borrow is that we have the only really big market. Investors overseas tend to prefer bonds denominated in dollars because such bonds are most readily marketable and because they have faith that the dollar will hold its value over the long pull as well as any currency in the world. We must be careful in whatever we do to protect this faith and the freedom and size of our money and capital markets.

An emotion can be aroused that it is unpatriotic for Americans to travel, buy and invest abroad. Yet this would be to tear the fabric of world prosperity. For we prosper and grow out of economic interdependence. Private business, like government business, is international. The world has gotten too small for insularity.

### Underdevelopment of Overseas Capital Markets

Foreigners are not only attracted to our market because it is big. They are also attracted because our Treasury and Federal Reserve are keeping long-term interest rates down for the benefit of our homebuilders, corporations, states and political subdivisions. They are attracted, too, because Europe has given too little attention to the development of correspondingly free capital markets. Abroad, foreign borrowers, and sometimes domestic borrowers too, require official approval and must wait in line before they are allowed to raise needed funds.

As a distinguished banker, Dr. E. Reinhardt of the Swiss Credit Bank, wrote recently:

> . . . it must not be forgotten that convertibility, as it exists today, represents full convertibility in the

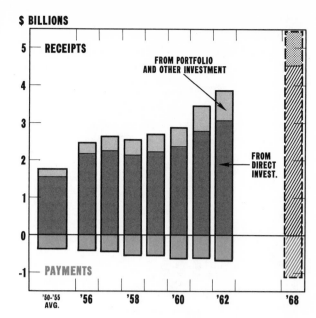

**International Private Investment Income Flows of the United States**

Source: The Brookings report.

classic sense in only a few countries, for example the USA, Switzerland and the Federal Republic of Germany. . . . Whereas the new currency systems facilitated the development of close inter-dependence on the . . . short-term . . . market, a similar degree of cohesion has not yet been achieved on the long-term market.

The Treasury and the Federal Reserve have undertaken, for balance-of-payments reasons, to encourage a rise in our short-term open market money rates, as dramatized by the July increase in discount rate from 3 to 3½ per cent. The effort is being made to avoid rises in long-term interest rates "while the economy operates below capacity without inflation." Yet narrowing the gap in long-term borrowing rates is fundamentally more important than narrowing the gap in short-term rates, from the standpoints both of improving the balance of payments and of encouraging the development of sensibly interrelated capital markets throughout the Free World.

The conflict between domestic and international objectives may be eased or even resolved, as numerous foreign observers have noted, by substituting income tax rate reductions for cheap money as a stimulus to dynamic expansion. People can have more of their own money to spend and rely less on borrowings. We can let our interest rates respond to international forces as indeed they must if we are to perform our role as banker for the world.

### FIRST NATIONAL CITY BANK

# First National City First in Geneva

**Citibank Makes Significant Addition To Its Extensive Overseas System.** Pacing the progress of business activity around the Free World, First National City adds another full-fledged banking office in a key financial center. △ Our new Geneva branch marks the first appearance of an American bank in Switzerland. This latest milestone typifies the attention Citibank is giving to the entire European business front. We maintain four branch offices in the Common Market area, two others in England, staffed by more than 600 experienced bankers. △ Here is a concrete projection of First National City's *total banking*—complete facilities, resources, experience everywhere from Manhattan to Malaya to Montevideo, ready to serve every kind of business. Wherever *your* company's interests lie, you will find First National City the right bank in the right place! **FIRST NATIONAL CITY BANK**

399 PARK AVENUE, NEW YORK 22, N.Y. • MEMBER FEDERAL DEPOSIT INSURANCE CORPORATION

*Brussels—Common Market capital— another Citibank branch office is at your service here.*

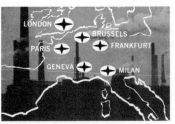

*Map pinpoints strategic locations of First National City's European branches.*

*One of First National City's busy London branches, serving many U.S. corporations doing business in Britain.*

# Monthly Economic Letter

1812    FIRST NATIONAL CITY BANK NEW YORK    1963

## General Business Conditions

As we move into the final quarter of 1963, the volume of incoming orders and profits supports expectations of sustained activity through the end of the year. Initial production schedules for autos have been set at new high levels, and retailers generally are confident of record fall and Christmas seasons. According to Department of Commerce surveys, manufacturers plan to enlarge their investments in inventories and capital equipment.

Tax reduction, discussed in greater detail elsewhere in this issue, continues to be the key to the 1964 outlook. The bill approved by the House on September 25 would add $5.6 billion to disposable income of individuals in 1964 and an additional $3.1 billion in 1965. The corporate share of the total $11.1 billion tax cut—$2.3 billion—would be spread over the next two years, but accelerated tax payments would postpone the full benefits from corporate rate reductions until 1971.

A bit of slack appeared in industrial production in August, as the Federal Reserve index (seasonally adjusted, 1957-59 = 100) eased off a point to 125.6, following seven consecutive monthly advances which had carried the index from 119.1 to 126.5. The unusually concentrated shutdowns of auto plants for model changes and a continued decline in steel production were the decisive August influences, offsetting further strength in output of machinery and other capital goods. Both steel and autos resumed an upward course in September and further increases are scheduled for October.

### Metalworking Activity

By the week ended September 28, steel output had been rising for six straight weeks to an annual rate of 98 million tons, up 8 per cent from mid-August. Industry sources look for October to show a better-than-seasonal increase of 10 per cent over September. Sustained demand, based on a high rate of metalworking activity in the closing months of the year, is expected to bring output for 1963 as a whole up into a range of 105-110 million tons, the highest since 1957 and well above the 98 million tons for 1962.

Output of passenger cars has been accelerated from the unusually low level of 156,400 in August to about 500,000 in September—the highest rate for that month since 1950. By late September two thirds of the industry's 46 assembly plants were working two shifts. Even so, extensive overtime will be required in October when schedules call for production of more than 800,000 cars. If realized, this will be the biggest monthly total in the industry's history.

The enthusiastic scheduling of '64 model production reflects the industry's high hopes for the new models. Spokesmen for the various makes have been unanimous in their forecasts of another good auto year in 1964, with sales somewhere around the 7-million mark. According to estimates by *Ward's Automotive Reports*, total sales of domestic cars are heading toward 7.2 million for 1963. Sales of imported cars, after slipping off from the peak of 614,000 vehicles in 1959 to 339,000 in 1962, are up moderately and are expected to exceed 350,000.

This year may challenge an old record for production of trucks. Fourth quarter output schedules point to an annual total of about 1,400,000, compared with the record of 1,412,149 in the Korean war year of 1951. Exports are running below the swollen 1951 rate, and chances are that domestic truck sales will reach a new high.

### Plant and Equipment Spending Strong

The good market for trucks emphasizes the growing demand for a wide variety of capital goods. Some persons tend to equate capital investment with machinery purchases, but in actuality this type of demand also covers construction of plants and a broad spectrum of electrical apparatus, professional and scientific instruments, tools and vehicles as well—everything from jet planes to office desks, from huge earthmoving equipment to intricate computers. Business is planning to spend $39.1 billion dollars this year on new plant and equipment, a 5 per cent increase over 1962's record outlays, according to the latest survey by the Department of Commerce and the Securities and Exchange Commission. The projected 1963 rate is 6 per cent greater than in the capital spending boom of 1957.

Corporate appropriations for new capital programs were up 20 per cent in the second quarter from the temporarily reduced first quarter level. The McGraw-Hill index of new orders for nonelectrical machinery was at a seasonally adjusted peak in July, while preliminary Commerce Department data on new orders received for machinery and equipment in August remained close to the record rate in the preceding three months.

Furthermore, the brisk rise in manufacturing activity has increased the proportion of capacity being utilized. This is a difficult concept to measure statistically, but several independent estimates agree that the gap between current operating rates and the level at which management prefers to operate has been narrowed considerably. In some lines, the optimum rate may already have been achieved. This is the sort of situation that intensifies management consideration of modernization or expansion, especially when next year's markets—given the stimulus of a tax cut—could well be decisively greater than in 1963.

Another major factor stimulating increased capital investment programs is the favorable trend in corporate profits. Confirming the preliminary results reported in this *Letter* two months ago, government sources have officially estimated a marked increase during the second quarter in profits and profit margins. The Department of Commerce puts after-tax earnings of all corporations at an annual rate of $26.8 billion, up 9 per cent from a year earlier and the highest on record. These estimates reflect the more rapid depreciation allowed under last year's revised guidelines, which many firms accepted for tax purposes but not for reports to shareholders. However these earnings are measured, they are helping to encourage and finance more capital spending.

The generally good level of business has also been felt in record high levels of employment. The unemployment percentage edged down slightly to 5.5 per cent, seasonally adjusted, in August. This was the lowest point this year, down from the peak rate of 6.1 in February, but almost equal to the 1962 average of 5.6.

It is also worth noting that the seasonally adjusted unemployment rate for adult males, at 4.1 per cent in August, was significantly below the 1962 average of 4.6. For married men, the rate was only 3.0 in August against 3.6 in 1962. Thus, the impact of unemployment on heads of families —which generally causes the greatest hardship— has been on the downgrade. What is keeping the over-all rate high is the increased unemployment rate among workers who are generally not the main support of families.

Unemployment among teenagers, seasonally adjusted, was 14.1 per cent in August, or one in every seven of this age group in the civilian labor force. This was an improvement over the average of 16.0 per cent in the preceding six months, but higher than the 13.4 per cent rate during 1962. For adult women, the unemployment rate in August was 5.7, compared with 5.4 in 1962. Both women and teenagers have been coming into the labor market at a faster rate than men, which partially explains their greater difficulty in locating work. Newcomers to the labor force are generally inexperienced and often unskilled.

## Russian-Canadian Wheat Deal

The momentous announcement on September 16 of Russia's $500 million deal to buy 228 million bushels of wheat and flour from Canada gave cause for fundamental reappraisal of U.S. trade policy.

Russia, once the "breadbasket" of Europe, is having to go abroad for food for its people. The Soviet shortage is partly attributable to some lack of success in the much-publicized "new lands" program but is more directly attributable to disastrous weather affecting yields and qualities of grain in most countries of Europe and Asia.

"Ill blows the wind that profits nobody." Strong

demand for wheat in the world market is helping the economies and balance-of-payments positions of Australia and Argentina as well as Canada. The situation invites reconsideration of a number of our policies. The opportunity is offered:

1. To reduce U.S. Government spending by hundreds of millions of dollars a year through scrapping export subsidies as well as putting the price-support system on the basis of an emergency floor. By their vote in the referendum last May, wheat farmers rebelled against the trend toward more and more regimentation to keep crop production down and prices up. Meanwhile price-support operations have choked storage bins with 1.2 billion bushels of wheat. The new crop, estimated at 1.1 billion bushels, is near double our annual consumption. Rather ironically, the Russians are giving us the opportunity to restore our grain trade to a free market basis.

2. To welcome inquiries from Soviet trade representatives with a view to consummating a sale from our accumulated stocks. Added exports will reduce our balance-of-payments deficit; sales of wheat out of government bins will reduce the budget deficit. Payment would have to be negotiated on a businesslike basis.

3. To reconsider our policy of attempting to check the growth of Russia's competing economic system by including that country on a selected list of countries with which trade is officially discouraged if not totally suppressed. As vividly illustrated by the Canadian wheat deal, our policy is one that our allies are unwilling to accept. Thus we become driven into a position of isolation.

The main objections to reopening trade with Russia are political and emotional. Americans have in mind Cuba, the missile crisis of no more than a year ago and the Berlin Wall. On the other hand, all peoples reject nuclear war as unthinkable. They recognize that the central problem of our day is to keep the peace even while embracing quite different ideas of appropriate political and economic organization. Rapprochement, as evidenced in the test ban treaty approved by the Senate last month, is eagerly to be desired.

All economic considerations favor normalization of East-West trade, with understandable exceptions. Trade among the nations, to mutual advantage, is a good way to keep rivalry on a peaceful basis.

| U.S.-Soviet Bloc Trade (In Millions of Dollars) | | | | |
|---|---|---|---|---|
| | U.S. Exports to Soviet Bloc | | U.S. Imports from Soviet Bloc | |
| | Countries | U.S.S.R. | Countries | U.S.S.R. |
| 1956 | 11.2 | 3.8 | 65.5 | 24.5 |
| 1957 | 86.1 | 3.5 | 61.3 | 16.5 |
| 1958 | 113.1 | 3.4 | 63.5 | 17.5 |
| 1959 | 89.3 | 7.4 | 80.9 | 28.6 |
| 1960 | 193.9 | 38.4 | 80.9 | 22.6 |
| 1961 | 133.3 | 42.7 | 81.1 | 23.2 |
| 1962 | 125.1 | 15.3 | 78.9 | 16.2 |

Source: Department of Commerce, *Overseas Business Reports*, April 1963.

## The Debate on Fiscal Responsibility

The House Ways and Means Committee, after eight months' study, reported out the income tax rate reduction bill on September 10. Although the bill departs in many respects from the President's specific proposals, submitted January 24, it has received his unqualified endorsement. Over a nationwide radio and TV hookup on September 18, he described the bill as the most important legislation before the Congress this year. Indeed, "no more important domestic economic legislation has come before the Congress in some 15 years." On September 25, the House passed the bill.

Indications are that, in the Senate, the tax bill will run into opposition, and not only from conservatives, who feel that the budget should be balanced before consideration is given to tax cuts, but also from spenders concerned over the alleged impoverishment of the public sector. It is such strange alliances—from both ends of the political spectrum—that have kept us wedded to emergency, war-level income tax rates all these years.

The fate of the bill hangs in doubt. The long months required by the Ways and Means Committee, explained by the controversial nature and complex language of the reform proposals, do not allow corresponding time for Senate consideration. Moreover, strong opposition has developed on the ground that, while major income tax rate reductions are widely recognized as long overdue and highly desirable, it is fiscally irresponsible to cut taxes at a time when the budget is running $9 billion in the red and major reductions in government spending are not in the program. The bill as it now stands is expensive in calculated annual revenue loss—$11 billion without regard to "feedbacks"—and encompasses many objectionable or incomprehensible provisions in its 304 pages. Thus many businessmen are confused as to whether they should support the bill or oppose it pending major spending cuts and a fresh approach on reform proposals.

### Bogged Down by Reforms

The snail's-pace progress of the bill confirmed fears many observers had expressed that inclusion of complex reforms would forestall any action whatever on income tax rates this year. Reforms in the tax system are needed but this objective is secondary to getting the rates down to less unreasonable levels.

When reforms are enacted they should be required to conform to two acid tests: do they simplify obedience to the law on the part of the tax-form-weary citizen; do they enlarge the base of taxable income?

These objectives got lost in the welter of discussion of confusing new complications proposed by the President or Committee members. Instead, the bill would free around 1½ million persons from paying any federal income taxes at all while adding to the burden of tax homework for tens of millions of others. The controversial petroleum depletion allowances provide an illustration. New methods of calculation are introduced, adding to the numbers of accountants and lawyers the companies must hire. Many people in the industry would have preferred a simple reduction in the allowance.

The Senate could save time, accelerate action and spare millions of manhours of tax-drudgery for conscientious citizens if it laid aside the reform package and simply enacted appropriate rate cuts for January 1, 1964 and January 1, 1965. Simplifying, base-broadening reforms could be tied to a later, third step of major rate reductions.

In this context, we quote the following comment from a reader, aroused by the article in our August issue on "The Invisible Costs of Government":

I do not mind paying my tax so much as the slavery of calculating it.

### Take It or Leave It?

As the President said:

The federal income tax is one of those subjects about which we talk, about which we complain, but about which not very much is done. Perhaps we've heard too long about the certainty of death and taxes. Perhaps other national and other international issues now seem more pressing.

Yet the fact is that the high wartime and post-war tax rates we are now paying are no longer necessary. They are, in fact, harmful. These high rates do not leave enough money in private hands to keep this country's economy growing and healthy.

Politics is the art of the possible. Many businessmen are inclined to support the bill, fearful that, if the present opportunity is not accepted, major income tax reduction will be put back on the shelf for more years of theoretical discussion and political inaction. The bill, for all its faults, *would* do a major job on income tax rates, including the higher rates which deter people from seeking additions to their taxable income and induce them instead to seek out channels for avoidance.

### Republican Opposition

The Ways and Means Committee reported out the tax bill by a vote largely along party lines. The Republican minority report, while agreeing that the excessive tax burden and steeply progressive tax rates should be reduced, objected to the addition of so many structural reforms which produce no revenue and add to the complexities and inequities of the law. So far as substantive changes are concerned, the report objected that:

. . . the structural reforms increase the taxes of the sick, of those who itemize deductions, and of those who invest in dividend-paying stocks, while giving a gratuitous "handout" of billions to big business by doubling the benefit of the investment credit. The tax system as a whole will be better if this bill is rejected by the Congress.

The main Republican objections, however, struck at a point of widespread concern—the "fiscal irresponsibility" of cutting taxes at a time when the budget is unbalanced and government spending on the rise. Congressman John W. Byrnes of Wisconsin, ranking Republican member of the Ways and Means Committee, in a broadcast on September 20, said "the President was dead right when he pointed out the urgent need for reduction in our taxes." But he went on to cite the background of $5 to $6 billion federal spending increases in each of the last three years, and forecast a further $4 billion rise next year:

Try as we may—try as the President may—neither he, nor you, nor I, can divorce our runaway spending and our mounting debt from his appeal for an immediate 11-billion-dollar tax cut.

\* \* \*

They are making a bet that this tax cut will give us a non-inflationary, continuing economic growth at a rate far beyond any we have ever before achieved. If this long shot does not come through, what surely lies ahead is an unending parade of huge deficits.

### Administration Reassurances

The Administration has offered a number of reassurances on this point:

• because of resultant economic stimulation, growth of the tax base, and the spacing out of the tax cuts, revenues will continue on a rising trend and the deficits will gradually be wiped out;

• deficits, unavoidable in any case over the short run, will be financed in a noninflationary manner, with the offer of bonds at rates of 4¼ per cent or more if necessary;

• the rise in expenditures will be vigorously curbed.

To many people, these reassurances are good so far as they go but are not sufficiently explicit. The Republican minority, reflecting such doubts, suggested that tax cuts be made conditional, for example on the size of the net federal debt on June 30, 1964, or on the magnitude of spending recommended by the President in his January budget message for the fiscal years ending June 30, 1964 and June 30, 1965.

In the debate on the floor of the House of Representatives, Congressman Byrnes proposed that the cuts become effective only if proposed budget spending for fiscal '64 does not exceed $97 billion and for the 1965 fiscal year, $98 billion. (Last January the President had proposed $98.8 billion for fiscal '64. A re-estimate for fiscal '64 and the first estimate for fiscal '65 will be incorporated in the President's January budget message.)

This proposal, defeated on a fairly close vote, has much to recommend it in principle. But it is open to objections. It would turn over to the Executive effective power to decide whether or not taxes should be cut and meanwhile leave future rates in doubt.

### An Expenditure Limit

It would be better if we went further and set a flat annual limit on expenditures.

Congress needs to regain control of expenditures in the exercise of its Constitutional responsibilities and has been struggling to do so. But methods attempted are indirect and ineffectual. For example, strong effort was made this past summer to get rid of so-called "backdoor spending": the operations of the Export-Import Bank were impeded for some weeks because of House objections to its financing through borrowings from the Treasury rather than through direct appropriations.

Yet most spending is straight out the front door. The Congress has been appropriating so much each year that there are huge carryovers of unexpended balances. For example, about two fifths of federal spending during the current fiscal year is being financed out of an estimated $87 billion carryover of unused spending authority from prior fiscal years. In his budget message last January, the President requested $108 billion in new obligational authority for fiscal '64. The House has made some cuts; nevertheless, it is clear that there will be another huge carryover as of June 30, 1964.

For effective control over spending, the Congress has relied on the public debt limit. The national legislature is privileged to make tax reductions dependent upon the fact that the public debt is less than some stated amount on some stated date. But this would leave uncertainties about future tax rates and still fail to provide any firm limit to expenditures. If revenues are good, the invitation is offered to increase spending; if they are poor, the Treasury is embarrassed

to meet contractual obligations.

The time has come to stop beating around the bush and meet the problem squarely, with a statutory limit on annual expenditures.

### Chairman Mills' Statement

Many worries about the future value of the dollar are based on impressions that the United States Government has little respect for money when it comes to spending. Tax reduction which compels retrenchment can help eradicate this image. It is reassuring to read what Congressman Wilbur D. Mills, Chairman of the Ways and Means Committee, has to say about the need to get away from "wasteful, inefficient government activities, merely because they incidentally give employment":

> The purpose of this tax reduction and revision bill is to loosen the constraints which present federal taxation imposes on the American economy. . . .

> Increases in economic activity, in the use of our resources, in personal and business incomes, and in federal revenues might be also realized if, instead of reducing taxes, the Congress and the Administration increased expenditures of government. In other words, there are two roads the government could follow toward a larger, more prosperous economy—the tax reduction road or the government expenditure increase road.

> There is a difference—a vitally important difference—between them. The increase in government expenditure road gets us to a higher level of economic activity with larger and larger shares of that activity initiating in government—with more labor and capital being used directly by the government in its activities and with more labor and capital in the private sector of the economy being used to produce goods and services on government orders.

> The tax reduction road, on the other hand, gets us to a higher level of economic activity—to a bigger, more prosperous, more efficient economy—with a larger and larger share of that enlarged activity initiating in the private sector of the economy—in the decision of individuals to increase and diversify their private consumption and in the decisions of business concerns to increase their productive capacity—to acquire more plant and machines, to hire more labor, to expand their inventories—and to diversify and increase the efficiency of their production. . . .

> When we, as a nation, choose this road we are at the same time rejecting the other road, and we want it understood that we do not intend to try to go along both roads at the same time. . . .

> There is no further justification for an indifferent attitude toward wasteful, inefficient government activities, merely because they incidentally give employment —tax reduction will also create job opportunities and in lines of activity which better satisfy the character and demands of the people for an enriched life.

> \*   \*   \*

> If I were called upon to give a definition of the phrase "fiscal responsibility," this is just how I would define it. It means conducting the finances of the Federal Government in such a way that a balanced

budget can be and is achieved in an economy which is growing rapidly, providing adequate employment and investment opportunities, making full use of its capital and human resources, and giving the fullest possible play to the initiative and venturesomeness of the private sector. Tax reduction and revision will make it possible for us to achieve these objectives—to be fiscally responsible—with minimum direct intervention by the government in the decisions of individuals and business concerns.

## Check-up on International Liquidity

This is the time of the year when chief financial officers of 90-odd member countries gather together for the joint annual meetings of the International Monetary Fund and World Bank. At this year's meetings, which open in Washington as this *Letter* goes to press, the finance ministers and central bankers will be discussing, among other things, the adequacy of international liquidity—i.e., whether there is, or is likely to be, enough international money and credit to support expanding world trade and investment. This idea has a natural appeal in the United Kingdom, which has faced a succession of balance-of-payments crises since World War II, and also in the United States, which—while incomparably stronger in reserves—has been suffering chronic balance-of-payments deficits; these have involved important losses in gold reserves and have led the U.S. Government to enter into complicated special borrowing arrangements with Continental Western Europe.

Meanwhile, there has been no evidence in statistics on world trade—growing in recent years at an annual rate of 8 per cent—to indicate a general lack of international liquidity. Existing gold and foreign exchange reserves of governments and central banks, supplemented by an elaborate network of international credit facilities, are greater than ever. The International Monetary Fund, centerpiece of the international financial system designed at the Bretton Woods Conference in 1944, had its resources sizably enlarged in 1959. Last year, ten major industrial countries agreed to a plan to supplement Fund resources "to forestall or cope with an impairment of the international monetary system." Nevertheless, there exists an uneasiness in some quarters as to whether present arrangements are sufficient to keep the world economy functioning smoothly in all contingencies that may arise.

The problem focuses on the inadequacy of gold and the reluctance of some countries to accept other nations' currencies as reserves in lieu of gold. Yet there is not, and never will be, enough gold to finance the world's trade. Credit is easier to supply, and also ever so much more efficient and convenient. There must be enough to finance trade expansion but not so much as to breed worldwide inflation.

Some observers, such as the authors of the recently published Brookings report discussed in last month's *Letter*, worry about inadequacy of international liquidity if, by 1968 as they expect, the basic international transactions of the United States should come into balance or move into surplus. The U.S. payments deficit has been the main source from which Europe has been building its gold and dollar reserves; if and when the United States succeeds in bringing its payments into better shape, this source will be dried up. The resulting pinch in international liquidity, it is asserted, might force Europe into restrictive monetary and fiscal policies, even at the cost of slower economic growth, and to cut imports and reduce foreign aid.

### A Dilemma Seen by the Brookings Report

The Brookings report sees the United States —and, indeed, the whole Free World—as facing an awkward dilemma:

> On the one hand, U.S. balance-of-payments deficits make the rest of the world increasingly reluctant to go on accumulating liquid dollar claims, and they hamper pursuit by the United States of vital domestic and international objectives.

> On the other hand, large and sustained surpluses may not be attainable; even if attained, they would not be desirable since they might not free the United States from undesirable constraints and they would impose constraints on other Free World countries.

By *constraint*—a term which repeatedly occurs in the Brookings analysis, sometimes accompanied by adjectives like *undesirable* or *perverse* —the authors mean preoccupations with the balance of payments that threaten four "higher priority" objectives: "Sustained growth at full employment," military strength, foreign aid and "the greatest possible freedom of economically productive international transactions in the Free World."

In the view of the Brookings team, future imbalances of payments between major advanced nations are less likely to arise from inflationary pressures, as they did in earlier postwar years. From now on, the report holds, structural factors —such as changes in technology, in productivity or in world markets for individual countries' or individual industries' exports—will be more and more responsible for disturbances in international payments. But the existing monetary mechanism does not provide enough liquidity to give countries experiencing such structural deficits time to make needed adjustments.

The report rests its analysis on the idea that international trade depends directly on global external liquidity, as measured by aggregate official monetary reserves. In 1961, such reserves totaled $61 billion. Since by 1968 international trade might be expected—according to the report's "conservative" projections—to increase by 35 per cent, the needed growth in world reserves would also have to be 35 per cent, i.e., $21.4 billion. Gains to official gold stocks from new output during 1963-68 are put at no more than $4.7 billion; on the other hand, declining U.S. balance-of-payments deficits would add only $3 billion to reserves of other nations. The rise in gold and dollar reserves of the rest of the world in the five years would thus total only $7.7 billion, and fall far short of the calculated $21.4 billion.

The time has come, the report concludes, to create a more "satisfactory" international monetary mechanism. While details are not provided, the study visualizes a new or revamped International Monetary Fund in which member nations would be required to hold some of their reserves and which would, through the acceptability of its obligations, be able to finance "substantial" imbalances in international payments of major advanced nations. The institution would issue some new, yet unnamed, currency unit; this is reminiscent of Lord Keynes' proposed "bancor" or Harry White's "unitas," rejected in favor of the dollar at the Bretton Woods Conference.

The Brookings report recommends that the U.S. Government should "immediately" begin to press for an "agreement to strengthen international liquidity along the lines just outlined."

### World Liquidity Quest

In recent years, a great variety of similar proposals have been offered. The scheme that has received most attention has been advanced by Professor Robert Triffin. It has been followed by many other proposals, but none of them has elicited widespread support. The fundamentals of complex and delicate issues involved were reviewed in these pages in March 1961, soon after the debate had begun.

At the IMF meetings a year ago, Britain's Chancellor of the Exchequer, Mr. Reginald Maudling, sketched out another realm of ideas to reform the international monetary structure. Also looking towards a more "automatic" system, "capable of expansion to the extent necessary at any time," Mr. Maudling proposed an arrangement whereby a country accumulating dollars or sterling would deposit them in special accounts at the IMF, carrying a gold guarantee; it could then draw on such deposits when it ran itself into payments deficits. Mr. Harold Wilson, leader of the British Labor Party, also called a few months ago for a reform of the international monetary machinery, which he described as "archaic" and as placing "artificial restrictions" on the ability of

nations to expand. Today, all too often, *expand* is a euphemism for *inflate*.

Government officials and central bankers over the past two years have worked out cooperative arrangements directed at strengthening "the monetary defenses of the Free World" against threats of instability arising from "disruptive" or "undesirable" movements of funds across national boundaries. The United States is participating in a gold pool to steady the price of the metal in the London market. The Federal Reserve has gone into the foreign exchange market, and the Treasury has arranged borrowings in Europe to limit fluctuations in foreign exchange rates, influence short-term capital movements and reduce our gold losses. Previously chary of using the IMF, the United States in July entered into a $500 million stand-by credit from that institution. Characterizing these cooperative arrangements as "a permanent reinforcement of the international financial machinery," central bank officials* have pointed out that "truly impressive resources can now be mobilized in support of any currency under attack."

The chief architect of these arrangements, Under Secretary of the Treasury Robert V. Roosa, writing in the October 1963 issue of *Foreign Affairs*, believes that the time is now ripe for a "systematic and searching appraisal" of "whether a continuation of recent evolutionary changes, or more sweeping reforms, will be needed for the probable dimensions of future requirements" for world monetary reserves.

Mr. Roosa invites "wide-ranging governmental consideration," adding: "There is not, of course, any reason to presume that daring or revolutionary approaches will in fact emerge for the future. The process of evolution may very well take us where we want to go."

President Kennedy, in his balance-of-payments message last July, indicated that the Administration is studying possible improvements in the international monetary system, with minds open to "initiatives" of our friends abroad. "At the same time," he wisely observed, "we do not pretend that talk of long-range reform of the system is any substitute for the actions that we ourselves must take now."

### Making Inflation Internationally Comfortable

Some people, here as well as abroad, are concerned lest shortage of gold once again threaten the sort of spiraling deflation that led to the worldwide depression of the 1930's. And they are certainly right when they argue that—save against a background of a threatened total loss

* "Conversations on International Finance" by C. A. Coombs (Federal Reserve Bank of New York), M. Iklé (Banque Nationale Suisse), E. Ranalli (Banca d'Italia), and J. Tüngeler (Deutsche Bundesbank), *Monthly Review* of Federal Reserve Bank of New York, August 1963.

of confidence in money—deflation is politically untenable and economically undesirable, with all the unemployment and business failures involved.

There have been dramatic examples—France in 1958 and Spain in 1959—of nations which have accepted some measure of retrenchment in order to set a firm base for flourishing expansion. But deflation is not a pleasant medicine. The way to avoid need to deflate or devalue is to combat inflation.

It is all too easy in this world to institutionalize inflation, as by government edicts or union contracts to escalate wages. As the authors of the Brookings report recognize, wage increases unwarranted by productivity increases either reduce profits and employment or require expansion of money supplies to support price advances. Hence what seems "archaic" about the international monetary system is that it does not accommodate itself too easily to the inflationary pressures of our time. What is disquieting about proposals for increasing international liquidity is the implicit idea that wasting away of the values of money is inevitable and irresistible.

### How Much Is Enough?

In the forthcoming scrutiny of the fundamentals and operation of the international monetary system, the views of M. Pierre-Paul Schweitzer, who took up his appointment as Managing Director of the International Monetary Fund on September 1, carry special weight. He said in an interview last summer:

> . . . I would not be immediately worried if the pump of the American deficit were to run dry. I am not at all sure that we need regular additions to liquidity on the scale produced by recent American deficits. Certainly the use of reserve currencies, as an addition to gold, must be maintained, and it may be that some new reserve currencies are needed. But I do not believe that we need to go on increasing liquidity at the recent rate.
>
> Indeed, it seems to me that there is some confusion between two concepts of international liquidity. Considered in the same way as domestic liquidity, as a means of financing the normal flow of trade, there is clearly no shortage: I do not hear of any exports or imports that cannot be financed. Quite another problem is that of dealing with balance-of-payments deficits. And, here, the expression "liquidity" is misleading. It is rather a question of resources being made available to finance such deficits. . . .

It would certainly be helpful if the conceptual confusion about international liquidity to which M. Schweitzer refers could get cleared away. The business that a company does is not controlled by the amount of cash it has in the till but by the credit it commands from suppliers and lending institutions. In the area of international trade, there is no shortage of credit to creditworthy merchants in creditworthy countries.

Global external liquidity is a pretty phrase, and it is possible for statisticians to figure, in the light of historical relationships, how many units of money may seem necessary to support some given volume of international transactions. Such calculations have little practical usefulness if only because the definition of assets counted as "liquid" is subject to arbitrary judgment. There is a revolution going on in the world in concepts of "money" and "reserves." Arithmetic out of past experience lacks present meaning.

Precision in the definition of money has been impaired by the activities of what economists call "nonbanks" which, in the process of raising money to lend, borrow by the issuance of short-term obligations that people consider as "money in the bank."

Precision in the definition of international reserves has been impaired by the evolution of the gold standard into a gold exchange standard under which greater varieties of credit instruments are counted as official reserves. Official currency reserves get increased as a result of deficits in the U.S. balance of payments. They also get increased by the achievement of convertible status by other currencies and, in particular, by decisions of the IMF to release reserves to give help to particular countries which are experiencing strains in their balances of payments but, nevertheless, seem creditworthy because they are pursuing proper policies to correct their situations.

At times, of course, the shoe may pinch, particularly if nations indulge in inflation; but in that event something ought to pinch to remind governments of their responsibility to protect the value of money and to awaken business and labor leaders to the follies of wage-price spiraling.

For these reasons, payments deficits must be "cured"—not merely "financed," as the Brookings report postulates. No international payments system can relieve a nation of its individual responsibility to achieve a balance in its international payments over a period of time. As Mr. Thorkil Kristensen, Secretary-General of the OECD, has stated:

> In the first place it is necessary to ensure that countries possess sufficient monetary reserves to finance, where necessary, what may be a substantial deficit over a certain period. In the second place countries must find themselves *constrained* [italics supplied] to embark upon internal policies designed to restore equilibrium. . . . The countries which find themselves in a strong position can help the others to strengthen their reserves, but in doing so they can also require the assisted countries to satisfy the conditions which seem to them to be proper.

The core of the world monetary problem is to find, in Mr. Kristensen's words, "a suitable combination between the necessary financing and the necessary discipline."

### Cutting Loose from Gold

Suggestions are offered in the Brookings report that the United States should sever such ties to gold as still remain, including the 25 per cent legal gold reserve requirement against Federal Reserve note and deposit liabilities. One curious idea advanced is that the United States should use $3-5 billion of its $15½ billion gold stock for purchases of foreign currencies to finance future U. S. payments deficits and thus dramatize its determination to use its gold to defend the dollar. If we did want to be rid of gold, it would be simpler to sell it more freely to cover current deficits and discard all the special borrowing arrangements set up to limit gold losses.

Admittedly, the place of gold in world money systems is ambiguous. Nowhere in the world today does gold serve as legal tender; yet the metal is valued by many peoples, and by many central banks, as a store of enduring value superior to paper money and claims for paper money. Many governments have found it necessary to coin and sell gold in their free markets not only to realize the premiums people are willing to pay but also to support confidence in paper. While the American people have not insisted upon restoration of freedom to hold gold, taken away in 1933, the international prestige of what Keynes once called "a barbarous relic" has been enhanced in the world by the inflationary environment of the past quarter of century.

A question which the Brookings report provokes but does not analyze is whether, if we were to cut the tie between gold and the dollar, the dollar as a currency and the United States as an international banker could maintain their world positions.

People in much of the world retain their traditional respect for gold. To disregard this fact of life, deeply anchored in monetary experiences, attitudes and ideas of other nations, is singularly unhelpful. To recognize that, in our complex and suspicious world, the alignment of currencies to gold gives a certain stability and cohesion to the monetary system and also provides an increment, as far as it goes, to international liquidity is an act of realism. The problem of insufficient gold, if it is ever to be mastered, will have to be mastered by repression of inflation so that people will have trust in the future values of money claims and make their savings available for loan and investment, financing economically productive projects.

There is little sentiment to turn the clock back and return to the traditional gold standard. By the same token, however, there is—in the world of today—no practical possibility of cutting loose from gold altogether. There are times and circumstances when no other "money" is acceptable. Recognition of this helps reinforce monetary discipline—something we must have if we want an orderly society.

### Where Are We Heading?

Granted that we are sailing on uncharted seas, our international monetary system as it has developed since World War II, the liberalization of trading policies, and the responsibilities accepted by nations to keep their balances of payments in order, have succeeded in lifting world trade to levels previously unknown. The record has been so much better than that following World War I that we should be hesitant to alter course.

This process of evolution has not been completed. Certainly, we should think twice about going down the road toward what Oscar Altman of the IMF staff calls "proliferation of agencies and techniques"—inter-central bank and inter-government borrowings, the special fund within the IMF, and the Maudling plan designed as yet another IMF appendage. Writing in the *Quarterly Review* of the Banca Nazionale del Lavoro, he warns that this trend "may lead to inefficiency and political misgivings." It assuredly does compound confusion. The experts who fully understand are few indeed.

In all the commotion over international liquidity, it sometimes gets forgotten that the world has a going institution with specific responsibilities for helping nations over balance-of-payments hurdles. The International Monetary Fund, although lacking formal power to create money, has abundant supplies in its warehouses. It may be useful to overhaul the statutes of the IMF, to align them with present practices and visible future needs, and also to revise quotas and voting rights. But the Fund exists and has proved its value under difficult circumstances.

## Neddy and Nicky

Countries of the Free World are faced with a stubborn problem: how to reconcile price stability with full employment. The outbreak of wage-price spiraling in Western Europe* has provoked intensive discussion of "incomes policy." The challenge is to preserve free market principles and at the same time keep the lid on wages demanded by employes and offered by employers. This is hard when business is prosperous, competent workmen are in scarce supply, strikes are costly and price advances are acceptable under prevailing market conditions.

The French stabilization program invoked last month incorporates a broad range of elements.

---

* See May 1963 issue of this *Letter*, "Wage Inflation in Europe."

Although official French gold reserves are the highest in a generation—$3.0 billion, to which may be added $1.3 billion in convertible currencies—it is well understood that continuance of wage-price spiraling will sooner or later bring balance-of-payments strains, drain off gold into private hoards and weaken respect for the franc abroad as well as at home. A committee within the Planning Council has been reactivated to study incomes policy.

### The British Approach

The United Kingdom has combined its search for an incomes policy with a concerted effort to improve the slow growth rate experienced in the 1950s.

Beset by recurrent foreign exchange crises between 1950 and 1962, the British Government last year set up two new organizations to assist in developing economic policies for more rapid growth within a framework of price stability. One, the National Economic Development Council (*Neddy*), consists of representatives from government, industry, the trade unions and the universities.

The other organization, the National Incomes Commission (*Nicky*), was established to deal with questions of pay or other conditions of employment in both government and private industry. *Nicky* took over the job of maintaining the "pay pause" instituted by the government in the 1961 sterling crisis. Broadly speaking, *Neddy's* task is to lay down the principles for more rapid growth, while *Nicky* stands as the interpreter of the public interest in particular wage settlements.

The basic guideline for the NIC is to keep ". . . the rate of increase of the aggregate of monetary incomes within the long-term rate of increase of national production." The Commission has suggested that the "guiding light" for wage increases be between 3 and 3½ per cent annually, assuming attainment of the GNP growth target of 4 per cent. Money incomes during the Fifties increased faster than output, leading to a finding of the Organization for European Cooperation and Development (OECD) that "the Government's policies in respect of incomes and profits are . . . of cardinal importance for the future expansion of the United Kingdom economy."

### Guiding Light Violated

*Nicky's* first two reports reviewed five wage settlements negotiated between industry and labor in 1962 and the first part of 1963. All but one of the agreements reviewed were found to be "contrary to the national interest." The increases granted in hourly rates were substantially beyond the guidelines.

In an effort to secure the cooperation of the trade unions, *Nicky* has also been charged with the difficult and controversial task of including profits in an incomes policy. Despite this inclusion, the trade unions have thus far boycotted *Nicky*, while participating actively in *Neddy*. The NIC has found it ". . . far from easy to formulate the general rules by which profits may be made to conform with an incomes policy." The attempt to include profits in an incomes policy is politically understandable. But the nature of profits is fundamentally different from that of wages and salaries. The latter are costs. The former is a residual after a business meets its expenses.

As *Nicky* has observed: "Profits are the contingent reward for the capital invested in a business, for the risks that have been accepted in earning the profits and for the skill and enterprise with which the affairs of the business have been conducted." Tampering with profits is a hazardous enterprise. It is profits that provide the incentive for the offer of abundant employment opportunities, a principal base for the realization of revenues to government and money for financing investments in labor-saving equipment. Profits, of course, do get limited in regulated public utilities and, unlike wages, are subject to antitrust investigations. Finally, there is the policing power of fiscal and monetary policies pursued by government which, in combination with international competitive conditions and the liberality of import policy, affect the price and profit realizations of business.

*Nicky* is approaching profits control in a gingerly fashion. The only principle on profits the NIC has enunciated to date is that firms whose

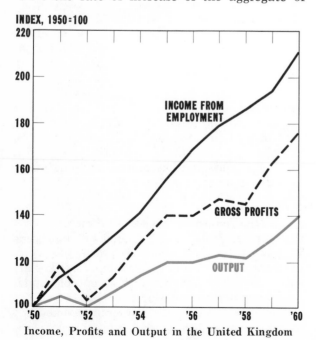

INDEX, 1950=100

INCOME FROM EMPLOYMENT

GROSS PROFITS

OUTPUT

'50 '52 '54 '56 '58 '60

Income, Profits and Output in the United Kingdom

productivity increases are greater than the national average should reduce their prices.

### Neddy's Comprehensive Approach

Chaired by the Chancellor of the Exchequer and restricted to an advisory role, *Neddy*, at its first meeting in March 1962, set a target of 4 per cent annual average growth in GNP for the period 1961-66. It has issued three reports to date: *Growth of the United Kingdom Economy to 1966, Conditions Favorable to Faster Growth* and *Export Trends*. A fourth, dealing with incomes policy, will appear soon.

*Neddy's* reports have covered the entire economy. They have set out the rates of growth that will be required to achieve the annual 4 per cent target.

| Selected NEDC Annual Percentage Growth Targets | | |
|---|---|---|
| | Actual 1955-61 | Targets 1961-66 |
| Productivity per worker ................. | 2.5 | 3.5 |
| Consumer expenditures per capita ........ | 2.1 | 2.8 |
| Education expenditures ................... | 4.5 | 8.0 |
| Exports ............................... | 3.0 | 5.0 |
| Investment ...........................n.a. | | 5.3 |

n.a. Not available.

The Council stresses the importance of education and training (especially management education), labor mobility, technological advances and regional development. Two key factors are singled out for special treatment as fundamental to the achievement of the 4 per cent target.

**INDEX, 1957=100**

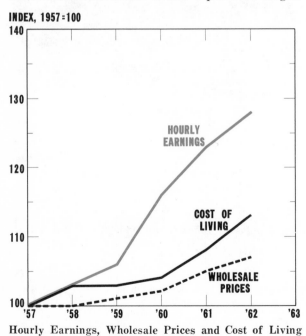

Hourly Earnings, Wholesale Prices and Cost of Living in the United Kingdom

One is export expansion. According to *Neddy*, achieving an annual increase of 5 per cent "is clearly a formidable task." Closely related—indeed, fundamental to achieving the export target—is Britain's ability to hold down costs and prices relative to those of other industrial countries. "Unless costs and prices go up considerably more slowly than in the past," the NEDC points out, "it is unlikely that the United Kingdom can maintain her competitive position in world markets."

Neither *Neddy* nor *Nicky* has authority to direct any action stemming from their policy recommendations. Yet such has been the impact of their reports on public opinion that negotiations in the building trades—an industry basic to the nation's cost structure—ended last month in a three-year agreement holding increases within the limits of the "guiding light."

### Encouraging Signs

The British economy is moving forward, although private capital investment is still down. The Chancellor of the Exchequer attributes no small part of this to a successful incomes policy:

> Because we have controlled our costs, because we have become more competitive at home, because the rise in incomes has been restrained, we are able to sell more and more overseas. . . . The prospects of expansion without inflation will clearly be undermined if incomes start once again to rise too fast.

*Neddy* and *Nicky* are too young to warrant a judgment on their contribution to policies that will speed Britain's economic growth. So far their work has been more diagnostic than curative. And should they determine a combination of policies that will contribute to growth, it will remain the responsibility of government to adopt the proposals and secure the support of industry and labor in carrying them out.

*Nicky* and *Neddy* have increased public understanding of cost-push inflation sufficiently to influence a major wage settlement. There is a lesson here for all free nations. As the Working Party on Costs of Production and Prices of the OECD reported a year ago, "in our kind of societies a successful incomes policy must derive its ultimate sanction from the understanding and cooperation of all those concerned." Further, as Under Secretary of the Treasury, Robert V. Roosa, wrote in the October issue of *Foreign Affairs*: "National policies for incomes, as well as for interest rates and credit availabilities, seem to be, or to be becoming, a normal part of the responsibilities which all governments now acknowledge in varying degrees for promoting growth, avoiding instability and achieving external balance."

**FIRST NATIONAL CITY BANK**

*"They only dive for First National City Travelers Checks*
*— they're better than money."*

Why should the divers—or you—settle for less than FNCB Travelers Checks? They're better than money because you can get an on-the-spot refund if they're lost or stolen. You'll get a prompt refund through any of FNCB's global network of thousands of refund agents. They are spendable anywhere—here and abroad—but only by you. And they are backed by First National City, best-known name in world-wide banking. Ask for them by name at <u>your</u> bank.

**Fastest refund in case of loss or theft—** Checks missing? Anywhere in the U.S. except Alaska and Hawaii, simply phone WESTERN UNION OPERATOR 25 for nearest refund location. For information concerning refund points in other countries, Alaska and Hawaii, ask at principal hotels.

# FIRST NATIONAL CITY BANK
# TRAVELERS CHECKS

Member Federal Deposit Insurance Corporation

*November 1963*

# Monthly Economic Letter

## General Business Conditions

Business expansion is moving ahead encouragingly in the closing months of the year. The high level of stock market prices, responding to a strong profits trend, is giving a further lift to business confidence. Although in September production slowed and retail sales declined, the current success of initial '64 model car sales is easing any doubts about the near-term outlook. The general feeling of buoyancy is also influenced by the continuing anticipation that Congress will enact a tax cut, either this year or next, but effective on January 1, 1964.

While the outlook is highly favorable, there are some sobering aspects; auto sales, strong as they are now, and construction, particularly of housing, may be hard put in the coming year to top this year's performance. These are among the reasons why tax reduction may become a needed stimulant, though the longer-term influence of lower individual and corporate rates on economic growth should not be overlooked.

It is important to remove uncertainties clouding economic prospects, for both business and government will soon be facing decisions about budgets and expenditures, the results of which will influence economic activity in the year ahead. Both Administration spokesmen and business leaders have recently commented on the need next year for the stimulus of tax reduction.

A group of more than 2,600 business executives —the Business Committee for Tax Reduction in 1963—expressed the view in a letter to members of the Senate on October 14 that "the economy is now approaching a critical juncture." They warned that "delay and doubts created by failure to enact the tax bill this year could entail serious economic risks."

### A $600-Billion Economy

Treasury Secretary Dillon, testifying before the House Ways and Means Committee on October 29, revealed that the Administration expects gross national product in the current quarter to reach a $596 billion rate. If the tax cut is passed effective January 1, an accelerated rise to $608 billion in the first quarter of 1964 and $620 billion in the second is anticipated. But even without a tax cut, the economy is expected to cross the line to a $600-billion GNP, reaching an estimated rate of $603 billion in the first quarter and $608.5 billion in the second.

Throughout this year the economy has performed better than expected. This was true again in the third quarter, as gross national product reached a record seasonally adjusted annual rate of $588.5 billion. The main reason the increase in GNP exceeded expectations was that over-all inventory accumulation did not decline as expected with the rundown of steel inventories. The increase in GNP of nearly $9 billion over the second quarter was the best advance this year, even allowing for the fact that roughly one third of the rise was due to higher prices. The rise covered most major areas of the economy, including business capital investment, state and local government expenditures and consumer outlays for nondurable goods and services.

The industrial production index was virtually unchanged in September at 125.7 (seasonally adjusted, 1957-59 = 100), thus extending the plateau which started in June. This index had moved ahead all during the first half of the year, but has remained in the 125.6-126.5 range since June. However, industrial production does not include the construction and service activities that have played a substantial role in the GNP rise. In October, industrial production apparently increased, as the declines in the automobile and steel industries, which largely accounted for the recent leveling off in the production index, were reversed.

Auto output, which dropped more sharply than usual during the model changeover, is back on an overtime basis. Assemblies in October appear to have exceeded 800,000 for the first time, and about 1.4 million are scheduled for November and December. During October, steel mills were pouring steel at an annual rate of 100 million tons, up 5 per cent from the average September rate.

In addition, output of business machinery and equipment rose in September for the fifth straight month. The volume of new orders received by machinery and equipment industries, which was on a high plateau from April through August, moved up 3 per cent to a new record in September.

### Autos Sustaining Retail Sales Total

Retail sales experienced an apparently temporary lull in September, as they sagged to within 2 per cent of the year-earlier level after average year-to-year gains of better than 5 per cent in the first eight months of 1963. But preliminary figures for the first three weeks of October show sales again running 5 per cent ahead of a year earlier. Some merchants have complained that the prolonged spell of warm, dry weather in many parts of the country has cut into sales of apparel and other fall lines.

Retail sales are being buoyed by auto sales during the introduction period for '64 models. In the 30 days through October 20, dealers sold over 650,000 cars, most of them '64s, for a gain of 12 per cent over the very successful introduction period for the '63s. (See also the article "A Seven-Million Car Market?" elsewhere in this issue.)

Consumers are still in a mood to buy, according to recent surveys. Their buying plans are backed up by a rising level of after-tax income. During the third quarter, consumers received, at an annual rate, $17.9 billion more disposable income than a year earlier. Of this gain, nearly all—$17.6 billion—went into enlarged personal consumption. Increased spending for consumer services absorbed approximately half of the rise, and stepped-up nondurable goods purchases took $6 billion more. Despite the excellent sales year for '63 model cars, durable goods outlays advanced only $2.8 billion over a year earlier, or about 6 per cent. With expectations of continued high and rising incomes, particularly if tax cuts put more pay in consumers' hands, retailers are looking forward to continued good sales.

## Third Quarter Corporate Profits

The current business upswing, already more than two and a half years old, continues to produce good corporate profits. Although third quarter results for 901 nonfinancial corporations were down from the high second quarter level because of seasonal declines in the automotive and steel industries, they topped the year-earlier quarter by 14 per cent. For the first nine months of this year, profits were up 12 per cent. In profits, as in many other measures of business activity, gains thus continue to surpass earlier expectations.

Aggregate profits after tax as reported to shareholders by the 901 corporations were $3.6 billion, down 10 per cent from the second quarter. Results for manufacturing companies alone (which account for about three of four firms reporting to date) are quite similar to those for all companies taken together. Manufacturing earnings for the third quarter, at $2.7 billion, were down 13 per cent from the preceding quarter and up 15 per cent from a year ago. For the first nine months of 1963, manufacturing earnings rose 13 per cent.

Of the manufacturers reporting, 56 per cent (seasonally adjusted) achieved better profits than in the previous quarter. This was off a bit from 59 per cent in the June quarter but still close to the best level obtained in the last four years. This percentage is regarded as an indicator that tends to foretell the course of general business.

Profits benefited in the third quarter from stepped-up buying by consumers, business and government alike, as reflected in the sharp rise in GNP. Earnings also drew continued support from successful management efforts to hold down production costs. Despite some rise in wage rates in the third quarter, unit labor costs in manufacturing held within the narrow range that has prevailed during the past two years, and below earlier highs. At the same time, a number of industries benefited from a fairly wide scattering of price increases. While a number of announced price advances have been nullified by competitive conditions and reductions continue to be the order of the day in some industries, the over-all price picture was somewhat firmer in the third quarter.

Profit margins were a bit wider than a year ago, but, as in recent years, were lower than in the second quarter. For manufacturers that report sales figures, the average profit margin in the third quarter was 6.0 cents on the sales dollar, down from 6.7 cents in the June quarter, but above the 5.6 cents of a year ago.

### Industry Trends

The third quarter results are all the more encouraging in view of the special boost to second quarter profits from hedge buying against a possible steel strike and the catching up on losses sustained in the dock strike. While steel continued its erratic earnings pattern with a sharp third quarter drop, its profits were more than double those of a year ago. For the nine months as a whole, the steel industry's showing this year has been its best since 1960. The sustained strong sales pace for autos and trucks led to good earnings gains as compared with a year ago for the automotive industry and, as might be expected, helped haul along many of its supplier industries. Thus, the rubber industry, which is headed toward a peak production year, benefited from high sales and firmer prices to show a gain of 27 per cent from a year ago. Production of several nonferrous metals moved closer to capacity and prices also moved up, with salutary effects on profits. Results for aluminum companies were below average, however, as

prices, though up somewhat recently, remained generally below those of a year ago.

The resurgence in capital goods buying aided machinery manufacturers to achieve a 17 per cent gain over a year ago. In heavy electrical equipment, where competition continues intense, year-to-year gains were smaller than for the electrical group as a whole. Good appliance sales, particularly for higher-priced items, along with further market expansion by color TV and stereophonic equipment, led to significant pluses for some firms in the electronics group. In chemicals, where results are closely tied to general business activity, gains were widespread though relatively moderate.

Sporadic price cuts for gasoline during the third quarter held back petroleum industry gains, but did not prevent a good year-to-year showing. Premium gasoline sold well, and demand for the full range of oil products continued strong.

Despite record construction expenditures, stiff price competition continued to restrain profit gains for some cement and glass companies. In the paper industry, it has been a case of running hard but virtually standing still in terms of profits. Even though paperboard operations, for example, were recently back to 100 per cent of capacity for the first time since the spring of 1956, earnings for the paper group were little changed from 1962, mainly because of depressed prices.

In consumer soft goods lines, year-to-year gains in beverages and food products were held back

## Net Income of Leading Corporations for the Third Quarter and First Nine Months
### (In Millions of Dollars)

| No. of Cos. | Industry Groups | Reported Net Income Third Qr. 1962 | Reported Net Income Second Qr. 1963 | Reported Net Income Third Qr. 1963 | % Change from Third Qr. 1962 | % Change from Second Qr. 1963 | Reported Net Income First Nine Months 1962 | Reported Net Income First Nine Months 1963 | Per Cent Change |
|---|---|---|---|---|---|---|---|---|---|
| 33 | Food products | $ 63.8 | $ 64.8 | $ 68.8 | + 8 | + 6 | $ 186.4 | $ 201.7 | + 8 |
| 13 | Beverages | 41.7 | 37.2 | 44.7 | + 7 | +20 | 104.3 | 109.4 | + 5 |
| 7 | Tobacco products | 71.4 | 71.4 | 76.8 | + 8 | + 8 | 198.3 | 206.9 | + 4 |
| 34 | Textiles & apparel | 25.0 | 25.5 | 28.6 | + 14 | +12 | 77.5 | 79.0 | + 2 |
| 15 | Rubber & allied products | 14.3 | 20.5 | 18.1 | + 27 | −12 | 46.5 | 53.3 | +15 |
| 29 | Paper & allied products | 55.1 | 58.7 | 55.0 | − ..* | − 6 | 166.8 | 164.4 | − 1 |
| 22 | Printing & publishing | 17.7 | 15.3 | 26.4 | + 49 | +73 | 35.6 | 47.7 | +34 |
| 48 | Chemicals, paint, etc. | 248.1 | 315.3 | 271.9 | + 10 | −14 | 791.0 | 840.2 | + 6 |
| 37 | Drugs, soap, cosmetics | 130.5 | 111.3 | 150.1 | + 15 | +35 | 351.7 | 390.6 | +11 |
| 36 | Petroleum prod. & refining | 699.1 | 772.0 | 825.9 | + 18 | + 7 | 2,052.7 | 2,437.8 | +19 |
| 39 | Cement, glass & stone | 92.5 | 90.0 | 95.5 | + 3 | + 6 | 228.5 | 221.8 | − 3 |
| 37 | Iron & steel | 58.1 | 232.3 | 129.6 | +123 | −44 | 334.4 | 475.0 | +42 |
| 20 | Nonferrous metals | 47.9 | 63.4 | 53.6 | + 12 | −15 | 180.8 | 167.8 | − 7 |
| 52 | Fabricated metal products | 74.0 | 72.0 | 74.7 | + 1 | + 4 | 193.5 | 201.1 | + 4 |
| 82 | Machinery | 146.1 | 180.8 | 170.4 | + 17 | − 6 | 446.2 | 491.8 | +10 |
| 67 | Electrical equip. & electronics | 118.7 | 125.5 | 129.5 | + 9 | + 3 | 351.2 | 373.1 | + 6 |
| 26 | Automobiles & parts | 285.6 | 687.0 | 320.4 | + 12 | −53 | 1,382.4 | 1,597.9 | +16 |
| 14 | Aerospace equipment | 33.3 | 40.6 | 35.7 | + 7 | −12 | 96.8 | 107.6 | +11 |
| 68 | Other manufacturing | 115.1 | 113.6 | 124.5 | + 8 | +10 | 309.1 | 321.8 | + 4 |
| 679 | Total manufacturing | $2,337.9 | $3,097.3 | $2,700.1 | + 15 | −13 | $7,533.5 | $8,488.8 | +13 |
| 19 | Mining & quarrying | 19.6 | 26.6 | 23.6 | + 20 | −11 | 73.0 | 76.8 | + 5 |
| 52 | Trade (retail & wholesale) | 58.3 | 60.0 | 62.1 | + 7 | + 4 | 165.4 | 180.7 | + 9 |
| 25 | Service & amusement | 11.5 | 14.4 | 14.1 | + 22 | − 2 | 34.4 | 41.3 | +20 |
| 40 | Railroads | 107.4 | 134.4 | 116.2 | + 8 | −14 | 267.0 | 314.6 | +18 |
| 20 | Common carrier trucking | 9.2 | 9.1 | 11.3 | + 23 | +25 | 21.1 | 23.9 | +13 |
| 11 | Other transportation | 16.6 | 23.4 | 29.3 | + 77 | +25 | 42.8 | 56.4 | +32 |
| 49 | Electric power, gas, etc. | 177.4 | 190.2 | 193.4 | + 9 | + 2 | 609.5 | 652.9 | + 7 |
| 6 | Telephone & telegraph | 383.9 | 396.0 | 416.8 | + 9 | + 5 | 1,119.8 | 1,190.1 | + 6 |
| 901 | Grand total | $3,121.8 | $3,951.3 | $3,566.9 | + 14 | −10 | $9,866.6 | $11,025.5 | +12 |

* Decrease of under 0.5%.

by lower earnings for a few companies. Results were highly mixed in the textile industry. Increased acceptance of new products brightened the profits picture for the drugs, soap and cosmetics group. Almost all tobacco companies improved their earnings as lower production costs and higher prices for nonfilter cigarettes generally offset a slowdown in sales gains.

Outside manufacturing, there were seasonal declines from the second quarter in a few groups, but gains across-the-board as compared with a year ago and for the nine months of 1963 to date.

## A Seven-Million Car Market?

Reports on the initial public reception of the '64 passenger cars have been glowing. The basic question now to be answered is: Will they sell as well as the '63s? Auto industry officials say yes and they are backing their optimism by scheduling the largest fourth quarter output in history—nearly 2.2 million cars, about 7 per cent above last year's record fourth quarter.

If these production schedules are maintained, about 7.5 million cars will have been turned out in calendar year 1963, making it second only to the exceptional 7.9 million produced in 1955. Excluding cars exported or added to dealer inventories, sales of U.S. cars appear headed for a calendar year total of about 7.2 million, compared with 7.4 million in 1955. In addition, Americans this year are buying about 375,000 imported cars, as against only 58,000 in 1955.

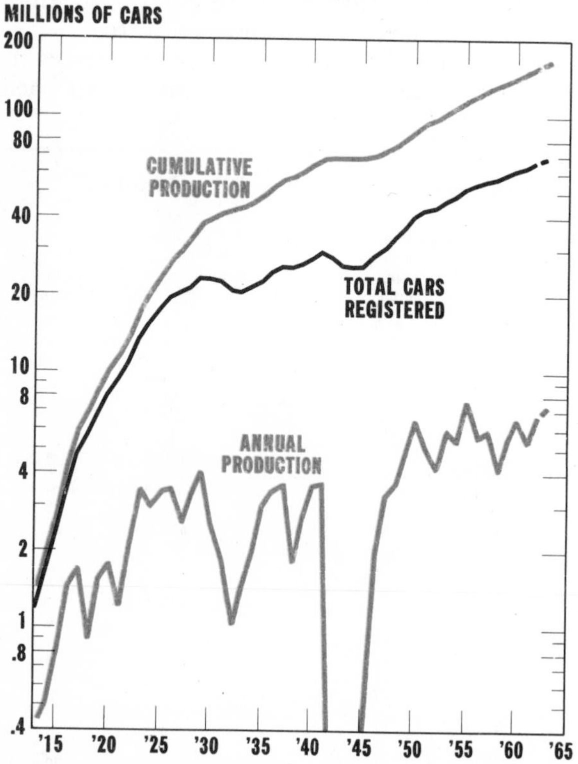

Auto sales in the neighborhood of 7 million have generally been regarded by the industry as "good." By that standard the industry is now having two such years in a row. While auto officials believe they can put together three "good" years in a row, pessimists outside the industry have expressed doubts. On the other hand, optimists are raising a question about the definition of a "good" year. They now consider the sale of 7 million new cars in a calendar year as normal—not exceptional.

But even if 7 million were normal, this would give no assurance for any particular year. The history of the automobile market, as shown in the accompanying chart, argues against extended plateaus. Production and sales in the auto industry are notoriously volatile. Demand reflects not only consumers' purchasing power and needs for transportation but also individual preferences toward styling, the desire to achieve and maintain a certain standard of living, and other human fancies and impulses. If a customer does not like the lines of this year's cars, he can, and often does, wait to see what next year's models look like.

The industry has had its ups and downs ever since the first few thousand horseless carriages were turned out in the closing days of the nineteenth century. Through 1917, production rose without interruption, but of the hundreds of firms which entered the field only a fraction survived. These survivors, however, expanded spectacularly. During the first decade after World War I, the rise in output, from less than a million cars in 1918 to over 4 million in 1929, played a key role in the expansion of the economy. Yet twice in that decade, in 1921 and 1927, production dropped more than 20 per cent from the preceding year. In the Great Depression, annual output dropped to one fourth of its 1929 peak, while under World War II restrictions passenger car production virtually vanished. In both periods, consumers managed by making their old cars do for a few years longer.

After World War II, the rapid upsurge in the auto industry was again a major factor in the postwar expansion, culminating in the extraordinary sales year of 1955. Even the 7-million level that the industry today looks to as a new norm is somewhat below the 1955 peak.

**MILLIONS OF CARS**

Growth of the Passenger Automobile Industry, 1913-1963
(Production figures exclude cars for export;
ratio scale to show proportionate changes.)

Source: Automobile Manufacturers Association; U.S. Bureau of Public Roads.

| Calendar Year | Domestic Cars | | Imported Car Sales | Total Sales |
|---|---|---|---|---|
| | Production | Dealer Sales | | |
| 1950 ....... | 6,675 | 6,310 | 16 | 6,326 |
| 1955 ....... | 7,942 | 7,408 | 58 | 7,467 |
| 1956 ....... | 5,802 | 5,851 | 98 | 5,949 |
| 1957 ....... | 6,115 | 5,827 | 207 | 6,034 |
| 1958 ....... | 4,244 | 4,286 | 379 | 4,665 |
| 1959 ....... | 5,594 | 5,488 | 614 | 6,102 |
| 1960 ....... | 6,696 | 6,142 | 499 | 6,641 |
| 1961 ....... | 5,516 | 5,556 | 379 | 5,935 |
| 1962 ....... | 6,935 | 6,753 | 339 | 7,092 |
| 1963 ....... | 7,541e | 7,200e | 375e | 7,575e |

e. Estimated.

Note: Dealer sales differ from production because of exports and changes in dealers' inventories.

Source: *Ward's Automotive Reports* and R. L. Polk & Co. (further use of import data prohibited without Polk's permission).

### Rising Replacement Demand

During the nearly seven decades it has been in business, the domestic automobile industry has assembled over 170 million passenger cars. Of these, a total of 68.5 million cars will still be on the road at the end of this year, according to estimates by the U.S. Bureau of Public Roads. Wear and tear and obsolescence have taken their toll; over 100 million cars have been scrapped or otherwise withdrawn from use.

In recent years, cars have been moving into automobile scrapyards at an average of more than 4 million a year. Unofficial estimates indicate that now the rate may have moved up to about 5 million. This figure is a measure of basic automobile demand—the number of cars which must be produced each year just to keep the same number of cars on the road.

Few cars are scrapped before they are six years old, usually no more than 5 per cent. By the ninth year, over 30 per cent have disappeared from the road, and by the twelfth year over two thirds have been scrapped. Less than 1 per cent of the 68 million cars produced for domestic markets before World War II is still in use.

As the second chart illustrates, the number of cars seven or more years old was about as high in the late Forties as it has been in recent years, but scrappage was far lower then because of the war-induced shortage of newer cars. Expanding postwar output soon began to reduce the backlog of orders for cars, but it was not until the late Fifties that scrappage of postwar cars became large. Since 1955, the number of older cars (seven years or more) has nearly doubled, but the number of "newer" cars (six or less years old) has inched up less than 10 per cent.

The growing number of older cars on the road has encouraged the belief that scrappage rates will rise and provide a firm base for an expanding car market. But it is also possible that a rising number of older cars indicates that consumers want to run their cars longer and spend their money on something else. Scrappage depends on many factors other than age.

Many observers attach great importance to the number of cars less than six years old as a major influence on the *new* car market. Most new car buyers—some studies indicate as many as four out of five—are people whose cars are six years old or less. Once a family has reached the economic level at which it can afford a new car, it tends to continue buying new cars rather than used ones, trading them in within six years. The person who trades in a car ready for the scrap heap is not ordinarily the same one who bought it when it was new, nor is he likely to replace it with a new car.

The average growth in the number of newer cars (0-6 years old) on the road was less than 1 per cent a year from 1956 to 1962. As a result, the ratio of newer cars to the number of households declined during these years, despite the marked rise in multi-car ownership at a rate of 8 per cent a year. At the same time, the number of older cars in use grew nearly 9 per cent a year. The nation's automobile population is being increased each year by new car production. But an even more important factor is the utilization of cars

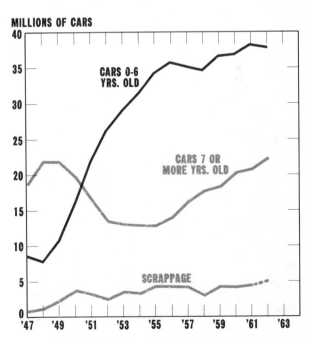

Cars on the Road by Age Group vs. Scrappage

Source: *Automotive News 1963 Almanac* (based on data compiled by R. L. Polk & Co.; further use prohibited without Polk's permission). Cars tabulated by model years as of July 1 each year; scrappage estimated for calendar years.

for a longer period before scrappage. These older cars are used increasingly as the second or third car in the family.

### The Two-Car Family

There has been a pronounced increase in ownership of second—and even third—cars by today's families. Several forces are behind this rise. One is the growing number of families in the middle- and upper-income brackets. As shown in the chart on the next page, families with incomes over $5,000 a year—which includes the bulk of automobile owners—have more than tripled in the postwar period. Families with incomes over $10,000—over half of them owning more than one car—are five times as numerous as in 1947. A special tabulation of 1960 Census data by the Department of Commerce shows that ownership of two or more cars ranges from negligible proportions in the lower-income brackets to 64 per cent among households with incomes over $15,000.

The large growth in the teenage population has also increased demand for second and third cars. The postwar babies are now turning 16 in large numbers. In 42 states, the minimum age for

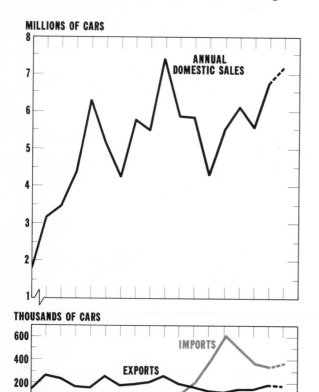

**Domestic Passenger Car Sales, Exports and Imports**

Source: *Ward's Automotive Reports*, Automobile Manufacturers Association, R. L. Polk & Co. (further use of import data prohibited without Polk's permission). Figures for 1963 are for 12 months ended August 31, 1963.

a driver's license is 16 or less, and all states license drivers at 18. The number of drivers in the younger age groups is expected to climb sharply in the next few years. Their buying is likely to center chiefly on older used cars. However, a vigorous used car market supports prices for trade-ins. Since new-car prices have been stable in recent years, the firmness of used-car prices has meant good deals for new-car purchasers.

Also contributing to demand for more than one car per family is the continued population shift to sprawling suburbs, bringing with it the need for an extra car for commuting, as well as for shopping and chauffeuring family members from one activity to another.

### A Question of Credit

The question has been raised whether the rise in consumer credit in the last couple of years may have left consumers unable — or unwilling — to take on the additional instalment obligations needed to support another 7-million car year. On August 31, consumer instalment credit outstanding totaled $51.4 billion, of which $21.5 billion was automobile paper. Total instalment payments are now taking up more of people's income than ever before. What is not so well-known, however, is that the burden of auto instalment payments on family budgets remains below earlier highs, despite the heavy borrowing in 1962 and 1963. Repayments of auto credit have been taking 4.7 per cent of after-tax income this year, compared with 5.0 per cent in 1956 and 1957.

Even more important is the high volume of repayments on auto paper that takes place every month. Such payments have recently been running at a seasonally adjusted annual rate of some $19 billion. Assuming that 40 per cent of new cars will continue to be bought for cash, and that two used cars will continue to be bought for every new one, a rough guess may be made at how many new car sales could be accommodated without any further rise in auto credit outstanding. So long as repayments on existing debt are merely rolled over into new debt—without any rise in the total credit pool—they can support over-all sales of well over 6 million new cars. With income continuing to rise, and with a tax cut that leaves more of these earnings in people's pockets, a 7-million car year could be financed with little rise in the burden of consumer credit.

### The '64 Market

The basic influences of scrappage, income, age distribution, population shifts and readily available credit all make another good automobile year possible. But, as the auto industry has found several times in the past, the basic long-term forces are not enough; it is also necessary to gain the confidence and enthusiasm of the customer.

Without confidence in the business outlook and in their financial future, many consumers are unwilling to make the substantial long-term commitment involved in a new car purchase. Undoubtedly, the prospect of a tax cut has been supporting retail sales this year, not so much through anticipatory spending of money not yet received as through the widespread confidence that the tax proposals inspire in continued growth and prosperity.

Enthusiasm over the new models is also essential, as is the sales effort put forth by the thousands of dealers in cities and towns across the country. Reports from the showrooms have been encouraging. Not only are crowds of people looking at and interested in the new cars, but more are buying. Starting with September 20 when the first '64s were introduced, sales in the first 30 days of the new season have run 12 per cent ahead of the corresponding period last year, which was also a most successful introductory period. These early reports are often distorted by large sales to auto rental firms and other car-fleet buyers and by backlogs of new-model orders built up when stocks of old models ran low. But by any standard the '64s are off to a good start. To make a good year, however, sales must be brisk in spring and summer as well as at model introduction time. The final answer rests with the consumer.

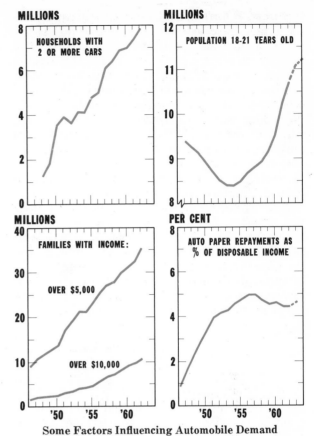

Some Factors Influencing Automobile Demand

Source: U.S. Department of Commerce, Automobile Manufacturers Association, Federal Reserve Board.

## Wheat and Cotton Subsidies

Many citizens were startled to learn that the sale of $250 million (some 150 million bushels) of American wheat to the Soviet Union, if consummated, will involve payment of an export subsidy amounting to around 60 cents a bushel. This looks like a gift by American taxpayers to the Russians. Yet people in the trade see the export subsidy as part of the cost of our wheat price-support program. As the *Prairie Farmer* writes in its issue of October 19:

> It has been said that the American taxpayer will be subsidizing the communists if we sell wheat for less than the supported price within the United States. This is pure foolishness. Neither Russia nor anyone else will buy wheat at more than the going world price. The difference between the world price and our price is of our own making. . . . In the wheat referendum last May, American wheat growers showed considerable dissatisfaction with the system we have saddled on ourselves.

In simple terms, domestic wheat prices are supported by the Commodity Credit Corporation at levels which are about 60 cents above the world market; subsidies in this amount become necessary to make American wheat salable through regular commercial channels in the international market.

Actually, the subsidy is acting to depress the world price. This is because the United States is so important a supplier to the world market. The subsidies, variable in amount according to the quality and location of the grain, establish differences between what American and foreign millers have to pay.

The combination of plenty here and shortage abroad offers a providential opportunity not only to market surplus grain but also to get away from export subsidization. If there were no subsidy, world and U.S. wheat prices could find equality, somewhere within the existing artificial spread. We could save the taxpayers' money and increase our export trade surplus at one and the same time.

### The Cooley Bill

Subsidy schemes have a way of creating more problems than they solve. The 8½ cents per pound export subsidy on cotton, like the export subsidy on wheat, is intended to keep a place for American cotton in the world market. Here the effects are even worse to behold. The subsidy sets up a difference in raw material costs between American and foreign textile manufacturers. Efforts to relieve this competitive disadvantage have led into a morass of quotas restricting imports of cotton textiles according to country of origin and type of fabric. But despite this elaborate machinery, which makes our claims to a liberal import trade policy seem quite insincere, the subsidy to overseas manufacturers is imperiling our textile manufacturing industry, which employs nearly 900,000 persons and turns out products valued at over $14 billion per year. It is also a factor in leading our industry to turn increasingly to synthetics, thus reducing the domestic market for cotton fiber.

Responding to well-justified complaints from the industry, Congressman Harold D. Cooley, Chairman of the Committee on Agriculture in the House of Representatives, has come to the conclusion that the only way to restore the international competitive power of the American cotton textile industry is to subsidize the price of cotton to domestic mills. He has reintroduced

a bill which, assuming the maintenance of the 8½-cent export subsidy during the season beginning August 1, 1964 and domestic mill consumption of approximately 8,500,000 bales (500 lbs. each), would provide subsidies equal to an annual cost of $360 million. The subsidy would be in the form of cotton acquired by the CCC in the course of its price-supporting operations.

Certainly the cotton export subsidy imposes an unjust burden on our cotton textile industry, its employes and investors. The Cooley bill's enactment would further expose the sorry state of the whole farm policy and, perhaps, help to bring an end to the subsidies that cost so much and so distort the economy. The better solution would be to go to the source of the evil and work gradually to reduce supports and to eliminate subsidies on the general principle that our industries should stand on their own feet and neither suffer special handicaps nor enjoy special benefits.

## International Liquidity—Whither Now?

The highlight of the annual meetings of the International Monetary Fund and the World Bank last month was the mutual agreement on a top-level review of the functioning of the international monetary system, with especial attention to the adequacy of international liquidity. To be sure, the conviction is widespread that there is at present no over-all shortage of money and credit to support expanding world trade and investment.* But, as the Fund's new Managing Director M. Pierre-Paul Schweitzer noted, "it is wise and prudent to look into the future to consider what difficulties might arise and to devise ways of meeting them."

Today, the concern is focused on oversupplies of dollars stemming from our persistent balance-of-payments deficit. But once the United States has succeeded—as it must sooner or later—in bringing its payments into better shape, the main source from which other nations have been building their gold and dollar reserves will dry up. Surely, the world does not need additions to liquidity on the scale produced by the heavy U.S. deficits of the past six years; furthermore, needs for currency reserves would diminish in a state of better international equilibrium. Nevertheless, restoration of a sustainable balance in U.S. payments, when achieved, will mark a new phase in international financial relationships.

President Kennedy, addressing the world's finance ministers and central bankers, stated the U.S. position on international liquidity as follows:

We recognize that the reserve position of other countries is a mirror image of our own; and as the

United States moves toward equilibrium, it will be more difficult for others to increase their reserves. Some nations will be more handicapped than others, but no nation should be forced to make drastic alterations in its domestic and trading policy because of short-run movements in its reserve position. The United States, therefore, stands ready to support such measures as may be necessary to increase international liquidity.

Two studies are to be undertaken—independently though cooperatively: one by the IMF and the other by a group of ten nations, sometimes called the Paris Club. This group represents all principal currencies and is already committed —though at the individual participant's discretion—to provide $6 billion of international credits in case of need to cope with possible threats to the stability of the international payments system.† The real problem is not to arrive at a theoretically perfect solution—desirable as it is to know what this may be—but rather to find practical answers that the governments providing funds may be willing to accept. The studies, it is expected, will result in appropriate recommendations for discussion at the IMF-World Bank meetings in Tokyo in September 1964.

### The Established Price of Gold

The studies will be directed toward improving the present monetary system, not at replacing it by an entirely new one. Our international monetary mechanism, as it has developed over

† See "A Fund Within the IMF" in the February 1962 issue of this *Letter*. The participants are Belgium, Canada, France, Germany, Italy, Japan, the Netherlands, Sweden, the United Kingdom and the United States; Switzerland, though not a member of the IMF, takes part under a separate agreement.

* For background, see the October 1963 issue of the *Letter*.

the past two decades, has served the world well, having helped restore meaningful currency convertibility and lift trade and investment to levels previously unknown. According to a statement issued, on behalf of the Ten, by Treasury Secretary Dillon:

> In reviewing the longer-run prospects, the Ministers and Governors agreed that the underlying structure of the present monetary system—based on fixed exchange rates and the established price of gold—has proven its value as the foundation for present and future arrangements.

To take the established price of gold and the present foreign exchange parities as given is a sensible approach. President Kennedy, in announcing the U.S. position on international liquidity, reaffirmed the U.S. determination—"in the interest of this country and, indeed, in the interest of all"—to protect the dollar "as a convertible currency at its current fixed rate" and to maintain the $35 gold price.

It is difficult to visualize any improvement in the present international monetary system that would be preceded by a gigantic devaluation. Repudiation by governments of the fixed price of gold would disqualify the dollar or any other currency as an instrument in which nations can hold part of their international reserves. Devaluation must also be avoided for the sake of reasonable monetary stability.

Flexible or variable exchange rates must similarly be discarded as a means of adjusting deficits in balances of payments. If losses of gold—and losses in the foreign exchange market value of currencies—were to become matters of little importance, resistance to inflation would certainly be greatly weakened. What the gold outflow does is to communicate a sense of harsh reality to the need for a nation to keep its economic and financial house in order. Moreover, fluctuating exchange rates among the leading currencies would hamper trade and investment and might lead to competitive currency depreciations to enlarge national export markets, as in the 1930's.

While retaining the established price of gold and fixed exchange rates, the Ten find it "useful" to undertake "a thorough examination of the outlook for the functioning of the international monetary system." This examination should be made with "particular emphasis" on the possible magnitude and nature of the future needs for reserves and for supplementary credit facilities which may arise "within the framework of national economic policies effectively aiming at the objectives" the Ten have set for themselves.

### Distinguishing Two Problems

"The most important objective to be pursued over the near future" is "the removal of the im-

balances still existing in the external accounts of some major countries"—a diplomatic way of describing the present position of the United States. A sharp separation is thus drawn between the provision of funds to cover the U.S. payments deficit pending the restoration of a sustainable balance and the intergovernmental review of the prospects and arrangements for international liquidity.

European delegates at last month's meetings made no secret of their dislike of any ideas, attitudes and devices that might submerge the U.S. balance-of-payments deficit in the sea of international liquidity. The Brookings report, which had surprisingly little to say about what to do to cure the U.S. deficit and greatly emphasized the need for liquidity, did not pass unnoticed. Both the President and the Secretary of the Treasury, however, endeavored to distinguish between the present U.S. problem and the concern over future liquidity—as evidenced in the President's Balance-of-Payments Message and in the Congressional hearings last July. Secretary Dillon, speaking before the world's financial officials, wanted once again to make "crystal clear" that:

> ... The United States does not view possible improvements in the methods of supplying international liquidity as relieving it of the compelling and immediate task of reducing its own payments deficit. Indeed, it is largely the prospect of the elimination of the United States payments deficit that makes it necessary and advisable to undertake these studies.

The U.S. payments deficit has, of course, its main counterpart in the surpluses of Continental Europe, and this is why the statement issued by Secretary Dillon on behalf of the Ten welcomes, along with the efforts of deficit countries to improve their balances of payments, "actions" by other nations to reduce or remove surpluses. The common objective is to reach "a better basic international equilibrium" and high levels of economic activity with a "sustainable" rate of economic growth and "in a climate of price stability."

### Monetary Reserves, Owned and Borrowed

The core of the problem is *not* any lack of means of financing the normal flow of exports or imports. Such financing is done by commercial banks of the principal trading nations, and the keen competition among them will assure enough credit for expanding world trade.

Concern about international liquidity centers around actual reserves of governments and central banks, and access to reserves through borrowings from other central banks and governments or from international financial institutions. Such reserves are needed to finance balance-of-payments deficits and thus provide time for needed adjustments.

Reserves held by governments and central banks are the most definite and easily measurable form of international liquidity. The accompanying charts trace the evolution of official reserves over the past decade both by countries and by types of assets—gold, dollars and sterling, in particular. The United States still has a healthy but not excessive share of the world's monetary gold stock; but having settled a large part of its balance-of-payments deficits in dollars, it also has large short-term liabilities to other nations. Our debts are other nations' reserves.

The problem focuses on the inadequacy of flows of newly mined gold into official stocks. Reserves in the form of currencies are easier to supply and, as the chart shows, constitute a growing portion of monetary reserves—though gold still represents some three fifths of the total.

Nations acquire currency reserves through surpluses in their balances of payments; but they do also borrow them. The chart includes amounts that members can borrow from the IMF almost automatically; these are equivalent to members' gold subscriptions and are regarded by the Fund as being virtually as freely available as the countries' own gold and foreign exchange holdings. Additional borrowings from the Fund require

justification, which becomes more stringent as a member seeks to borrow more. The Fund's resources in gold and convertible currencies total $9 billion; as already mentioned, arrangements have been made among the ten leading nations to enable the Fund to borrow currencies from members gaining reserves to lend them (along with its regular resources, and subject to certain conditions) to those whose currencies are under pressure.

Nations can also borrow reserves directly from other central banks and governments. This is exemplified by reciprocal extensions of credit between central banks, such as the currency swaps arranged by the Federal Reserve System, or medium-term borrowings by one government from another, such as sales of special obligations by the U.S. Treasury.

The statement issued by the Ten mentions no particular plan, institutional arrangement, policy or technique to provide additional international reserves. It merely notes that the study should evaluate "various possibilities" for covering future needs for reserves. At last year's IMF meetings, the British Chancellor of the Exchequer, Mr. Reginald Maudling, proposed an arrangement whereby a country accumulating dollars or sterling would deposit them in special accounts at the

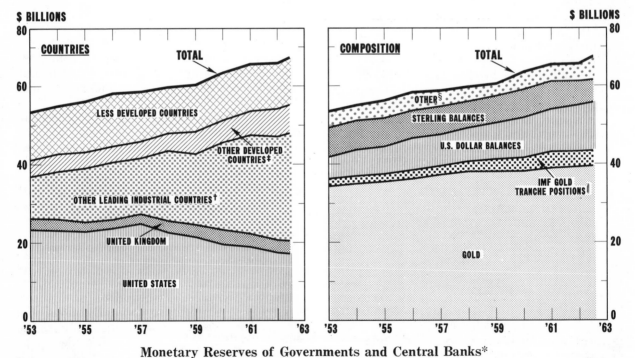

**Monetary Reserves of Governments and Central Banks***

(End of year, except data for 1963 which are for June.)

* Excluding U.S.S.R., Mainland China and countries in their spheres. † Belgium, Canada, France, Germany, Italy, Japan, Netherlands, Sweden, Switzerland. ‡ Other European countries, Australia, New Zealand, South Africa. || Amounts equivalent to the gold portion of members' subscriptions, which they may draw "essentially automatically" under the Fund's policy as developed over the past decade. Subscriptions to the Fund have been made, as a rule, 25 per cent in gold and 75 per cent in members' currencies; these subscriptions are called quotas, which in turn govern drawings on—i.e. borrowings from—the Fund. § Including, prior to 1959, credit balances with the European Payments Union.

Note: Based on data published in International Monetary Fund's *International Financial Statistics*.

IMF and then draw on such deposits when it ran itself into payments deficits. This year, he noted in his address that other possibilities would be "increases of Fund quotas and more flexibility in the use of the Fund resources. These possibilities are not exhaustive or mutually exclusive. All should be considered."

### The Core of the Problem

The core of the problem is to determine safe limits for creating international money and to devise practical working rules for its control. The discussions at last month's meetings show the complexity and delicacy of the problem.

Germany's chief delegate, Mr. Ludger Westrick, stressed that in a dynamic world, "and as long as we are not able to achieve a complete coordination of national policies," there will always be balance-of-payments problems. The question of how best to *finance* the deficits is important but even more important is the question of "how to provide sufficient incentives for *curing* them." We should not waste our time chasing the will-o'-the-wisp of international liquidity.

Behind international credit, there must be tangible goods and services provided by individual nations that find themselves in positions of surplus. The surplus nations will, understandably, be reluctant to grant to deficit countries automatic credits of indeterminate amounts for indeterminate duration. Looking at it from this vantage point, Governor Holtrop of the Netherlands Bank concluded: "Any newly created exchange holding and any monetary credit given potentially will represent a draft on the real resources of other countries and, therefore, merits to be husbanded with great care."

The French Finance Minister, M. Valéry Giscard d'Estaing, asked that the new study lead to "positive conclusions" on "three essential points." First, under the gold exchange standard as it operates today, there is no "spontaneous mechanism" permitting a prompt return to equilibrium. The surplus nations "congratulate" themselves on the increase in their foreign exchange holdings "while overlooking some of the unsound aspects of these gains;" on the other hand, the deficit country is relieved by such easy financing from losing gold. This was a veiled allusion to the fact that the United States, in its role as world banker, has received from the rest of the world aggregate short-term credits of $12 billion over the past five and a half years.

In the process, noted France's spokesman, money supplies are expanded—in the surplus nations as a result of increases in foreign exchange reserves, and in the deficit country because of the use made by surplus nations of their newly acquired foreign assets. For, "in their legitimate desire to earn interest on these holdings," the surplus nations normally invest them on the markets of the deficit country. "Without overrating the size of this phenomenon in relation to the evolution of the money supply, one must admit that it tends to offset one of the spontaneous corrective mechanisms."

The second point about which the French Finance Minister asked that a conclusion be reached was that while countries in surplus positions are holding large amounts of reserve currencies, if they themselves ran into deficit the countries now supplying reserves "might not accumulate so readily the currencies of their new debtor. To say the least, full reciprocity is not achieved." This raises the serious question of how far the United States may be prepared to move in the direction of holding other currencies—not in relatively small amounts as today, but in sizable amounts at times when other nations experience difficulties in their international accounts.

The third point concerns the proportion of gold in total official gold and foreign exchange reserves—a proportion which works out at 99 per cent for the United States; about 90 per cent for the Netherlands, Switzerland and the United Kingdom; 80 per cent for Belgium, and 70 per cent for France and Italy; and approximately 60 per cent for Germany, the largest holder of gold outside the United States and, presumably, Russia. This state of things, noted the French Finance Minister, does not reflect "an equitable distribution of the burdens of international monetary cooperation."

M. Giscard d'Estaing asked that the new study clarify policies regarding the three means of international settlements that may supplement payments in gold: (1) credits among central banks; (2) credits granted "on a more durable basis" within international monetary organizations; and (3) long-term loans—a type of assistance "more appropriate in nature and duration" than the short-term credits so generally used in recent years to cover continuing deficits.

Considerations like these go down to the fundamentals of the international monetary system as it operates today. They will, no doubt, be explored fully in the forthcoming re-examination of the international monetary system—the first comprehensive review since the Bretton Woods Conference twenty years ago.

**FIRST NATIONAL CITY BANK**

IT'S A SMALL WORLD...

# ...WHEN YOU DO BUSINESS WITH FIRST NATIONAL CITY BANK

Your business interests may be global or local. Wherever they are, chances are First National City is there too. For Citibank is as global as banks on-the-scene in 34 countries on five continents (plus correspondents all over the world) can make it . . . and as local as 118 offices in metropolitan New York and correspondents coast-to-coast can knit it. △ When you deal with the people at First National City, you do business with a corps of ex-perienced professionals. And through them you can draw on our complex of world-wide facilities. Here is *total bank-ing* at your disposal. △ It certainly *is* a small world . . . when you deal with people at First National City.

**FIRST NATIONAL CITY BANK**
399 PARK AVENUE, NEW YORK 22, N.Y. • MEMBER FEDERAL DEPOSIT INSURANCE CORPORATION

*December 1963*

# Monthly Economic Letter

## General Business Conditions

The nation and the world were jolted by the sudden and tragic death of President Kennedy on November 22. The public's shock and anxiety were mirrored in the stock market, which had to be closed after prices were sent plummeting by a wave of selling. When business resumed on Tuesday, following a day of mourning which closed banks and businesses across the country, stock prices more than made up for the losses on Friday. This reflected not only confidence in the new President but also confidence that the basic policies advocated and pursued by his predecessor would not be changed.

Throughout the world, exchange markets maintained their poise in the wake of the President's assassination. Indeed, immediately upon news of the shooting, central banks everywhere offered assistance to our monetary officials to counter any possible weakening in the dollar. Such co-operation among central banks was developed by the Kennedy Administration over the past three years to minimize disturbances at times of international uncertainty.

President Lyndon Johnson, in his address to the joint session of the Congress on November 27, combined an expression of the nation's sorrow at the recent tragic events with an appeal to Congress for prompt action on the late President Kennedy's legislative proposals. He called especially for passage of the civil rights and tax reduction bills. The new President promised that the government will manage expenditures "with the utmost thrift and frugality," and pledged "the defense of the strength and the stability of the dollar."

### Basic Strength of the Economy

President Johnson comes to office at a time when the economy is at record levels with a good deal of momentum for further growth. Production and profits have never been higher.

Just in the last couple of weeks, a wave of favorable business statistics has given fresh evidence of the advances which have taken place and the potential for further gains. The gross national product in the third quarter achieved an annual rate of $588.7 billion, up $9.1 billion from the second quarter. Corporate profits before taxes were estimated at a third quarter rate of $52.0 billion, a new record. Industrial production, personal income, retail sales and housing starts set all-time highs in October. New orders for machinery and other durable goods, construction contracts and corporate appropriations for new capital investment showed marked increases, foreshadowing higher industrial activity in 1964.

The strength of business reflects, at least in part, the hopes aroused by the late President's tax program. In his speech to the joint session of Congress, President Johnson urged time and again that Congress translate the Kennedy proposals already before it into effective action:

. . . no act of ours could more fittingly continue the work of President Kennedy than the early passage of the tax bill for which he fought all this long year. This is a bill designed to increase our national income and Federal revenues, and to provide insurance against recession. That bill, if passed without delay, means more security for those now working, more jobs for those now without them, and more incentive for our economy.

With the new President's long experience in legislative leadership, as well as the sympathetic support he is receiving in this transitional period, action on the tax program may indeed be more prompt than seemed likely earlier.

In terms of the business outlook, the greatest danger inherent in the changeover was that it might lead to loss of confidence and thus to vacillation and inaction, slowing down the economic expansion currently under way. If the President can continue to revitalize confidence and inspire Congressional action, there will be no danger of hesitation arising from uncertainties that had already begun to appear before the death of President Kennedy.

### Cautious Business Spending Plans

The delays and disappointments in the progress of tax legislation this year seem to have created a wait-and-see attitude among businessmen. This is suggested by their relatively cautious and conservative plans for capital expenditures next year. According to an October survey by McGraw-Hill, businessmen were planning at that time to spend 4 per cent more on new plant and equipment in 1964 than in 1963. This would raise outlays to $40.7 billion, compared with the $39.1 billion scheduled for 1963.

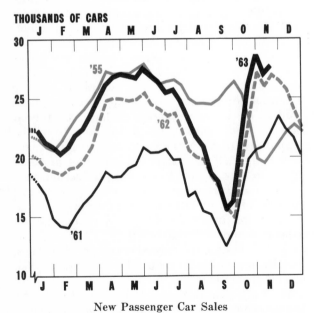

**THOUSANDS OF CARS**

New Passenger Car Sales

Daily average sales of domestic autos for preceding 30 days, plotted on 10th, 20th and final day of month.
Source: Computed from data in *Ward's Automotive Reports.*

These figures, taken at face value, are disappointing since capital expenditures in the fourth quarter are already expected to reach a seasonally adjusted annual rate of $41.2 billion. However, it is worth noting that such early sampling of plans usually understates the magnitude of an increase or decrease. This was the case in six of the last eight McGraw-Hill fall surveys, in which the percentage change anticipated fell short of the final results by an average of 4½ percentage points. Thus, it would not be surprising to see actual capital outlays once again exceed the levels anticipated in the fall survey.

### Expanding Production

Industrial production moved forward to a new high in October and apparently continued upward in November. The Federal Reserve index (seasonally adjusted, 1957-59=100) moved up 0.7 in October to 126.6, but remained within the narrow range of fluctuations (only 0.8 from high to low) which has prevailed since June. The rebound in October was largely attributable to the record rate of auto production, up 9 per cent on a seasonally adjusted basis, aided by a continued rise in output of business equipment and household durable goods.

Steel production increased about seasonally in October and maintained a contraseasonal advance in November. By the end of the month, 1963 output had topped 100 million tons—the first time the industry has reached this mark since 1957. For the year as a whole, output may be in the neighborhood of 109 million tons, up 11 million tons from 1962 but still short of the record 117 million tons poured in 1955.

Most automobile assembly lines have been running nights and Saturdays trying to keep up with the surging consumer demand for '64 models. In the 30 days ended November 20, as shown in the accompanying chart, dealers' sales of new passenger cars were at a daily rate 4 per cent above the corresponding 1962 period. In the first two months the '64 models have been on the market, sales have averaged 6 per cent higher than in the record introductory period for the '63 models. For the year through November 20, dealers' sales of domestic cars are only 2½ per cent behind the exceptional 1955 sales pace; if imported cars are included, this year so far is about 2 per cent ahead of the corresponding 1955 period.

In retail stores generally, as well as automobile showrooms, the hiatus in sales during the period of mourning for President Kennedy has naturally depressed sales figures and other business statistics for November. Yet there is reason to believe that sales will eventually match or exceed last year's figures and bring the total volume for 1963 to new peaks in most lines. According to recent surveys, consumers—with record incomes and ample credit at their disposal—are planning a high level of spending in the next six months. With widespread confidence in the future, and with a blend of fiscal and monetary policies dedicated to achieving economic growth without inflation, the economy can advance to new heights in the months ahead.

## Turning Point in Fiscal Policy

President Johnson has inherited a fiscal situation clouded by continuing uncertainties over the proposed tax cut and an unprecedented slowdown in the passage of spending legislation by Congress. While getting ready to put the finishing touches on the fiscal '65 budget for presentation to Congress next January, the Administration under the late President Kennedy had been in the unusual position of running government operations almost halfway through the '64 fiscal year with eight out of twelve appropriation bills still pending in Congress. The impasse in fiscal decisions had already been causing considerable headshaking among businessmen and economists seeking to forecast the shape of the business curve for the year ahead.

The key questions still remain: Will there be a tax cut, and if so, when and how big? How much money will the government spend in the years ahead and how much tax revenue will it give up? How large will be the deficit resulting from the tax cut and spending decisions for fiscal '64 and '65?

Answers to these questions have been delayed as both tax cut and spending decisions have become enmeshed in the legislative bargaining process. It is no secret that the delays are at least partly traceable to the strong sentiment in Congress for lower spending and smaller deficits than the Administration had envisioned. While Congressional actions have also been slowed by consideration of other issues—including civil rights, the test-ban treaty and the rail strike threat—deliberations have been prolonged, as in the foreign aid debate, by a heightened desire to limit federal spending and eliminate waste. All this is leading to one of the longest Congressional sessions in history.

### Solid Improvement in Budgetary Outlook

But despite the appearance of confusion and the impossibility of making precise estimates pending Congressional decisions, the fact is that the actual fiscal situation has improved a good deal since last January when the late President Kennedy's tax and budget proposals were first unveiled. Requests for authorizations and new appropriations are being examined with a critical eye by committees of both Houses and several bills have undergone further trimming on the floor. Spending is not only being cut for the current fiscal year but authorizations for future

**Original Estimates and Actual Results for Fiscal Years 1955-64, Administrative Budget Basis**
(In Billions of Dollars)

| Fiscal year | Expenditures Orig. est. | Expenditures Actual result | Receipts Orig. est. | Receipts Actual result | Surplus (+) or Def. (—) Orig. est. | Surplus (+) or Def. (—) Actual result |
|---|---|---|---|---|---|---|
| 1955 | 65.6 | 64.4 | 62.7 | 60.2 | — 2.9 | — 4.2 |
| 1956 | 62.4 | 66.2 | 60.0 | 67.9 | — 2.4 | + 1.6 |
| 1957 | 65.9 | 69.0 | 66.3 | 70.6 | + 0.4 | + 1.6 |
| 1958 | 71.8 | 71.4 | 73.6 | 68.6 | + 1.8 | — 2.8 |
| 1959 | 73.9 | 80.3 | 74.4 | 67.9 | + 0.5 | —12.4 |
| 1960 | 77.0 | 76.5 | 77.1 | 77.8 | + 0.1 | + 1.2 |
| 1961 | 79.8 | 81.5 | 84.0 | 77.7 | + 4.2 | — 3.9 |
| 1962 | 80.9 | 87.8 | 82.3 | 81.4 | + 1.5 | — 6.4 |
| 1963 | 92.5 | 92.6 | 93.0 | 86.4 | + 0.5 | — 6.2 |
| 1964 | 98.8 | 97.8* | 86.9 | 88.8* | —11.9 | — 9.0* |

*Latest estimate of the Bureau of the Budget, assuming that the House-approved tax-cut bill becomes effective Jan. 1, 1964.

expenditures are being held considerably below original requests. As a result of these decisions, as well as economies effected by the Administration, Budget Bureau Director Kermit Gordon a month ago estimated that expenditures this fiscal year would be held to $97.8 billion—$1 billion below the $98.8 billion estimated in January.

Meanwhile, both individual incomes and corporate profits have risen more than expected, yielding $1 billion in additional taxes. The six-month postponement to January 1, 1964 in the anticipated effective date of the tax cut will mean about $900 million more in revenues. Thus, Treasury Secretary Douglas Dillon now figures revenues for the year ending next June 30 at $88.8 billion—$1.9 billion more than projected last January.

The improvement in revenues, combined with the lowered spending estimates, has reduced the projected deficit for the current fiscal year by $2.9 billion. Assuming that the House bill calling for a two-stage $11 billion tax cut becomes effective January 1, 1964, Secretary Dillon now places the deficit at $9.0 billion, compared with the $11.9 billion figure of last January.

Thus, the prolonged deliberations and heated debates over fiscal legislation have not been in vain. The more that spending bills have been slashed, the more likely it has become that we can reduce tax rates without running undue risks of inflation. In terms of fiscal fundamentals, the developing decisions are giving substance to a new policy based on closely controlling government spending while providing tax relief to improve incentives and spur the private economy.

### Economy Pledge Being Fulfilled

It may be recalled that the Administration's fiscal proposals last January, which coupled a big tax cut with a $4.5 billion rise in expenditures and an $8.6 billion boost in new obligational authority, were sharply challenged from both sides of the aisle. Chairman Clarence Cannon of the House Appropriations Committee —which originates all money bills in Congress— vowed to do his best to trim the budget: "We will look for and find places to cut it substantially without impairing national security."

With sentiment for economy gaining strength in both Houses as the session has progressed, Representative Cannon has been true to his word. The complexities of the government spending mechanism make precise estimates difficult, but Representative Cannon recently expressed the opinion that Congress would chop "some-thing like $5.4 billion" from the Administration requests for appropriations, holding them about $2.9 billion below what was granted last year.

Cutting appropriations, however, is not the same thing as cutting current expenditures. It takes a long time after the spigot is turned off before the money stops flowing. Some $42.4 billion of this year's budget expenditures were authorized by Congress in years past. Another $11.8 billion recur automatically under permanent law, the most important item in this category being interest on the public debt. (With money rates rising this year, Budget Director Gordon has estimated that interest costs have risen by $500 million since the January projection of $10.1 billion.) Thus, only some $44.7 billion out of the $98.8 billion in expenditures originally requested were subject to action by Congress in this session.

Spending is also being held down by the unprecedented delay in voting new appropriations. In the interim since July 1, many agencies—including the Defense Department until mid-October—have operated under "continuing resolutions." This means that agencies must restrict their spending roughly to the same rate as in fiscal '63 or to that provided in pending appropriation bills, whichever is lower.

With almost half the year gone, many agencies that were slated to raise their spending this year have been forced to hold their expenditures below original budget estimates. While this creates practical difficulties for government agencies, it shows the intimate relationship between taxes and spending that exists in the minds of Congressmen.

---

#### The Budget Process

*New obligational authority.*—Since no Federal funds can be spent without specific authority from the Congress, the budget presents the President's recommendations as to the amounts of budget authorizations (new obligational authority) necessary to carry out the planned programs. The Congress then considers and acts on these requests for new obligational authority.

New obligational authority is composed of three kinds of authorizations which allow Federal agencies to incur obligations requiring the payment of money.

*Appropriations* are the most common form of new obligational authority; they authorize the agencies not only to order goods and services but also to draw funds from the Treasury and make expenditures to pay for the goods and services when delivered.

*Contract authorizations* are occasionally given to agencies which allow them to contract for the delivery of goods and services but not to make expenditures to pay for them. . . .

*Authorizations to expend from debt receipts* permit agencies to borrow money (usually through the Treasury), to contract for its use and to pay the amounts authorized.

\* \* \*

*Relationship between new obligational authority and expenditures.*—Not all of the obligational authority enacted for a fiscal year is spent in the same year. Appropriations to pay salaries or pensions are usually spent almost entirely in the year for which they are enacted. On the other hand, the bulk of appropriations to buy ballistic missiles or to construct an airfield are likely to be spent 2 or 3 or more years after enactment. . . . Therefore, when the Congress reduces or increases the amount of new obligational authority requested by the President for a given year, it does not necessarily change the budget expenditures *in that year* by the amount of the increase or decrease.

—Excerpted from *The Budget in Brief, 1964 Fiscal Year,* Bureau of the Budget.

---

### Reductions in Spending Authorizations

Seasoned observers, however, are not so much impressed with the reduction in fiscal '64 expenditures as with the sharp paring of requests for new obligational authority. Though the phrase sounds like a prime example of bureaucratic gobbledygook, new obligational authority—which may be viewed as charge accounts for government agencies—constitutes the key to all future spending. As shown in the accompanying box, which explains budget terminology, the government cannot enter into contracts or spend money unless authorized by Congress.

Appropriations being the most important kind of obligational authority, the $5-6 billion that Congress is cutting from the Administration's appropriations requests is highly significant in slowing the spending trend. Originally, the Kennedy Administration had requested $107.9 billion in new obligational authority, but later cut this by $620 million. With these changes, as well as the $500 million rise in interest costs, the Congressional reductions would leave the new authorizations some $6.1 billion below the amount requested last January.

In the four appropriation bills which had won final approval by late November, initial requests amounting to $61.9 billion had been slashed by $2.2 billion. The largest of these requests—$49 billion for National Defense—was trimmed back by $1.8 billion. The National Institutes of Health—which for years have been voted more money than they asked for—for once were given less than the $980 million originally requested.

An additional $3 billion have been cut from seven other appropriation bills by the House of Representatives. At the end of November, the only regular appropriation bill still to be acted on by the House was Foreign Aid. But even here, sharp cuts in the foreign aid authorization bill by both Houses had set an upper limit of about $3.6 billion—some $1.3 billion less than what the Administration had originally requested. Among other actions, both Houses chopped $600 million out of the $5.7 billion requested for the space program, reflecting less urgency felt for the moon race. Even the $4.6 billion Public Works bill—known as the "rivers and harbors" bill—was pared by $286 million in the House.

Progress to date, of course, could be substantially nullified if large supplementary appropriations are voted later on. Legislators must continue to exercise restraint in order that the balanced fiscal formula thus taking shape is not upset.

### Conditions Ripe for a Tax Cut

It now seems that the fiscal conditions for a sound tax reduction are on the way to being met. Not only are current expenditures being held down, but new authorizations for future spending are being tightly controlled. The rising trend in obligational authority has been moderated. For his part, President Johnson has ordered an

| | | | | Congressional Actions on Spending Authority, 1955-64 (In Billions of Dollars) | | | |
|---|---|---|---|

**Congressional Actions on Spending Authority, 1955-64**
(In Billions of Dollars)

| Fiscal year | New Obligational Authority | | | Total Obligational Authority Year-end balances |
|---|---|---|---|---|
| | Administration requests* | Actual authorization | Change from previous year | |
| 1955 | $56.3 | $ 57.1 | $ -5.7 | $79.6 |
| 1956 | 58.6 | 63.2 | +6.1 | 73.0 |
| 1957 | 66.3 | 70.2 | +7.0 | 68.9 |
| 1958 | 73.3 | 76.3 | +6.1 | 72.1 |
| 1959 | 72.5 | 81.4 | +5.1 | 71.8 |
| 1960 | 76.8 | 79.6 | -1.8 | 72.5 |
| 1961 | 79.4 | 86.7 | +7.1 | 76.4 |
| 1962 | 80.9 | 92.9 | +6.2 | 79.3 |
| 1963 | 99.3 | 101.5 | +8.6 | 87.2† |
| 1964 | 107.9 | 101.8‡ | +0.3 | n.a. |

*Requested in January budgets. †Current estimate. ‡Estimated on the basis of Congressional actions to date on 11 appropriation bills and on the foreign aid authorization bill, and allowing for $500 million increase in estimated costs of the public debt.

economy drive in government agencies and among defense contractors.

It should be recognized, however, that economy sentiment has prevailed in Congress largely because of the widespread desire to cut taxes in a responsible manner. Failure to act on taxes would not only mean that many legislators would no longer feel constrained in their spending decisions but it would give the spending forces the upper hand in the event of any pause or dip in business. In that event, the prospective deficits are certain to be much larger than any now envisioned with a tax cut.

Now that so much has been accomplished to minimize interim deficits and keep the lid on inflationary forces, it would be fitting for Congress to get on with the job of reducing taxes. Nothing else could so effectively remove the uncertainties hanging over the business situation than for Congress to cooperate with the new President in bringing long-awaited tax relief to the American people.

## A New Chapter in Silver History

This year's trends and developments in silver have added significantly to the checkered history of the white metal. As a result of a widening gap between world output and consumption of silver, the price of the metal has risen to the highest level in 43 years—slightly above $1.2929 per fine ounce, the monetary value of silver. At this price, the slightly more than ¾ ounce of silver contained in a standard dollar coin has a market value of one dollar; if the price were to move higher, the metal content of the coin would be worth more than its value as money. This is also the price at which the U.S. Treasury is legally required to redeem, in the metal, paper money in the form of silver certificates.

Furthermore, Congress—passing the first silver legislation since 1946—has authorized an arrangement that permits silver stored in Treasury vaults to be disposed of to the public in bar form at the statutory monetary value. Since September, the Treasury has been busy redeeming silver certificates and supplying the metal thus released to meet market demands.

The earlier chapters of this dramatic story were told in these pages in December 1961 and 1962. At the end of November 1961, the Treasury suspended the silver sales to industrial users it had been making at $0.91 an ounce from its "free" or "nonmonetized" stocks, i.e., stocks not required as backing for silver certificates; the decision had been precipitated by threatened exhaustion of these stocks, absorbed by constant growth in our silver currency circulation and rising sales for use in domestic arts and industry. The price of silver in the New York market increased from $0.9162 an ounce prior to the suspension of Treasury sales to an average of $1.0453 in January 1962. Thereafter, the market held more or less steady for about six months, but beginning with August 1962 the price rose further until it reached $1.2930 last September; it has since remained unchanged. In less than two years, and at a time when prices of most other metals have increased moderately, the price of silver has risen by 41 per cent.

To take care of the requirements for coinage following the virtual exhaustion of "free" stocks, the President in November 1961 directed the Treasury gradually to retire $5 and $10 silver certificates, with additional Federal Reserve note issues filling the gap. At the same time, the President asked Congress to authorize Federal Reserve Banks to issue $1 and $2 bills to replace silver certificates in these denominations, which tie up no less than 1.3 billion ounces of silver for backing. The legislation came into effect in June 1963 and the Federal Reserve began issuing $1 bills at the end of November.

Withdrawals of $5 and $10 certificates to re-

## CENTS PER FINE OUNCE

U.S. Treasury and Open Market Spot Silver Prices
1955-63
(Monthly Averages)

* The "monetary value" of silver is the value at which the metal content of the standard silver dollar, established in 1837 at 0.7734375 fine ounce, is worth $1; this makes a full fine ounce of silver worth $1.2929. . . . † Price at which the Treasury, at the San Francisco Mint, sold silver prior to November 28, 1961.

Note: The New York price is that quoted by Handy & Harman.

lease silver have been rapid. From the end of November 1961 through September 1963, 250 million ounces were so freed, with 189 million remaining as currency backing. Together with 1.3 billion ounces behind $1 and $2 silver certificates, and counting also 38 million ounces of "free" silver and a few other items, the Treasury silver stocks now total 1.6 billion ounces.

### Demonetizing Silver

This year's silver legislation also eliminated certain provisions on the statute books requiring the Treasury to purchase silver and to hold it in monetary reserves, and putting a government price floor of $0.905 an ounce under newly mined domestic silver. As may be seen from the chart, this price has been below the market price for the past few years and the purchase requirements have, therefore, been virtually inoperative.

The basic purpose of the new legislation was —in Treasury Secretary Dillon's words—"to afford the government a sure and substantial supply of silver for its coinage needs." The shift from silver certificates to Federal Reserve notes is intended to be gradual.

Under the new legislation, the Treasury remains obliged to redeem—in standard silver dollars or in silver bullion, at its option—silver certificates presented for redemption. It may not dispose of any silver to the public at a price lower than the $1.2929 monetary value (when the price is under that level, it may use silver only for sale to other government departments or for coinage); but it is expressly allowed to dispose of silver when the market price stands above $1.2929, as is the case today. Last July, the Treasury announced that it would meet all orders for silver at the $1.2929 monetary value while simultaneously redeeming equivalent amounts of silver certificates.

The $1.2929 monetary value goes back to 1837 when it was reduced slightly from that stipulated by the Act of 1792 providing for gold and silver coinage in the United States. The recent rise in the silver price has thus brought the metallic value of standard silver dollars to a level at which —disregarding costs of melting—the silver contained in the coin is worth the value of the coin as money.* Subsidiary coinage—half dollars, quarters and dimes—would not be worth their silver content unless the price of the metal rose above $1.3824.

Today, silver is thus at a point where the U.S. Treasury, through redemption of silver certificates, becomes a residual supplier for demand in excess of commercial offerings. Since exports from the United States are free, the $1.2929

* The silver content of certain five-cent coins minted during World War II is now worth 7¢.

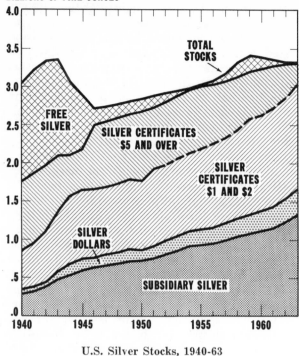

**U.S. Silver Stocks, 1940-63**
(As of June 30)

Note: Excluding silver content in five-cent coins minted during World War II, estimated at about 49 million ounces.

price, adjusted to cover freight and insurance costs, extends to markets outside the U.S.

### The Silver Gap

Underlying the rise in the price of silver are profound changes in world production and consumption of the metal. To place these trends and developments into proper focus, we have prepared a chart showing the statistical position of silver in the United States separately from that in the Free World outside the United States.

As appears from the top section of the chart, silver output in the United States has held at around 35 million ounces annually for the past three years. Industrial consumption (net) has been running at about 110 million ounces—nearly three times current domestic production. With coinage requirements in 1963 estimated at 86 million ounces—up 10 per cent from 1962—the U.S. silver gap is now somewhat in excess of 150 million ounces a year. Although complete figures are lacking for a full accounting of supplies and uses, the table on the next page shows the changing picture.

From November 1961, when U.S. Treasury sales of "free" silver stocks were suspended, through the middle of 1963, the metal consumed by industry and the arts came mostly from current output and regular commercial imports. Recently, disposals of Treasury silver in exchange for silver certificates have become of

importance, reportedly totaling some 15 million ounces in the last three months. During the entire year 1961, it may be recalled, the Treasury sold 62 million ounces at $0.91.

The expansion of coinage in half dollars, quarters and dimes has, on the whole, kept pace with the rise in the value of the nation's output of goods and services—the gross national product. In addition there has occurred a notable growth in the use of coin-operated vending machines, toll collections and the like with the result that demands for subsidiary coinage have been rising. In certain areas, it has been necessary to ration the available supply. Until quite recently, silver dollars had been in overabundant supply and, in fact, none have been minted since 1935; of late, however, their circulation has increased—by $90 million from November 1961 through September 1963, when it stood at $432 million, with only $53 million left in Treasury and Federal Reserve vaults. The U.S. Mint is getting ready to strike 50 million new silver dollars.

The lower section of the chart portrays silver output and consumption in the Free World outside the United States. According to figures published by the U.S. Bureau of Mines, total consumption in industry and coinage has exceeded output since 1960; the gap averaged 15 million ounces a year during 1960-62.

**MILLIONS OF FINE OUNCES**

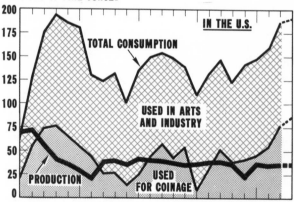

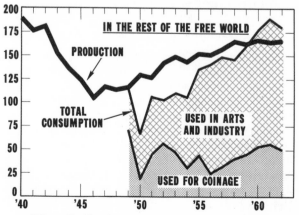

**Silver Production and Consumption, 1940-63**

Silver in the United States
(In Millions of Ounces)

| | 1959 | 1960 | 1961 | 1962 | 1963 |
|---|---|---|---|---|---|
| **Output** | 23.0 | 36.8 | 34.9 | 36.3 | 36.0* |
| **Consumption** | | | | | |
| Industry and arts (net) | 101.0 | 102.0 | 105.5 | 110.4 | 106.0* |
| Coinage | 41.4 | 46.0 | 55.9 | 77.4 | 86.0* |
| Total | 142.4 | 148.0 | 161.4 | 187.8 | 192.0* |
| **Excess of consumption over output** | 119.4 | 111.2 | 126.5 | 151.5 | 156.0* |
| **Imports** | | | | | |
| Commercial | 24.1 | 45.0 | 39.9 | 68.1 | 45.8† |
| Lend-Lease returns.... | 45.0 | 15.7 | 10.4 | 8.3 | ‡ |
| **Exports** | 9.2 | 26.6 | 39.8 | 13.1 | 15.9† |
| **Excess of commercial imports over exports** | 14.9 | 18.4 | 0.1 | 55.0 | 29.9† |
| **Changes in U.S. Treasury stocks:** | | | | | |
| "Free" stocks | −27.1 | −51.6 | −95.1 | +8.5 | +1.4¶ |
| Other stocks§ | −19.2 | −16.1 | −34.5 | −103.0 | −147.2¶ |
| Total change | −46.3 | −67.7 | −129.6 | −94.5 | −145.8¶ |

\* Tentative estimates. † Through September. ‡ Less than 0.02 million ounces through September; of the 411 million ounces of silver lent by the United States during World War II to the United Kingdom, the Netherlands and certain other countries, only 8.6 million remain to be returned. § Stocks securing silver certificates, and silver coins in the hands of the Treasury. ¶ Through November 22.

Sources: U.S. Bureau of Mines, U.S. Department of Commerce and U.S. Treasury Department.

In recent years, silver coinage has been resumed in a number of countries, including Austria, France, Germany, Italy and Japan, but with silver contents lower than in the United States; this makes newly issued foreign coins less vulnerable to melting than U.S. coins. Canada's coins have had a somewhat lower silver content than ours since 1920. Several countries, including the United Kingdom, withdrew silver coins from circulation after World War II.

Supplies abroad have been supplemented by releases from official stocks, recoveries of scrap and meltings of Mexican and other coins of older vintage worth more for their silver content than as money. Sales by Mainland China, considerable two years ago, have this year been conspicuous by their absence; like the Russians with gold, the Chinese sell silver only when they need foreign exchange badly.

### The Silver Problem Today

Since the U.S. Treasury is, by far, the most important source of silver apart from new production, the question naturally arises as to how long its existing 1.6-billion ounce stock may last. In Congressional hearings last spring, Secretary Dillon expressed the view that the passage of the proposed legislation would assure the government of adequate supplies of silver for coinage for the next 10 to 15 years. This expectation evidently rested on the assumption that the only demands for silver from Treasury stock, other than for coinage, would be for silver needed by other U.S. Government agencies.

With the market price slightly above $1.2929, disposals of Treasury silver may well be larger than would be indicated by the program suggested earlier this year for the withdrawal of silver certificates. The gap between production and consumption in the arts and industry, described earlier, provides some basis for believing that the Treasury may have to dispose of sizable amounts each year to keep the market price from rising above the monetary value.

Increased drawings on the Treasury stock would bring closer the time when the market price of silver would pierce through the monetary ceilings of $1.2929 and, ultimately, $1.3824. The risk of seeing people throw silver coins into the melting pot and thus denude themselves of change would necessitate either a replacement of existing coins by coins with lower silver content or by coins containing no silver.

The Treasury stated last May, in a memorandum submitted to the Senate Banking and Currency Committee, that it considered it "unwise to abandon silver coins before it is absolutely necessary to do so, if, indeed, it ever should be." It rested this view on the ground that "the United States has had a silver coinage since 1792 and its people, we believe, attach considerable value to having silver coins." Furthermore, a change from silver to a base-metal coinage would involve "great difficulties . . . for our large and expanding coin-operated vending machine industry."

In expressing the belief that existing Treasury stocks are adequate to meet coinage needs "for at least the next 10 to 15 years," the Treasury memorandum noted:

> During that period, new supplies of silver may be developed somewhere in the world as a result of the present price of silver, or the demand for silver for industrial use may decline as a result of changes in technology. For example, some other countries may abandon the use of silver in their coins, which would increase the available supply; or substitutes for silver in some of its uses may be developed, as seems quite possible in the case of the photographic industry.

No one can say for sure what supplies and demands for silver may be five or ten years hence. Granted the many uncertainties in the outlook for silver, this year's legislation—avoiding, as it has, drastic revisions in our coinage system—has been a sensible move. The recent level of demands for the metal is a warning that further steps to economize on usage may need to be taken. Without abandoning silver coinage, consideration may well have to be given to minting our coins with lower silver content than they have had traditionally or swinging to cheaper metals for some of them. Looking at silver in broader perspective, all we have done this year is to gain time.

# Our Merchandise Trade

Of the many remedies proposed for our balance-of-payments problem, the one that looks easiest on the surface is the expansion of exports. Further expansion of our sales abroad is, indeed, vital; yet it cannot be regarded as the only road toward balancing our international accounts. Continuing close attention to all of the items that make up our balance of payments is essential.

At the White House Conference on Export Expansion in September, Administration leaders set a 10-12 per cent target for export increases. This is a tough assignment to fulfill. There was a time when our exports were limited only by the amount of dollars that foreigners could earn by selling to us, plus what we were willing to lend or give to them. After World War II, when other industrial countries were prostrate, the term "dollar shortage" aptly described the world's financial problem. But now the shoe is on the other foot. Most other industrial countries now have more dollars than they need. Thus we have the job of inducing them to spend more of those dollars here, either to purchase goods or to invest in productive enterprise.

Enlarging U.S. exports hinges broadly on three conditions: (1) the maintenance of high-level prosperity abroad; (2) keeping down our costs and especially our export prices, while offering competitive delivery terms, servicing and styling; and (3) breaking down remaining tariff and other trade barriers and preventing new ones from being put up. On the first two counts, things have been going well. But on the third, the outlook is not as clear. Our negotiators will be hard pressed to achieve freer trade in the major trade discussions scheduled for 1964.

### Our Recent Trade Performance

Since 1960, our exports have set records in every year and, on the basis of results for the first nine months, seem certain to do so again in 1963. This year's exports are running 3 per cent ahead of 1962 and 11 per cent ahead of 1960. Imports—up 4 per cent over 1962 in the first nine months of this year—have also been growing, but not as fast as during the 1950s. As a result, our trade balance—the margin of exports over imports—has returned to the $4-5 billion range so far in the 1960s, after shrinking to less than one billion dollars in 1959.

The improvement has largely dispelled fears that our goods are being priced out of world markets. These fears had been aroused by declining surpluses in 1958 and 1959 compared with 1957. In retrospect, special factors seem largely responsible for that drop. The 1957 figure had been swollen by Europe's increased needs for fuel and other imports arising from the Suez crisis. The reaction in the ensuing two years reflected not only the loss of this special stimulus, but also a sequence of other disruptions that dealt a series of shocks to our trade position. Among these were the romance between American motorists and foreign cars, the temporary cutoff of aircraft exports in anticipation of the new jets and the long steel strike of 1959.

We must not be too impressed, however, with the size of the present surplus. More than a tenth of our exports consists of shipments financed by foreign aid and sales of agricultural products against inconvertible currencies. Looking at commercial trade only, our export surplus declined somewhat in 1962 and is slipping again this year.

### Capital Goods Pace Exports

Capital equipment sales constitute the brightest spot in our export picture. Because of our lead in technology, industrial expansion abroad is quickly reflected in rising purchases of "research-intensive" industrial materials and capital goods from us. Our strength in such exports since 1960 is traceable in part to business expansion in Canada and Japan as well as in most Western European countries.

Exports of capital goods—primarily indus-

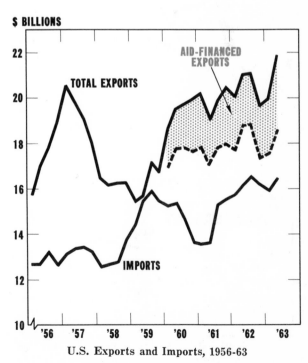

U.S. Exports and Imports, 1956-63

Note: Data on aid-financed exports not available before 1960.

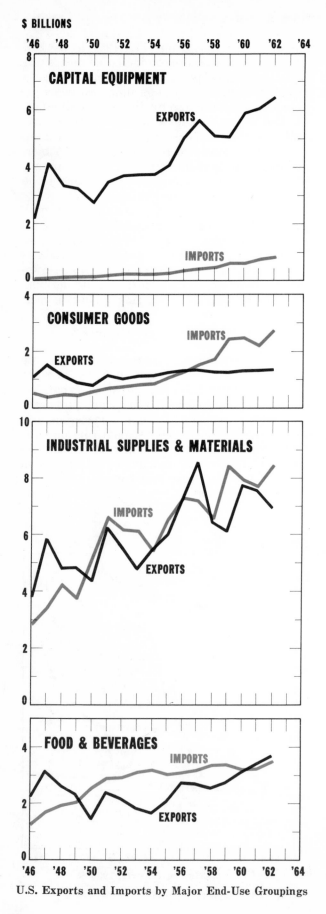

'46    '48    '50    '52    '54    '56    '58    '60    '62    '64

CAPITAL EQUIPMENT

EXPORTS

IMPORTS

CONSUMER GOODS

IMPORTS

EXPORTS

INDUSTRIAL SUPPLIES & MATERIALS

IMPORTS

EXPORTS

FOOD & BEVERAGES

IMPORTS

EXPORTS

'46    '48    '50    '52    '54    '56    '58    '60    '62    '64

U.S. Exports and Imports by Major End-Use Groupings

trial machinery and transportation equipment —recently have been outpacing imports by about eight to one. Particularly encouraging has been the rapid growth in shipments of such advanced types of capital equipment as computers, specialized industrial machinery and instruments. Exports of aircraft have been dropping since hitting a peak in 1960, but a decline in truck and bus exports has been reversed this year.

In contrast to capital goods, our consumer goods exports have not responded fully to the growth of foreign markets because of the rapid development of overseas production, differences in consumer tastes and needs and also import restrictions, especially those maintained by many less-developed countries for balance-of-payments and other reasons. Recent figures, however, show a considerable improvement in consumer goods shipments to Europe, particularly in electrical goods, photo equipment and books. Automotive exports have also been recovering.

Consumer goods imports, which nearly doubled between 1956 and 1959, leveled off in 1960 and dropped slightly in 1961. While they have since shown a renewed uptrend, it has been less rapid than in earlier periods of prosperity. The most striking development in consumer imports over the past decade was the eleven-fold rise in auto imports between 1955 and 1959. Detroit's compact cars have largely checked these inroads in the domestic market, although foreign car imports are again on the rise. Much of the recent growth in imports has been in such items as radios, apparel, cameras, footwear and gem diamonds.

### Shifting Balance in Industrial Materials

Public attention is most readily drawn to our competitive position in capital equipment and consumer goods, but trends in the industrial supplies and materials category are no less important. Though our export trade in industrial materials increased in 1960, the situation changed in 1961; last year exports declined further while imports rose. With other countries expanding capacities in such lines as steel, oil refining, petrochemicals, paper, cotton, aluminum and other nonferrous metals, this trend is likely to continue. Particularly dramatic has been the shifting balance in the oil and refined products category despite the imposition of import quotas in 1957. While exports last year were just slightly higher than in 1954 —at the $450 million level—imports had doubled to nearly $1.8 billion. Similarly, imports of steel and iron ore have tended to rise while exports have not. Dollar sales of raw cotton have been suffering from increased production abroad despite the 8½ cent per pound export subsidy we provide. But in contrast, there has been an encouraging rise in exports of such items as industrial chemicals, man-made fibers, plastics and synthetic rubber.

It seems likely that further expansion in economic activity at home will draw in more imports of industrial materials. The recent strengthening in prices for lead, zinc, aluminum, wood pulp and other materials will add to the import bill but will simultaneously add to the purchasing power of countries that are traditionally our good customers—Latin America and Canada. Thus higher prices for basic commodities will not necessarily change our trade balance with those countries.

### Problems in Farm Products

Trade in food and beverages looks encouraging, with exports overtaking imports in 1961 for the first time since 1949. Until recently, the actual situation was not as promising as the official statistics indicate because the improvement in exports included a sharp increase in sales of wheat for "soft" currencies. Last year, only 23 per cent of our wheat exports was sold for dollars, primarily to Western Europe and Japan. This year and next, however, poor grain crops in both Eastern and Western Europe and in Japan will result in a temporary spurt in dollar sales of wheat, particularly if the sale of $300 million worth of grain to the Soviet bloc goes through.

It is often overlooked that the United States is the world's largest exporter of farm products. In 1962 agricultural exports comprised 24 per cent of our total exports excluding military aid shipments—18 per cent if surplus sales for inconvertible currencies are deducted. But American agricultural productivity—embarrassingly high as our surpluses so visibly attest—cannot over the long pull be expected to maintain as wide a competitive edge over other countries. In the foreseeable future, however, the size of our agricultural exports will depend on the effects of farm support and protectionist policies of other countries. It is for this reason that trade in farm products will be the most difficult question facing negotiators next spring at what has come to be called the "Kennedy round" of trade discussions to be held under the auspices of the General Agreement on Tariffs and Trade (GATT).

### The Job Ahead

The United States Government is aiding exporters by stepping up its trade promotion efforts and by making available an array of export credit insurance and guarantees of bank credit comparable to those available to European and Japanese exporters.

What is also needed is a further reduction in tariffs and in nontariff trade restrictions around the world. As internal trade barriers go down within such regional groups as the European Common Market and the European Free Trade Association, exports of outside countries, and especially farm exports, will be facing entirely new competitive conditions. Not only will American exports be affected by the EEC common external tariff and agricultural policy, but discrimination against Latin America and Japan will also hurt our sales to them. Furthermore, there have been rumblings of new restrictions against American goods by our two largest customers, Canada and Japan.

Next year's trade negotiations are critical to the development of trade for the entire Free World. Given lower import barriers abroad, and provided that we maintain competitive prices for our exports, we could expect to see increases in sales of goods in all major categories—capital equipment, consumer goods, industrial materials and agricultural products. But even though an amicable solution to the unfortunate "chicken war" with Common Market countries is in sight, opinions as to the prospects for the success of next year's tariff negotiations range from outright pessimism to, at best, no more than hopeful optimism.

Whatever the outcome, we cannot afford to relax our efforts to make our industry more efficient. Vigilance with respect to costs and prices is essential. To safeguard our competitive position, we will have to moderate increases in money wages while stimulating further efforts to raise productivity and improve the quality and diversity of our products and of our salesmanship abroad.

We need an export surplus not for its own sake but rather to enable us to do internationally what the world wants us to do—in defense, aid, investment and development. Secretary of the Treasury Dillon has rightfully called for "heroic measures" to balance our international accounts. Addressing the White House Conference on Export Expansion, the Secretary laid great stress on the importance of a tax cut to achieve such a balance. But he did not stop there:

> . . . While the tax bill will provide the climate and the extra leverage to spur us on to greater efforts and to help make those efforts continually more productive, it will still be imperative that we step up our drive to expand our exports and widen our access to foreign markets—and that we maintain the kind of wage and price stability we have enjoyed over recent years. Above all, you in private industry must work ever harder to seek out, explore and develop export opportunities. For the tax bill will give us the more dynamic and growing economy in which any measures that you adopt can have maximum impact—and in which you will have the heightened incentives you must have if you are to mount an export drive of the scope and intensity we need.

December 1963

*"They only dive for First National City Travelers Checks
— they're better than money."*

Why should the divers—or you—settle for less than FNCB Travelers Checks? They're better than money because you can get an on-the-spot refund if they're lost or stolen. You'll get a prompt refund through any of FNCB's global network of thousands of refund agents. They are spendable anywhere—here and abroad—but only by you. And they are backed by First National City, best-known name in world-wide banking. Ask for them by name at your bank.

**Fastest refund in case of loss or theft—**
Checks missing? Anywhere in the U.S. except Alaska and Hawaii, simply phone WESTERN UNION OPERATOR 25 for nearest refund location. For information concerning refund points in other countries, Alaska and Hawaii, ask at principal hotels.

# FIRST NATIONAL CITY BANK
# TRAVELERS CHECKS

Member Federal Deposit Insurance Corporation